Lower-Class Families

LOWER-CLASS FAMILIES

The Culture of Poverty
in Negro Trinidad

Hyman Rodman
MERRILL-PALMER INSTITUTE

NEW YORK
OXFORD UNIVERSITY PRESS
LONDON 1971 TORONTO

For my families in Montreal, Detroit, and Trinidad

Preface

THIS BOOK presents an exceptionally detailed description of lower-class family life within a community. Although primarily ethnographic, it also attempts to be explanatory. Moreover, the explanation of data is offered as a first step toward a general theoretical statement of lower-class family organization. Some readers may be most interested in the descriptive material, as raw data for their own theories or interpretations. Others will be most interested in the explanation, in order to see how useful it is in explaining data on other societies.

Very few ethnographic studies have been published about lower-class Negro communities in the United States or the Caribbean. This is one reason for the sharp controversies about whether family life is organized or disorganized; whether the families reflect a culture of poverty or a poverty of culture; whether they represent strength or weakness; whether a war on poverty should focus upon the deficiencies of individuals and their families, or upon the deficiencies of a society which perpetuates poverty. I hope that the present study of a lower-class Negro community in Trinidad will help clarify these issues.

The book is based upon eleven months of field work which were spread out over the years 1956, 1959, 1962, and 1968. Most of the field work was done in a rural village in northeastern Trinidad (pseudonymously called Coconut Village), and most of the quotations used in the book stem from there. But many observations and interviews were carried out across the northern part of Trinidad, from Port of Spain to Sangre Grande and from Sangre Grande to Toco, and some of these data have been incorporated. The general features of lower-class family life in Coconut Village have been checked against lower-class family life in other parts of Trinidad, and an attempt is made in the book to report the essential characteristics of lower-class family organization throughout Negro Trinidad. In addition to a description of Coconut Village I have also included a more general account of the social, economic, and political background that impinges upon all Trinidadians.

Trinidad, however, has a highly varied population in terms of social class, race, religious affiliation, and national origin. A study which is based mainly upon a lower-class Negro village of approximately one hundred inhabitants is thus not a study of Trinidad as a whole. There are many differences to be found also among lower-class Negroes; this report will therefore concentrate upon the major trends and features of lower-class family organization, and will not point out repeatedly that there are exceptions to the patterns being described.

Let me anticipate one point. There are many observers who are quick to focus upon illegitimate births, non-legal marriages, female-headed households, and deserting fathers as the major problems of the lower class. Occasionally these observers are also morally outraged, and they may characterize the lower class with terms such as "promiscuous" and "immoral." My own intention is to avoid a moral stance and to describe the situation as objectively as possible. "Lower class" is therefore not used in its pejorative but in its scientific sense and it merely refers to individuals who are at the lower end of an educational, occupational, or income scale. In consequence, "lower class" and "poor" are sometimes used interchangeably. Other terms with pejorative connotations are avoided (and new terms such as "marital-shifting" and "child-shifting" have been used) in order to prevent middle-class moral judgments from creeping in. The result, as the reader will see in the theoretical chapters, is that family patterns which are frequently referred to as problems of the lower class are perhaps better seen as cultural solutions of the lower class to other, more basic problems.

In the past dozen years, I have been interested in the problems of race, poverty, and family organization in Trinidad, the United States, and other parts of the world. Stokely Carmichael, born in Trinidad and recently based in the

United States and Guinea, is one important person among many who symbolize the widespread fight against racism and poverty. What are the consequences of racial discrimination, poverty, and class injustice? For a long time powerlessness, self-derogation, and apathy were the dominant responses of those discriminated against. Recently Black Power, self-pride, and militancy have become the responses of many. The disadvantaged are more sharply aware of their human and civil rights, and they are becoming more determined to wrest them from their oppressors. For a long time the poor have been silent in the face of injustice, and their work has supported the position and privileges of others. Government subsidies for the rich have been lauded as part of the free enterprise system; government subsidies for the poor have been impugned for destroying incentive. *Noblesse oblige* is our ideology while *noblesse permet* is our policy.

There is, therefore, a spirit underlying this book which attempts to see beyond Trinidad to the world at large. Although I did my work on the larger island of Trinidad, Tobago is also part of the country, which is known as Trinidad and Tobago. Trinidad and Tobago became an independent nation in 1962. The government has been controlled by blacks since 1956, and the social and political situation, at least until 1970, has been highly stable. Poverty and unemployment, however, are still severe problems, and they continue to have an influence upon political developments as well as upon the structure of the nation's families. This book's focus upon the family should therefore not blind the reader to social, economic, and political forces, but should open a new perspective on the organization of the society as a whole.

The book's organization. The readers who are particularly interested in the social, economic, and political data of Trinidad and in a description of Coconut Village will want to read the chapters in the order presented. Other readers may be interested in the Trinidad material only insofar as it illuminates the general characteristics of lower-class families; after reading Chapter 1 these readers may want to turn to Chapter 4. The details of family relationships in Trinidad are presented in Chapter 4 through 7; some of the rules that influence and reflect family relationships are presented in Chapters 8 through 11. Finally, in Chapters 12 through 14, an explanation is presented for the Trinidad data. Chapter 12 discusses four general characteristics of lower-class family life, seeing them as part of a lower-class orientation toward circumstances. Chapters 13 and 14 present a comprehensive explanation of the major facts about lower-class family organization and values in Trinidad and, by implication, suggest that the facts and their explanation are widely applicable beyond Trinidad.

H. R.
Detroit, Michigan
Fall 1970

Acknowledgments

MANY INDIVIDUALS have helped me in completing this study. As a Canadian residing in the United States and doing field work in Trinidad I have tri-national debts, including some that I probably cannot recall. Above all, I want to thank the Coconut Villagers who suffered my presence and my questions; without them the study could not have been done. The names of the village, the villagers, and others who were interviewed must remain anonymous, in line with my pledge of confidentiality. But I do want to thank the following among those who facilitated my work in Trinidad: Michael H. Beaubrun, Andrew Carr, Richard Coombs, J. D. Elder, George E. Mose, Christopher Nath, Franklin Nath, C. R. Ottley, D. W. Rogers, and George Sinanan. Successive directors and staff members of the Central Statistical Office gave me a great deal of assistance and I particularly want to thank Vincent E. Bailey, I. W. Chinnia, Jack Harewood, and Frank B. Rampersad. Over the years I have also been aided by several librarians of the Central Library of Trinidad and Tobago, notably Marjorie Lumsden and Ursula Raymond.

Financial assistance has been received from the Social Science Research Council of Canada, the National Institute of Mental Health (U.S.A.), and the Research Institute for the Study of Man. In addition, I am greatly indebted to the Merrill-Palmer Institute for fostering an atmosphere that has encouraged the research and the writing.

I am grateful to Harriet Larkin and Hazel McCutcheon who typed several drafts of the manuscript for me, and to Cecilia Pack who checked the references.

Jon Clark, Stephenie Clark, Albert K. Cohen, Jo Lynn Cunningham, Talcott Parsons, Vera Rubin, Betty Sarvis, David M. Schneider, Audrey Smedley, Raymond T. Smith, and Patricia Voydanoff read earlier drafts of the manuscript and helped me to improve it.

My wife, Barbara, a citizen of Trinidad and Tobago, has provided help at all stages of the project. Our son Ken, also born in Trinidad, along with U.S.A.-born Rick, Dave, and Gail, have had to bear periods of absence occasioned by the work on the book. A melange of dual citizens of Trinidad and Tobago, the United States, and Canada, they have been closely involved in the book's preparation.

I am also greatly indebted to my wife's family, the Mahases, of Guaico, Trinidad, whose help and hospitality contributed in numerous ways to the completion of the study.

Contents

When you asked him why he was so black,
he would answer with serious conviction: "Just
as I wus goin' to born the light went out." The
light, we admitted, had gone out for many
of us.   GEORGE LAMMING
                                    1953 (Barbados)

Trinidad is the land of the humming bird.
The birds who does have the feed will hum;
those that isn' got the feed wouldn' be able
to hum.   COCONUT VILLAGER
                                    1956 (Trinidad)

What if we're weary?
What if we're bent?
This is the harvest Heaven has sent!
Dance in a ring, dance in a row,
This is the land of the rich cocoa.
                        OLGA W. COMMA MAYNARD
                                    1960 (Trinidad)

Black people will not be stopped in their
drive to achieve dignity, to achieve their share
of power, indeed, to become their own men
and women—in this time and in this land—
by whatever means necessary.
                        STOKELY CARMICHAEL AND
                        CHARLES V. HAMILTON
                                    1967 (U.S.A.)

If a soul is left in darkness, sins will be
committed. The guilty one is not he who com-
mits the sin, but he who causes the darkness.
                                    VICTOR HUGO
            quoted by Martin Luther King, Jr., 1967

Calls for peace, justice and equality, and
economic and political progress for all peo-
ples are empty and meaningless if some racial
groups continue to be oppressed by others
who find themselves in positions of power by
chance or by political manipulation. Economic
prosperity for the few must not be attained
through the degradation of the many.
                    PRIME MINISTER ERIC WILLIAMS
                            1970 (Trinidad and Tobago)

PART ONE

SOCIAL, ECONOMIC, AND POLITICAL DISADVANTAGES

1. *Lower-Class Families: An Introduction*

*The histories of mankind that we possess are
histories only of the higher classes.*
ROBERT MALTHUS

THREE MAJOR QUESTIONS that can be used in studying
lower-class families are: (1) How do lower-class conditions
influence family organization? (2) How does the organization of lower-class families influence the socialization and
development of children? (3) What practical steps can be
taken in order to deal with the problems represented by
lower-class families? [1] This book takes its orientation from
the first, and perhaps the fundamental, question. A great
deal is still unknown about how families are shaped by
lower-class conditions. Do the deprivations of lower-class
life give the lower-class family a certain form of organization, regardless of whether we are talking about American
families or Trinidadian families, black families or white
families, Mexican families or British families?

Once we know something about the organization of lower-
class families, it becomes possible to consider the consequences of this organization for individual development and
behavior. It is within the lower classes that we find more
crime and delinquency; lower educational motivation and
more school drop-outs; more schizophrenia; higher rates of
divorce, separation, and desertion; more common-law marriages and illegitimate births; more health problems and a
shorter life-span; greater difficulties in remaining in professional treatment; and a host of other "problems." [2] To what
extent will information about family relationships help us
to explain these phenomena? To what extent will it help us
to alter them? This book does not directly take up these
issues. Nevertheless, considering lower-class family organization in detail provides a good deal of background infor-

3

mation that will be of interest to those who are primarily concerned with personality development of, or professional work with, the poor.

LOWER-CLASS CONDITIONS

Within a society, one set of conditions that influences behavior and values is a family's position in the system of social stratification. Depending upon this position, the money, prestige, and power resources available to the family vary. The family's status and resources are importantly influenced by the man's occupation. In the lower-class family, however, we are dealing with men who are unemployed, underemployed, or poorly paid in unskilled or perhaps semi-skilled employment. Where the lower-class man is expected to be the breadwinner in the family, as in countries like Trinidad and the United States, he frequently is unable to meet this expectation adequately.[3] A number of consequences can be expected from the man's inability to fulfill this basic role, as well as from the family's lack of resources. Conditions in the lower class may therefore be more powerful in shaping behavior and values than in other social classes, and the lack of resources may lead to the development of cultural patterns that are widely shared among the poor.

THE CULTURE OF POVERTY

It is therefore not surprising that most of the recent discussions of class culture are about lower-class culture or the culture of poverty.[4] The term "the culture of poverty" encapsulates the patterns of value and behavior of the poor, and views them as a comprehensive way of life.[5] In summarizing the characteristics of the poor, the concept is useful; but it may also be harmful by promoting a stereotyped view of the poor. This is particularly the case if the major components of the culture of poverty turn out to be merely a catalogue of undesirable traits, such as apathy, intolerance, lack of motivation, disorganization, and fatalism.[6]

What does a study of lower-class families have to do with the culture of poverty? First, because family behavior and values are an important part of a people's culture, the study of lower-class families provides essential information on one aspect of the culture of poverty. Second, the family represents the major group in which adaptations to poverty are made and transmitted. The study of poor families therefore, although not a study of the total way of life of a group, reveals a crucial slice of that life. If there really are many similarities among the poor families in the *vecindades* of Mexico, the rural villages and urban shanty-towns of Trinidad and Guyana, the *favelas* of Brazil, and the slums and ghettos of Britain and the United States, then we have really hit upon a fact of major importance.

Perhaps focusing upon a sensitive area like the family will also help us to illuminate several heated controversies about the poor. The controversy in the United States surrounding the "Moynihan report," *The Negro Family: The Case for National Action* (U.S. Department of Labor, 1965), is frustrating to follow, and leads us around in circles.[7] Daniel P. Moynihan, formerly Assistant Secretary of Labor, dealt with discrimination, unemployment, and poverty as basic causes of the difficulties of lower-class Negro families, and he wrote the report within a framework calling not merely for equality of opportunity between races, but for equality of results. At the same time, however, the report places heavy emphasis upon the deterioration of the Negro family, and upon the high incidence of illegitimacy, crime, female-headed families, and welfare dependency. The history of the report's development and publication accounts for its organization and emphasis.[8] The possibility of interpreting some passages within it as laying the blame for Negro failings upon the Negro family accounts for the sharp criticisms.

What light can we shed upon the substance of the controversy? In brief, Moynihan stressed cultural developments in the Negro family (brought about "by discrimination, injustice, and uprooting") that might impede it from taking advantage of opportunities. Others have stressed the adaptive quality of Negro family life that enables it to survive under harsh circumstances. Since the former view leads to an emphasis upon negative qualities, and the latter upon positive qualities, there has been a sharp exchange between advocates of the two different positions.[9] But the positions are not irreconcilable; as a matter of fact, they are readily compatible. The cultural developments of lower-class Negro families may be adaptive and creative in surviving under conditions of discrimination and deprivation, and yet a handicap in taking advantage of new opportunities under changing conditions.

Because of the differences among the poor it is necessary to be cautious in applying labels to them. Hylan Lewis has documented a variety of life styles among the low-income people he studied and has cautioned against the indiscriminate use of the concept of a culture of poverty.[10] Others have suggested that we talk about the subcultures of poverty for two reasons: there may be important cultural differences among the poor, and we are not describing a way of life that is totally independent of the larger culture.[11] It should also be recognized that we may have a biculture of poverty. That is, poor people are influenced by the values of the larger society, and they typically share such values as work and achievement, and marriage and family unity. When such values cannot be realized they may "stretch" their values and become satisfied with lesser degrees of achievement and family unity.[12] These "stretched" or alternative values may co-exist with the conventional values. As a result, poor people may have a wider range of values in some areas. They may thus be able to take advantage of new opportunities, provided that the opportunities are really there, and that they know how to take advantage of them. Opening up opportunities, rather than changing the values of the poor, may therefore be the crucial practical problem in attacking poverty.[13]

Emphasizing the heterogeneity among the poor has been one line of argument that questions the validity of the culture-of-poverty concept. S. M. Miller has drawn a conceptual distinction based upon two factors—economic stability and family stability—and has used this to describe four types of lower-class families: the stable poor (economic and family stability); the strained (economic stability–family instability); the copers (economic instability–family stability); and the unstable (economic and family instability).[14] Jessie Bernard emphasizes the variety of cultural styles among all United States Negroes, including the lower class.[15] At an empirical level, however, it is not merely a question of demonstrating heterogeneity but of seeking relationships. The heterogeneity in the lower class is great enough that it is not possible to characterize the lower class in any simple way. But it is nevertheless possible to demonstrate that certain patterns are more characteristic of the lower class than of other classes.[16] It may also be possible to show that some family patterns cohere functionally within the lower class. In this way we can demonstrate the influence of lower-class status upon family life. Whether such evidence would substantiate the existence of a culture (or subcultures or a biculture) of poverty is a complicated question that would hinge upon our definition of class and of culture.[17] Without going into that question here (but see Chapter 14), it can at least safely be said that such evidence would demonstrate the process we are primarily concerned with in this book—the influence of poverty upon family organization.

CULTURE VERSUS CONDITIONS

There is no doubt that the escape from poverty is easier for some individuals and groups than for others. Similarly, the condition of poverty has less influence on the behavior and values of some groups than on others. Prior cultural forms may provide a kind of insulation against the conditions of poverty, making it more difficult for these conditions to lead to the characteristics subsumed under the culture of poverty. For example, there is a large "East Indian" [18] group in Trinidad, and the findings in this book apply only in small measure to lower-class Indians.[19] Despite a considerable degree of assimilation to Trinidadian culture, the Indian-Negro differences are still substantial; and this is especially pronounced for rural Indians living in predominantly Indian villages. Why do the conditions of lower-class status not have a similar effect upon the family organization of Trinidad's Indians? A major reason is the persistence of some aspects of Indian culture which have a stabilizing influence upon family life. The social and economic conditions of lower-class status are not all-powerful as determining factors of family organization. They interact with other factors, such as the historical and cultural background of a people, in influencing the family. Lower-class status is therefore a necessary, but not a sufficient condition for the existence of the kinds of family patterns we are going to describe. This point will be elaborated upon when we present our theoretical position, especially in Chapters 13 and 14.

NEW WORLD NEGROES

Given an interest in the impact of lower-class status upon family organization, there is an important advantage in studying New World Negroes (Afro-Americans). The ruthlessness of the slavery experience they have undergone effectively destroyed kinship, community, and tribal ties. Although there is evidence of African retentions,[20] most of the cultural life of the people was stripped away by slavery. Cultural values and forms of family organization cannot readily be transmitted from generation to generation unless they are acted upon, and the slaves did not have the freedom to do so.[21] There was some acculturation to the values and family forms of the white masters, but even this was limited by the impositions of slavery. With emancipation, therefore, we can observe the influence of lower-class status upon family organization with less intervention from prior cultural forms than occurred in other uprooted peoples. As E. Franklin Frazier states, "Probably never before in history has a people been so nearly stripped of its social heritage as the Negroes who were brought to America." [22]

Afro-Americans also had to make adaptations to the circumstances of slavery in different communities in the Americas. The slaves

> sought to make comprehensible the destinies imposed upon them by brute force. The daily job of living did not end with enslavement, and the slaves could and did create viable patterns of life, for which their pasts were pools of available symbolic and material resources. . . .
>
> When we speak of Afro-American cultures, we are speaking of mangled pasts; but those pasts were carried by successive generations of men, dealing with the daily challenges of oppression. The glory of Afro-Americana inheres in the durable fiber of humanity, in the face of what surely must have been the most repressive epoch in modern world history. It has depended upon creativity and innovation, far more than upon the indelibility of particular culture contents.[23]

At the time of emancipation, New World Negroes who had survived and adapted to slavery typically became lower-class members of a larger society. This called for new and continuing adaptations, not only to lower-class status but also to developing patterns of racial prejudice and discrimination. Discrimination made mobility much more difficult and perpetuated lower-class status through the generations for a great many Afro-Americans. By focussing upon a group that has endured lower-class status for several generations, we may find family patterns that show the influence of lower-class status in more fully developed form than found in groups more recently become lower-class. This suggests that lower-class Afro-Americans may reveal patterns yet to emerge in other societies.[24]

NOTES

1. Other major questions can also be used in studying lower-class families—for example: How did the families become lower-class? How does the organization of the family influence its acquisition and use of resources?

2. Some of these relationships have been disputed or have

been given alternative explanations. Is there more lower-class crime, or more stringent enforcement of laws broken by lower-class individuals? Is there lower educational motivation, or a realistic response to teaching that is inadequate for lower-class needs? Do lower-class people show higher rates of schizophrenia, or does mental illness lead to a decline of one's class status? Is a higher rate of illegitimacy in the lower class related to a greater use of contraceptives and abortion in the middle class? Are emotionally disturbed lower-class individuals untreatable, or is this a justification used by middle-class health and welfare professionals who do not know how to treat them?

See the discussions in the following: John P. Clark and Eugene P. Wenninger, "Socio-Economic Class and Area as Correlates of Illegal Behavior Among Juveniles," *American Sociological Review* 27 (December 1962): 826–34; N. Warren Dunham, Patricia Phillips, and Barbara Srinivasan, "A Research Note on Diagnosed Mental Illness and Social Class," *American Sociological Review* 31 (April 1966): 223–27; Frank Riessman, *The Culturally Deprived Child* (New York: Harper, 1962); Kenneth Clark, *Dark Ghetto* (New York: Harper & Row, 1965); Hyman Rodman, "On Understanding Lower-Class Behaviour," *Social and Economic Studies* 8 (December 1959): 441–50; Frank Riessman, Jerome Cohen, and Arthur Pearl (eds.), *Mental Health of the Poor* (New York: Free Press, 1964). John A. Clausen, "Mental Disorders," in Robert K. Merton and Robert A. Nisbet (eds.), *Contemporary Social Problems*, 2nd ed. (New York: Harcourt, Brace & World, 1966).

3. Elliot Liebow, *Tally's Corner: A Study of Negro Streetcorner Men* (Boston: Little, Brown, 1967); and Hyman Rodman, "Marital Relationships in a Trinidad Village," *Marriage and Family Living* 23 (May 1961): 166–70.

4. Hyman Rodman, "Class Culture," in *International Encyclopedia of the Social Sciences* (New York: Macmillan, 1968), XV, pp. 332–37.

5. Oscar Lewis, *The Children of Sanchez* (New York: Random House, 1961), pp. xxiii–xxvii; Oscar Lewis, *La Vida* (New York: Random House, 1965), pp. xlii–lii; Oscar Lewis, "The Culture of Poverty," in John J. TePaske and Sydney Nettleton Fisher (eds.), *Explosive Forces in Latin America* (Columbus: Ohio State University Press, 1964), pp. 149–73; Oscar Lewis, *Five Families* (New York: Basic Books, 1959), pp. 2–3; and Oscar Lewis, *A Study of Slum Culture* (New York: Random House, 1968), pp. 3–21.

6. Charles A. Valentine, *Culture and Poverty* (Chicago: University of Chicago Press, 1968); and Patricia Cayo Sexton, *Spanish Harlem* (New York: Harper & Row, 1965), pp. 176–79.

7. *The Negro Family: The Case for National Action* (U.S. Department of Labor, Office of Policy Planning and Research, Washington, D.C., 1957), popularly known as the Moynihan report

because Daniel P. Moynihan was the principal author. See also Laura Carper, "The Negro Family and the Moynihan Report," *Dissent* 13 (March–April 1966): 133–40; Herbert J. Gans, "The Negro Family: Reflections on the Moynihan Report," *Commonweal* 83 (October 15, 1965): 47–51; Nathan Glazer, "The Negro American: A Review Essay," *Public Interest* (Spring 1966): 108–15; and Elizabeth Herzog, "Is There a Breakdown of the Negro Family?" *Social Work* 11 (January 1966): 3–10.

8. Lee Rainwater and William L. Yancey, "Black Families and the White House," *Trans-action* 3 (July–August 1966): 6–11, 48–53; and Lee Rainwater and William L. Yancey, *The Moynihan Report and the Politics of Controversy* (Cambridge, Mass.: M. I. T. Press, 1967).

9. Valentine, *op. cit.;* and Lewis Coser, "Unanticipated Conservative Consequences of Liberal Theorizing," *Social Problems* 16 (Winter 1969): 263–72.

10. Hylan Lewis, *Culture, Class and Poverty* (Washington, D.C.: Health and Welfare Council of the National Capital Area, 1967). For other accounts of variation, see St. Clair Drake and Horace R. Cayton, *Black Metropolis* (New York: Harcourt, Brace, 1945), pp. 564–657; E. Franklin Frazier, *The Negro Family in the United States* (Chicago: University of Chicago Press, 1939); Jessie S. Bernard, *Marriage and Family Among Negroes* (Englewood Cliffs, N.J.: Prentice-Hall, 1966); Andrew Billingsley, *Black Families in White America* (Englewood Cliffs, N.J.: Prentice-Hall, 1968); Robert Staples, "Towards a Sociology of the Black Family: A Theoretical and Methodological Assessment," *Journal of Marriage and the Family* 33 (February 1971).

11. Catherine S. Chilman, "Child-Rearing and Family Relationship Patterns of the Very Poor," *Welfare in Review* 3 (January 1965): 9–19.

12. Hyman Rodman, "The Lower-Class Value Stretch," *Social Forces* 42 (December 1963): 205–15; "Illegitimacy in the Caribbean Social Structure: A Reconsideration," *American Sociological Review* 31 (October 1966): 673–83; and "Controversies about Lower-Class Culture: Delinquency and Illegitimacy," *Canadian Review of Sociology and Anthropology* 5 (November 1968): 254–62.

13. Hyman Rodman, "Family and Social Pathology in the Ghetto," *Science* 161 (August 23, 1968): 756–62.

14. S. M. Miller, "The American Lower Classes: A Typological Approach," *Social Research* 31 (Spring 1964): 1–22.

15. Bernard, *op. cit.*, pp. 27–66.

16. Raymond T. Smith, *The Negro Family in British Guiana* (London: Routledge & Kegan Paul, 1956), pp. 221–54; Allison Davis, "The Motivation of the Underprivileged Worker," in William Foote Whyte (ed.), *Industry and Society* (New York: McGraw-Hill, 1946), pp. 84–106; and Albert K. Cohen and Harold M. Hodges, Jr., "Char-

acteristics of the Lower-Blue-Collar-Class," *Social Problems* 10 (Spring 1963): 303–34.

17. Herbert J. Gans, "Culture and Class in the Study of Poverty: An Approach to Anti-Poverty Research," in Daniel P. Moynihan (ed.), *On Understanding Poverty: Perspectives from the Social Sciences* (New York: Basic Books, 1969); Hylan Lewis, 1967, *op. cit.;* Jack L. Roach and Orville R. Gursslin, "An Evaluation of the Concept 'Culture of Poverty,' " *Social Forces* 45 (March 1967): 383–92; Hyman Rodman, "Class Culture," *op. cit.;* and Valentine, *op. cit.* Cf. Steven Polgar, "Biculturation of Mesquakie Teenage Boys," *American Anthropologist* 62 (April 1960): 217–35.

18. See the Glossary of Trinidad Creole English Terms, Appendix 2, for definitions of Trinidad terms used in the book.

19. Morton Klass, "East and West Indian: Cultural Complexity in Trinidad," *Annals of the New York Academy of Sciences* 83 (1959): 855–61; and Morton Klass, *East Indians in Trinidad: A Study of Cultural Persistence* (New York: Columbia University Press, 1961), pp. 93–136, 230–49.

For comparable data on British Guiana (Guyana) see Chandra Jayawardena, "Family Organization in Plantations in British Guiana," in John Mogey (ed.), *Family and Marriage* (International Studies in Sociology and Social Anthropology, Vol. 1, Leiden: E. J. Brill, 1963), pp. 43–64; Raymond T. Smith, "The Family in the Caribbean," in Vera Rubin (ed.), *Caribbean Studies: A Symposium* (Seattle: University of Washington Press, 1960), pp. 74–75.

20. Melville J. Herskovits, *The Myth of the Negro Past* (Boston: Beacon Press, 1958), and Norman E. Whitten, Jr., and John Szwed, "Negroes in the New World: Anthropologists Look at Afro-Americans. Introduction," *Trans-action* 5 (July–August 1968): 49–56.

21. There was somewhat more opportunity to transmit and retain African cultural patterns in the West Indies than in the United States, but African retentions are of relatively little importance in both areas. Eric Williams has referred to the people of the West Indies as "deracinated by slavery . . . we have nothing indigenous." (*The Nation,* PNM Weekly, March 13, 1964, Trinidad, p. 7) Cf. Pierre L. van den Berghe, *Race and Racism: A Comparative Perspective* (New York: John Wiley, 1967), pp. 124, 135. Sidney W. Mintz, "Foreword," in Norman E. Whitten, Jr., and John F. Szwed (eds.), *Afro-American Anthropology: Contemporary Perspectives* (New York: Free Press, 1970), pp. 1–16.

22. E. Franklin Frazier, *op. cit.,* p. 21.

23. Sidney W. Mintz, *op. cit.,* pp. 8–9.

24. Anne Parsons ably reports such emerging patterns for lower-class Neapolitan families, and explicitly relates them to developments among lower-class Afro-American families. As she makes clear, despite a strong tradition of family stability and patriarchal

authority in southern Italian families there is evidence, especially in the lower class, of trends toward matrifocality, the father's marginality, marital instability, male peer group ties, and more generally, a strong individualistic pattern. Anne Parsons, *Belief, Magic, and Anomie: Essays in Psychosocial Anthropology* (New York: Free Press, 1969), especially pp. 52–53, 67–97.

2. The Social, Economic, and Political Background

They used Negroes they stole from Africa to work the land that they stole from the Indians.
ERIC WILLIAMS

THE FAMILY RELATIONSHIPS of the poor in Trinidad are intertwined with their position in the total society. It will therefore be helpful to examine the social, economic, and political forces of the island society before turning to a description of family life. I will not attempt a detailed analysis of these forces, but will concentrate instead upon highlighting their major features and presenting them in their historical setting.[1] I will also indicate their significance for the understanding of lower-class life.

EARLY HISTORY

Trinidad was discovered by Columbus in 1498 and remained in Spanish hands for approximately three centuries. The Spanish, however, ignored their West Indian possessions, being preoccupied with the gold and silver mines of Mexico and Peru, so that there was never any large Spanish settlement in Trinidad. When the King of Spain was persuaded, in 1783, to encourage Roman Catholic migration to Trinidad, so many French settlers came from the French West Indian islands that the French greatly outnumbered the Spanish. The French came in the 1780's because of the liberal grants of virgin land being made, and in the 1790's because of the revolutionary reverberations in the French West Indian islands. Many of the French settlers were sugar planters, and they brought their slaves with them. It was only after their arrival that sugar was grown in Trinidad on a large scale.

In 1797 the British captured Trinidad, and English planters came in on the heels of the French. The major motive was economic—the profits to be made in growing sugar cane —and a major problem was to obtain a labor supply for the sugar estates. The native Amerindian population was decreasing by this time, sufficient white European labor could not be obtained, and so other sources were tapped. The slave trade brought in Negroes until it was abolished in 1807. Following emancipation in 1834, and after four additional years of enforced apprenticeship, many Negroes quit estate labor, thus worsening the estates' labor shortage. Indentured laborers were then brought into the colony, mainly from India. In this way the actual population of the island was built up around an economic base, with the planters at one end of the social hierarchy, and the Negroes and "East Indians," [2] who were brought in as laborers, at the other end.

Due to the difficulty of obtaining labor, the position of the large planters was gradually undermined. Just after emancipation the price of labor rose, since many Negroes would not work on the estates, but preferred to squat on unappropriated lands which they worked. The price of labor having gone up, the Negroes who did work on the estates were sometimes able to buy land of their own, especially after the price of Crown lands was reduced in 1868. Moreover, after the Indians had worked as indentured laborers, grants of land were made to them in order to retain their labor beyond the period of their contract or in place of return passage to India. Consequently, some of the Negroes and Indians, brought in to work the planters' land, came to own land of their own. Unfortunately, however, as we shall see later on, many of them could not rely upon their lands alone for a living.

Aside from the problem of labor, a variety of other economic factors contributed to the weakening position of the planters.[3] They relied almost entirely on the sugar crop, which was protected in the British market, but absentee ownership and antiquated technological methods were weakening the competitive position of British West Indian sugar.

In addition, the rising tide of industrialization, linked with the abolition and emancipation movements, was beginning to overcome the influence of the merchants and planters upon British sugar policy. Foreign slave-grown sugar was admitted into Britain even after emancipation in the British colonies. Beet sugar production increased in France and elsewhere, aided by subsidies and high tariffs against sugar imports, and was displacing British West Indian sugar in many markets, including Britain. The revolution in France, and in its Caribbean colonies—in particular San Domingo (now the Dominican Republic) which was producing nearly as much sugar as all of the British Caribbean colonies combined—had aided the sugar economy of the British colonies for several decades. But in the latter half of the nineteenth century the large land holdings of the planters began to break up, just as earlier they had increased at a rapid rate as the large and successful planters bought out their smaller and less successful competitors.[4]

LAND AND WORK PROBLEMS

The lot of the former slaves and indentured laborers was a hard one even when they did acquire land. This is a problem that has continued to the present day. Since much of "the readily accessible agricultural land was alienated, many small farmers have no option but to cultivate land in hilly and mountainous regions which are not well served by roads."[5] Furthermore, the rule of equal inheritance tended to break up land holdings, so that the unit held was often very small, and "most small farmers have had to build up their farms in separate fragments as and when opportunities occurred and their circumstances permitted."[6] Therefore, there was not only the problem of transportation to market, but also the problem of transportation between land holdings, such that "in some flat land areas of Trinidad it was found that one of the first items of 'agricultural equipment' a farmer acquired was a bicycle."[7] The only agricultural tools are the hoe and cutlass for a great many farmers, and a lack of capital is also a common problem. Thus, the farmer cannot raise a more diversified crop, or own more livestock, which could help make farming a full-time occupation. In short, due to the poor land, the problem of transportation, the fragmented holdings, and the lack of capital, farming seldom becomes a full-time occupation, and a cash wage must usually be relied upon by these part-time farmers.

The need to work for a cash wage, the difficulties involved in getting work, and the problem of underemployment faced by the working man in all of the West Indian islands have led to a great deal of migration out of the West Indies, from one West Indian island to another, or from one area in an island to another. The presence of oil and, formerly, of United States military bases in Trinidad put that island in a better economic position than the other islands, and most of the inter-island migration has been to Trinidad. This does not mean that there is no economic problem in Trinidad, but simply that there the problem is less severe than in the other islands.

As George Cumper has said, "Migration is a characteristic of West Indian Society."

> In 1946 there were 80,000 British West Indians living in the area of the census who had been born in a colony other than the one in which they were then resident; that is, one person in twenty was living outside his native colony. Many more were living outside the British West Indies in the United States and elsewhere. Others in the larger colonies had moved considerable distances to new parishes or districts; in some colonies the proportion is as high as one in three of the population. In the whole census area the proportion of the population who have been emigrants from their own districts is perhaps one in five, and the proportion of families from which a member has gone away to find a job elsewhere is even higher.[8]

With a novelist's sensitivity, George Lamming refers to the unemployment problem of Barbados which leads to migration.

> *Old Man:* Time wus when money flow like the flood through these here hands, money as we never ever knew

it before. We use to sing in those times gone by 'twus money on the apple trees in Panama. 'Tis Panama my memory take me back to every now an' again where with these said hands I help to build the canal, the biggest an' best canal in the wide wide world. . . .
Old Woman: 'Tis a next Panama we need now for the young ones. I sit there sometimes an' I wonder what's goin' to become o' them, the young that comin' up so fast to take the place o' the old. 'Tis a next Panama we want, Pa, or there goin' to be bad times comin' this way.[9]

One major need in the West Indies today is greater mechanization of agriculture to increase the productivity of agricultural labor and its contribution to the national economy. There is also a need to slow down the population movement to urban centers through more effective use of agricultural resources, and to increase industrial expansion in order to absorb the displaced agricultural labor.[10] In Trinidad, oil and asphalt are the major industries, and in 1967 accounted for 359.2 million dollars of a total domestic product of 1258.5 million dollars.[11] These industries involve a large capital investment for each person employed, but the major need in Trinidad, and in the West Indies, is for increased employment, and hence for industries which use up little capital and much labor.[12] In the *Caribbean Economic Review* (1949–50), W. Arthur Lewis fully discussed this and such related problems as the need for a single customs union in the area and the need for an industrial development corporation to attract industry. The latter was established in Trinidad in 1959, but the idea of a customs union died with the Federation of the West Indies in 1962 and has only recently been revived. The more general idea of regional economic cooperation, however, remains very much alive throughout the Caribbean area, in large measure due to the efforts of Prime Minister Eric Williams of Trinidad and Tobago. He has encouraged regional support from the Commonwealth Caribbean areas for the University of the West Indies and British West Indian Airways, and he has also hoped for closer cooperative arrangements with the non-

British areas of the Caribbean and the Latin American countries.

SOCIAL CLASS AND RACIAL DISTINCTIONS

The social distinctions within the islands are closely bound up with the historical and economic factors outlined above. The white Europeans, who had been the masters of the slaves and the employers of the indentured laborers, retained their dominant social position, while the Negroes and East Indians were at the bottom of the social scale.[13] But there is another very important group within the island about whom nothing has so far been said—the colored group.[14] During the time of slavery they were referred to as "the free people of colour" and were subject to a variety of restrictions which set them off from the white group, particularly in the French and British islands. When the British captured Trinidad they retained the more liberal Spanish law for many years, and whenever there were attempts to introduce English law the "free people of colour" petitioned the governor to bear their rights in mind. However, despite their inferior social position vis-à-vis the whites, the colored people identified with the whites and in general did not take up the cause of the Negro slave or free man.

The fact that the colored group originated from the sexual relations between white and Negro, in particular between male white planter and female Negro slave, explains the intermediate social position of the colored group. The mulatto child was often freed and educated by his white father, and at times was able to inherit land and money from his father. Thus, when there was an influx of people to Trinidad from the French islands, many of the people who came over were colored, and they brought their slaves along with them as well. That is, Trinidad was settled later than most of the other Caribbean islands, and many of the white people and "free people of colour," as well as many of the Negro slaves, came from other islands. But the intermediate position of the colored group, their identification with the white group, and their rejection of the Negro group, did not change. As Williams says:

> Their concern with colour and lightness of skin was almost an obsession. It was not uncommon to find a British West Indian mulatto, thoroughly incensed at claims of white supremacy based on colour, going to the most fantastic lengths to prove his own superiority to a black man.[15]

The color of a man's skin always was, and still is, a factor to take into consideration in arriving at his social position.[16] Formerly, the separation between white planter and Negro slave was complete and was based upon economic and political position as well as skin color. With the growth of the colored group and of differences in skin color and economic position within that group, as well as with the introduction of other ethnic groups, principally the East Indians, who now constitute about 37 per cent of the island population, the system of social stratification became much more complex.[17] The racial composition of the population of Trinidad and Tobago can be seen in Table 1. The mixed group consists of individuals born to parents of different racial groups, and although this includes an increasing number who are Negro-Chinese, Negro-East Indian, and more varied mixtures, the bulk of the mixed group is still colored (Negro-white). Since we are interested here principally in the relationships among the white, colored, and Negro population we shall confine our analysis to these groups.

A major feature of the system of stratification is the wide gulf between the classes, especially between the lower class and the others; and the economic factors we have outlined help us to understand this. Thus Andrew Pearse has written: "Slavery and indentured labour within the colonial structure nurtured a status system with wide gaps between classes which were also ethnically different." [18] Due to the low level of industrialization there are few skilled jobs in the island; and a large majority of the Negro group, which consists of almost half of the population, is engaged in unskilled labor.

The colored group, which consists of about 15 per cent of the population, is largely in the professional and white-collar occupational groups, while many of the large-scale business enterprises and plantations are concentrated in the hands of a small group of whites. This is an overly simplified picture of the situation, but it does serve as a rough guide to the system of occupational stratification in the islands, and it does highlight the position of the lower-class Negro group, for whom upward mobility is extremely difficult.

Table 1

POPULATION OF TRINIDAD AND TOBAGO BY RACE AND SEX, 1960

RACE	MALE	FEMALE	TOTAL	PER CENT
Negro	176,380	182,208	358,588	43.3
White	7,873	7,845	15,718	1.9
East Indian	153,043	148,903	301,946	36.5
Chinese	4,709	3,652	8,361	1.0
Mixed	65,178	69,571	134,749	16.3
Other	4,228	4,076	8,304	1.0
Not Stated	169	122	291	—
Total	411,580	416,377	827,957	100.0

Source: *Population Census, 1960,* Vol. II, Part A, Table 5, Central Statistical Office, Government of Trinidad and Tobago, 1963; *Annual Statistical Digest 1968,* Table 15, Central Statistical Office, Government of Trinidad and Tobago, 1970.

Within the colored group, of course, there are many variations in skin color and occupational status. The considerations which enter into a marriage within this group illustrate the interplay of skin color and occupational factors in determining social status:

> A light-skinned girl of the lower middle class would be keen to marry a darker-skinned person who was high up on the professional scale—that is, a doctor or a lawyer. At the same time a doctor or a lawyer would seek to obtain

entree into a higher status group by marrying a light-skinned person.[19]

Moreover, many colored professionals have returned to Trinidad with white wives, having married in the country where they took their professional training, usually in Britain.

With the passage of time the approximate divisions of island society into an upper-class white group, a middle-class colored group, and a lower-class Negro group have become less and less accurate. Educational, economic, and political factors are all involved. But even though educational and economic opportunities have opened up for the lower-class person, he is still at a distinct disadvantage. For example, secondary school education was not free until 1961, and for most of the lower-class population, which was in rural areas, such schools were not accessible. Williams (1950) has discussed the disadvantages of the educational system which were especially severe for the rural and lower-class person.[20] Since 1956, however, when Williams the scholar also became the head of the Trinidad and Tobago government, there have been marked improvements in educational opportunities. From 1957 to 1966 the number of primary and intermediate schools has risen from 411 to 461, the teachers in them from 4,439 to 6,301, and student enrollment from 159,503 to 216,063. In secondary schools, as can be seen in Table 2, enrollment from 1956 to 1966 jumped from 14,310 to 39,003—a jump from 9.6 to 17.2 per cent of the total population aged 10 to 19 years. Since there are few students under thirteen in the secondary schools, these figures underestimate the percentage of youth who attend secondary schools, but they do indicate the sharp rise that has taken place in attendance.

A BRIEF HISTORY OF TRINIDAD'S POLITICS

The political situation, though intimately related to the economic and social situation, is, in a sense, the most important area to be considered. For here, ultimately, rests the power to effect broad changes in the social system. The policy of colonial powers to grant local self-government by degrees is often less a reflection of the inability of colonial people to govern themselves than of the desire of the metropolitan country to control the direction of change within the colony and to preserve certain advantages for itself. This is reflected in the common speed-up of the process leading toward self-government when there is local agitation about the hardships of colonial rule, and a real danger of alienating the local people if self-government is delayed. The extension of increasing degrees of local self-government in Trinidad offers a good example of this.

Table 2

STUDENTS ATTENDING SECONDARY SCHOOLS, 1952–1966

	TOTAL NO. OF STUDENTS	MID-YEAR ESTIMATE, TOTAL POPULATION 10–19 YEARS OLD	PERCENTAGE OF 10–19 YEAR OLDS IN SECONDARY SCHOOLS
1952	11,110	125,150	8.9
1956	14,310	149,650	9.6
1960	21,146	184,300	11.5
1966	39,003	226,250	17.2

Source: Computed from information supplied in issues of *Digest of Statistics on Education* and *Annual Statistical Digest,* published by the Central Statistical Office, Government of Trinidad and Tobago.

The British first captured Trinidad in 1797, and kept the colony under the Governor's rule. In 1831 a legislative council was first formed; however, all the members were nominated and it served only in an advisory capacity. Finally, in 1925, there was an elected minority in the legislative council. But both candidates and voters had to meet certain financial conditions, so that only a very small minority of the people of Trinidad could run for office or vote. Hewan Craig has said:

> The financial qualifications for elected members of the Council were designed to ensure that these members would be men of independent means with a substantial interest

in the colony's welfare, the assumption being that such persons would make the most responsible advisers to the government.[21]

It was natural that under such conditions the welfare of the working man would be ignored. There were, however, several elected members (Arthur Andrew Cipriani, Adrian C. Rienzi, and Timothy Roodal) who were supporters of labor, but they could not wield much influence within the Legislative Council due to the political restraints imposed upon them. Rienzi, for example, complained that the legislature was "nothing but a mock Parliament," and that crown colony government was "a subtle form of dictatorship." [22]

One of the avowed reasons for keeping political control in the hands of the imperial government was the concern for the rights of the mass of the people who would not be represented in the local legislature. Trinidad was acquired late by Britain, and the imperial government had already had much trouble with local governments in other colonies where the interests of the white planters were represented. Furthermore, the British were outnumbered by the French and Spanish, and they in turn were outnumbered by the "free people of colour," so that the extension of self-government would have involved problems beyond those faced in the other British colonies. Thus, the imperial government retained complete political control, and one of the things which this made possible was the institution of laws to improve the lot of the slaves—laws which were not adopted in the other colonies where the British planters controlled the legislative councils. Despite these efforts on the part of the imperial government, which continued after emancipation, the working man never was adequately represented, and his political and economic hardships finally led, in the 1930's, to a series of riots and disturbances throughout the British West Indies. In Trinidad the riots took place in 1937 among the oil workers who were led by T. U. B. Butler. As a result of these disturbances a commission was appointed to investigate conditions in the British West Indies, and in 1941, in Trinidad, its recommendations led to an extension of suffrage. Finally, in 1946, universal adult suffrage was instituted, and in 1950 there was an elected majority in the legislative council for the first time.

The gains which increased political participation have brought about for the laboring class have so far been small ones. One reason for this is that political action has been hampered because of the weakness of the political parties in Trinidad.[23] Although such parties have existed for a long time, none of them were effectively organized, all of them promised jobs, houses, water, and the like, and most of them claimed to represent the common man. The ease with which old parties were broken and new ones formed reflected the weakness of their organization. For the most part the elected members in the 1950 legislature acted as individuals, and they were therefore not able to deal with the island's economic problems in an organized way.

Traditionally, as I have already pointed out, the colored person did not ally himself with the lower-class Negro worker, either socially or politically. Nevertheless, since the colored people were, on the whole, better educated for political action, it was reasonable to expect that the initial steps to deal with the island's problems would be taken by them. Certainly they were handicapped in doing so for a long time due to constitutional limitations. But clearly this was not the only problem, as the difference between the 1950 and 1956 elections vividly testifies. One of the things that was needed was an effective political party, ably organized and led, which could capture the people's imagination and the people's votes. This was something that the People's National Movement (P.N.M.), led by Dr. Eric Williams, was able to do.

The P.N.M. was organized less than one year before the 1956 elections. Unlike the other parties in existence, it was well-organized and well-run, with an intelligent political program and with able leaders who were aware of the country's problems. One important virtue of the party was its multi-ethnic character, for it had the support of many white, Chinese, and Indian Trinidadians as well as a large majority of the colored and Negro people. In the 1956 elections the party received a majority of the total votes cast, despite the fact that there were seven other parties in the race and thirty-eight independent candidates. It won thirteen of the twenty-four elected seats. Although there was some initial confusion because the imperial government had not expected such a decisive victory by any party, instructions to the Governor were finally altered to permit the nomination of party members to the legislative council so that the P.N.M. could effectively control the government of Trinidad and Tobago.

Trinidad and Tobago also joined in the short-lived Federation of the West Indies which held its first elections in 1958. The West Indian Federal Labour Party, with which the P.N.M. of Trinidad and Tobago was affiliated, won control of the Government of the West Indies. In Trinidad, however, they could only win four of the ten seats. This reflected the need for more political work within many rural areas, where less was known about the P.N.M. and where rumors misinterpreting its aims spread easily. It also reflected the fact that the P.N.M. got most of its support from the Negro and colored population of Trinidad and Tobago, and that these groups were more urbanized than the Indians.

There is some tension between the Indians and the Negroes of Trinidad, which stems from the historical conflict imposed upon these groups by the colonial powers. Indians were brought in as indentured laborers to work on the sugar estates in order to complement the Negroes who remained on the estates, and to drive the price of labor down.[24] This tension has been exploited in recent political campaigns, despite the P.N.M.'s multiracial orientation. It has been characterized by its opponents as a "Negro party," and it has so far failed to win more than a small minority of Indian votes. The Democratic Labour Party (D.L.P.) has drawn its support primarily from the Indians in Trinidad, and it has in the past capitalized upon rumors about Government discrimination against Indians in order to consolidate its support. There have undoubtedly been instances of such discrimination at the local level on the part of Negro supporters—just as the Negroes had, in earlier days, been discriminated against by

Indians and whites. The instances of discrimination were, however, greatly exaggerated and the tension between the races was extremely high in 1961 and the early part of 1962.

The immediate cause of the tension between the Negroes and Indians was the Trinidad and Tobago election of December 1961. By this time a two-party system had been established, and the elections were being contested by the P.N.M., which was the party in power, and the opposition D.L.P. party. Both parties devoted a good deal of attention to presenting a multiracial image, and they both had a thoroughly multiracial slate for the 1961 elections. Yet the tradition of a "Negro" P.N.M. party and an "Indian" D.L.P. party had, unfortunately, already been established, and many party groups at a local level used racial antagonism as a means of winning support. The leadership of the P.N.M. deplored this, but such tactics were less noticeably discouraged by the leadership of the D.L.P. in an attempt to gain control of the government. The P.N.M., however, won twenty out of thirty seats. While racial tension did not immediately subside, the strength and temperance of the P.N.M. party's leadership during the 1960's provided a stability of government in Trinidad and Tobago that was not surpassed in other countries of Latin America or the Caribbean. This is all the more remarkable when compared to the political instability and racial antagonism in Guyana (British Guiana) during the same period.

In the early part of 1962, attempts to ease the racial situation in Trinidad were successful. The leaders of the D.L.P. and the P.N.M. were finally able to agree on the need to start dissociating racial from political loyalties. At the Independence Conference which took place in Marlborough House, London, from May 28 to June 8, 1962, bipartisan accord was achieved. Both parties agreed upon independence for Trinidad and Tobago, and upon the Trinidad and Tobago constitution. A significant degree of bipartisan consultation and accord was maintained from the Independence Conference until independence was granted on August 31, 1962. This statesmanlike bipartisanship has continued in some measure since independence, although dissension and leadership changes within the D.L.P. have hampered cooperation.

The emotion generated by election campaigns has also led to some tension, and this has been heightened by the presence of a small group of leftist, Cuban-oriented individuals. But the P.N.M. won twenty-four of the thirty-six seats in the 1966 elections, while the opposition D.L.P. party won the other twelve. In the local government elections of 1968 the P.N.M. won sixty-eight seats (D.L.P., twenty-eight, and independents, four) and took control of the three municipal areas and of four of the seven counties. The P.N.M. thus is firmly in control of the central government and of most of the bodies of local government, and the bipartisan agreement to avoid racial appeals and to stress racial harmony has been fairly well maintained. As a result there has been a good deal of stability in the country and a significant reduction in racial tension.

This does not mean that racial tension has been completely eliminated, though one of Trinidad's proudest boasts in tourist literature and to visiting dignitaries is the harmony that exists in the island between the diverse racial, religious, and national groups. There is a good deal of truth to such a boast, and Daniel Crowley has pointed out the way in which acculturation and Creolization have gone a long way toward providing "the common ground which makes it possible for Trinidad to function as a society." [25] Indeed, the racial situation is relatively harmonious when compared to most other areas of the world, including England and the United States, and perhaps that is the reason why so many visiting dignitaries speak as though the harmony were complete. The major problem in Trinidad and the West Indies is not a racial one but an economic one, and therefore the racial difficulties are rightly glossed over. But the tourist's myth of complete racial harmony does not bear close examination, and the friction between the races has always been one of the major sources of material for Trinidad's calypsonians.[26] Nevertheless, there is now a desire on the part of most of the political leaders to create unity out of diversity within Trinidad.

Many political leaders also desire to replace insularity by

cooperation within the West Indies, despite the breakup of the Federation of the West Indies in 1962. Several movements are currently underway that will undoubtedly lead to greater political and economic cooperation in the Caribbean. Prime Minister Eric Williams of Trinidad and Tobago has made such cooperation one of his special concerns. The establishment of a Caribbean Free Trade Association in 1968 was one important step in the development of economic cooperation and planning on a regional basis in order to enlarge the market for locally produced goods and to improve the economic position of the region.

THE POPULATION PROBLEM

There is a high population density in the West Indies, and also a high rate of natural increase because the birth rate has remained high while mortality has been sharply cut. Migration has always been one way in which some of the excess population has been handled, but it has never been anything but a makeshift solution. A number of investigators have stressed the need for a public policy to encourage the practice of birth control in the West Indies as a more appropriate solution to the population problem.[27] This sentiment has also been expressed by leaders of the opposition D.L.P. in Trinidad and Tobago. Roman Catholic feelings, however, tied the government's hands. During the 1956 elections, to offset rumors of a "Godless" party led by a man who would impose birth control upon the populace, the P.N.M. emphasized and reemphasized that birth control was a private matter in which no government had a right to interfere. For a long time they did not part from this position, and indeed took no actions that would lend government support to voluntary family planning agencies. Finally, in 1965, an Ad Hoc Committee was established by the government party "to consider and report on what should be the Party's attitude towards family planning. . . ." The report strongly favored family planning as "necessary to the social and economic development of our country." It recommended government support for voluntary efforts to promote family planning, and it also recommended that the P.N.M. institute an educational program on family planning.[28] The party's newspaper, *The Nation,* undertook an educational campaign to inform the people of Trinidad and Tobago of the Report's findings and recommendations. It also documented the increasingly favorable attitudes toward family planning in many countries throughout the world, including predominantly Roman Catholic countries. After further deliberation, the Government of Trinidad and Tobago instituted its own national program in family planning in 1967, coordinating it with the efforts of the voluntary organizations. Its aim was to lower the crude birth rate from approximately thirty per thousand to less than twenty per thousand in ten years.

BLACK POWER

Despite its political stability and economic progress, Trinidad is faced with a problem that has striking parallels to the situation in the United States. Between 1965 and 1967 its unemployment rate has been approximately 14 per cent; for those in the 15 to 19 age group unemployment has fluctuated between 30 and 36 per cent, and for the 20 to 24 age group between 20 and 27 per cent. These figures parallel the unemployment figures for youth in the Negro ghetto areas of the United States. The relative deprivation of the poor and unemployed in a society that is marked by economic advances poses a serious problem, and phenomena such as the world-wide Black Power movement indicate dissatisfaction with present conditions and an attempt to change them. It is noteworthy that Stokely Carmichael, born in Trinidad, and formerly a leading advocate of Black Power in the United States, was not permitted to enter Trinidad. Nevertheless, there is the beginning of a militant movement in Trinidad which looks to Cuba as a revolutionary model. Some of these militant individuals formed the Workers and Farmers Party in 1965 and contested the national elections in 1966. They received only 3 per cent of the total vote and did not win a single seat.

High levels of unemployment, however, have contributed

to the growth of the Black Power movement in Trinidad, and in 1970 their protests led to a short-lived rebellion against the government. Their rallying cry is not merely black power, but also economic power, and they are ideologically committed to define "black" so as to include East Indians as well as Negroes. Their threat to Trinidad's stability is thus far limited. The P.N.M. is strong nationally, and the government is making serious efforts to deal with unemployment. Moreover, Trinidad, unlike the United States, is characterized by a system of racial justice. It therefore seems that only if unemployment continues at a high level will disaffection from the government pose a serious threat to Trinidad's political stability. It is to be hoped that the coming years will mark the beginning of substantial economic and social advance for all people within the Caribbean area, as well as in Trinidad. This would relieve the pressure of deprived conditions and economic injustice upon lower-class families, and would undoubtedly lead to changes in the structure of these families. Perhaps better times really are in store for the lower-class person who has, until now, borne the brunt of the island's economic and social burdens.

NOTES

1. For more detailed background material on Trinidad see Eric Williams, *History of the People of Trinidad and Tobago* (Port of Spain, Trinidad: PNM Publishing Co., 1962); Lloyd Braithwaite, "Social Stratification in Trinidad: A Preliminary Analysis," *Social and Economic Studies* 2 (1953), Nos. 2 and 3; Hewan Craig, *Legislative Council of Trinidad and Tobago* (London: Faber and Faber, 1952); Lionel Mordaunt Fraser, *History of Trinidad* (Port of Spain, Trinidad: Government Printing Office, Vol. 1, no date, Vol. 2, 1896); Gertrude Carmichael, *The History of the West Indian Islands of Trinidad and Tobago, 1498–1900* (London: Alvin Redman, 1961); Ivar Oxaal, *Black Intellectuals Come to Power: The Rise of Creole Nationalism in Trinidad and Tobago* (Cambridge, Mass.: Schenkman Publishing Co., 1968).

2. This is the local term for Indians from India, or their descendants. See Appendix 2.

3. See Lowell Joseph Ragatz, *The Fall of the Planter Class in the British Caribbean, 1763–1833* (New York: Century Co., 1928); and Eric Williams, *Capitalism and Slavery* (Chapel Hill: University of North Carolina Press, 1944).

4. Eric Williams points out that the need for a large unit of production, labor supply, and capital investment had "led inevitably to the elimination of small scale farming and the emergence of the large sugar plantation operated by slave labour." "The Importance of Small Scale Farming in the Caribbean" (Trinidad: Conference on Education and Small Scale Farming, Caribbean Commission, 1954), pp. 1–2.

5. C. Y. Shepard, "Organization for the Processing and Marketing of the Products of Small Scale Farming," in *Small Scale Farming in the Caribbean* (Trinidad: Conference on Education and Small Scale Farming, Caribbean Commission, 1954), p. 40.

6. *Ibid.*, p. 41.

7. A. L. Jolly, *Peasant Farming* (Port of Spain, Trinidad: Central Secretariat, Caribbean Commission, 1954), p. 5.

8. George Cumper, *Social Structure of the British Caribbean*, Part 2 (University College of the West Indies, Extra-Mural Department, no date), p. 28.

9. George Lamming, *In the Castle of My Skin* (London: Michael Joseph, 1953), pp. 86–87.

10. W. Arthur Lewis, "Industrial Development in the Caribbean," reprinted from *Caribbean Economic Review* 1 (1949) and 2 (1950): 25–52, by Central Secretariat, Caribbean Commission, Port of Spain, Trinidad, 1951; *Policies for Faster Economic Growth in Trinidad and Tobago* (Committee for Economic Development of Trinidad and Tobago, January 1968), pp. 45–55.

11. These provisional figures refer to West Indian currency valued at factor cost, and were provided by the Central Statistical Office, Trinidad and Tobago. The oil and asphalt percentage of the total domestic product has remained at between 28 and 36 per cent for every year between 1952 and 1967. See *The National Income of Trinidad and Tobago 1952 to 1962* (1964), p. 2, and *Annual Statistical Digest 1966* (1968), p. 113, both published by Central Statistical Office, Trinidad and Tobago.

12. W. Arthur Lewis, *op. cit.*, p. 48.

13. Elsa V. Goveia, *Slave Society in the British Leeward Islands at the End of the Eighteenth Century* (New Haven: Yale University Press, 1965).

14. For a fuller account of this group's position in the Caribbean see Eric Williams, *The Negro in the Caribbean* (Washington, D.C.: Associates in Negro Folk Education, 1942), pp. 57–69; also, Fernando Henriques deals with the problem of color and class in Jamaica in detail: *Family and Colour in Jamaica* (London: Eyre & Spottiswoode, 1953).

15. Eric Williams, *Education in the British West Indies* (Port of Spain, Trinidad: Teachers Economic and Cultural Association, Ltd., 1950), p. 8.

16. Lloyd Braithwaite, *op. cit.;* also see calypsos on pp. 207–08, Appendix 1.

17. See Lloyd Braithwaite, *op cit.*, for a fuller account of the system of stratification than the one presented here. However, he too concentrates upon the white, colored, and Negro groups.

18. Andrew C. Pearse, "Vocational and Community Education in the Caribbean," in Wilgus A. Curtis (ed.), *The Caribbean: Its Culture* (Gainesville: University of Florida Press, 1955), p. 126.

19. Lloyd Braithwaite, *op. cit.*, p. 48.

20. Eric Williams, *Education in the British West Indies, op. cit.;* see also Williams's comments on social class discrimination in *The Nation*, PNM. Weekly, Oct. 29, 1965, pp. 1, 3, 12.

21. Hewan Craig, *op. cit.*, p. 39.

22. *Ibid.*, p. 88.

23. Eric Williams, *The Case for Party Politics in Trinidad and Tobago* (Port of Spain, Trinidad: Teachers Economic and Cultural Association, Ltd., 1955).

24. This tension was more severe in Guyana (British Guiana) than in Trinidad because the emancipated Negroes in the former colony faced more difficulty in cultivating land on their own. Donald Wood, *Trinidad in Transition: The Years After Slavery* (London: Oxford University Press, 1968), pp. 3–10; cf. Arthur Calder-Marshall, *Glory Dead* (London: Michael Joseph, 1939), pp. 237–38; Eric Williams, *History of the People of Trinidad and Tobago, op. cit.*, pp. 113–20, 223.

25. Daniel J. Crowley, "Plural and Differential Acculturation in Trinidad," *American Anthropologist* 59 (October 1957): 819.

26. See calypsos on pp. 206–11, in Appendix 1.

27. George W. Roberts, *The Population of Jamaica* (Cambridge, Eng.: Cambridge University Press, 1957); E. Gordon Ericksen, *The West Indies Population Problem* (Lawrence: University of Kansas Publications, 1962); direct and inferential support for such a policy is also to be found in the papers by G. W. Roberts, R. J. Harewood, L. Braithwaite, Robert T. McMillan, *et al.*, in *Research Papers*, No. 4, December 1967, Central Statistical Office, Trinidad and Tobago.

28. *Report on Family Planning*, prepared by a Committee of the General Council, People's National Movement, March 31, 1965, pp. 1, 64.

3. Coconut Village

Let not Ambition mock their useful toil,
Their homely joys, and destiny obscure;
Nor Grandeur hear with a disdainful smile
The short and simple annals of the poor.
                                    THOMAS GRAY

THE HIGHWAY in northeastern Trinidad runs along fairly close to the coast, and coconut palms grow on estate lands on either side of the highway for several miles' distance. At one point the highway dips to within fifty or sixty yards of the sea, and this is where Coconut Village is located. There are several beach houses on the land overlooking the sea, where middle-class colored and East Indian families spend their holidays at various times of the year. These houses are built of concrete, and have a pumped water supply. One of the houses, which has an electric generator in its garage, sometimes turns its lights on for an hour or two in the evening, and brightens a knot of villagers who gather to talk along the highway. But the villagers' houses are built up on the other side of the highway, and the life led by the villagers differs greatly from the life led by the people who come to the beach houses on their holidays. The people of Coconut Village are members of the lower class of island society, and most of the data for this study of families in poverty were gathered among them. Thus it is of greatest importance to know how the villagers live.

Coconut Village Street runs off the highway, and two streets run northwards off Coconut Village Street—East Street and West Street. The villagers all live within the boundaries set by the highway on the east, Coconut Village Street on the south, West Street on the west, and the small Roman Catholic church and burial ground on the north. The houses in the village are fairly close together, so that next-door neighbors can talk to one another from their houses. When an argument takes place in a household it is often a public affair, for it can be heard by any villager from the street in front of the house.

On most evenings there will be a group of villagers, usually only men, gathered about one of the cross-streets. Since Coconut Village Street is the only street leading to the village, the group usually gathers where Coconut Street meets the highway, or East Street, or West Street. A temporary Community Center, consisting only of wattled walls and a thatched roof,[1] is located at the junction of Coconut Village Street and West Street, and a game of draughts (checkers), with perhaps two or three onlookers, is frequently played there in the evening. Once it grows dark, after about six o'clock, the game continues to be played by the light of a flickering candle or a *flambeau*—a bottle of "pitch oil" which is turned upside down at intervals to soak the burning rags in the neck of the bottle. Steel band practices, usually held on Saturday evenings, also take place in the Community Center. After the evening's practice the band members, as well as several of the others who happen to be around, occasionally make a tour of the village, the bandsmen beating their pans in the front, and the others *jumping up* behind them to the music.

The village shop is another place where, on occasion, a group of men from the village gathers in the evening, drinking wine and beer, and talking.[2] The shop is located along the highway, with the shopkeeper's house beside it—the only house, besides the beach houses, that overlooks the sea. The shop is the major source for the villagers' provisions during the day—rice, saltfish, sugar, flour, and oil. There is also a *parlour* on West Street, where they can buy biscuits, bread, sweet drinks, cigarettes, and candies.[3] Although the shop sells these items as well, the villagers buy most of them from the *parlour* which is located closer to their homes.

The coconut palms growing on the plot of land around most households are useful to the villagers in a variety of ways. For a few, the leaves are used to thatch their houses, and for many, to thatch their kitchens, which are separate from the main house. Most of them use a *cocoyea* broom which is made of the dried central strips of the palm leaf.

Young coconuts, the so-called jelly nuts, are cut for their coconut milk and jelly, and the older nuts are used to make copra, which can then be sold or used to make coconut oil. And as we soon shall see, the coconut estates around the village also provide the villagers with their major source of work, so that there is good reason for calling the place "Coconut Village."

The people in the village are predominantly dark-skinned Negroes, although several are East Indians and *Douglas* (pronounced dō' glaz). Although in other parts of the island, where they are more numerous, the East Indians have retained their religion and way of life,[4] the few within the village and in the surrounding area have been *creolized*. The villagers walk about barefoot, the men generally wearing old pants and shirts, and the women wearing dresses. On special occasions, however, such as weddings or trips to town, the villagers appear in shoes and in their newest clothing.

The typical village house is a tapia (mud) house with a galvanized iron roof, although several are built of wood or sun-dried bricks, and several have coconut straw thatch roofs. Locally grown woods are used in building the house; the framework for the walls is made by wattling and then filling this in with mud mixed with a grass binder. After the walls have been completed, to whiten them and make them smooth they are *leepayed*, that is, white dirt dug from the seaside is mixed with water and applied to the walls in several progressively thinner layers. The majority of the houses consist of two rooms, and many of these are further subdivided by screen, or occasionally wooden, partitions. Several houses have in addition a small gallery at the back where the cooking is done. Most of the houses, however, have a kitchen behind and apart from the house, usually of wattled walls not completely plastered with mud, and of thatched roofs. Of the two house rooms, one is usually a bedroom, with a bed, table, and clothes hung up on the walls, and the other a drawing room with a table, some chairs, and a "safe" containing the best glasses and kitchenwares of the house. There would not usually be sufficient space at the table for everyone to sit, and, at any rate, the members of a household seldom eat together as a unit, but at different times and in various parts of the house. Every house has at least one "pitch oil" lamp which is lit in the evening.

Behind the house, besides the kitchen, there is also an outhouse or pit latrine and occasionally a pig pen. But pigs, chickens, and dogs can be seen wandering about the village at any time of the day, scavenging for whatever food may be available. There are also one or two water barrels behind each house, which catch the rain water in order to cut down on the number of trips to the river.

Land is owned by someone in a little over half of the households in the village, ranging from a small house lot to five acres in a trace more than a mile's distance from the village. But the land is poor, the hoe-and-cutlass farming is antiquated, and the problem of transportation is a serious one. No vehicle can drive all the way up the trace where some of the villagers own land, and this makes it extremely difficult for them to sell their produce. Only two villagers own donkeys, which they use to transport their crops from their land holdings; the possession of a donkey is a mark of some standing within the village. For example, one of the villagers would sometimes be referred to as "the man with the donkey" in much the same tone that might be used by middle-class people to refer to "the man with the Chrysler Imperial."

Another problem has already been mentioned as common to the West Indies: many of the land holdings of the villagers are very small, and several villagers are working as many as three separate plots of land. The net result is that no villager can rely upon the land alone for his living, and they all must seek work of one kind or another. A large majority of the working villagers do estate labor on one of three nearby coconut estates. Some of them are paid by the day— $2.48 (Trinidad dollars) for a day's work at one estate, and $2.00 at another. Others are paid by the amount of extracted coconut meat they bring in, and work as individuals or as a team in picking, gathering, cracking, and extracting the nuts. The actual job done by any person may vary a good deal from day to day, the employment is irregular, and no work is carried out or pay collected when it rains or when the overseer decides to lay a villager off for several days. For instance, on one estate over a four-week period, day workers averaged only a little more than three working days per week.

Several women of the village do estate labor, but most of them are not employed. A few get part-time domestic work at the beach houses, when these are occupied, and one woman occasionally gets some sewing to do. One man is a part-time caretaker of one of the beach houses. There are also a few men in the village who work on road repair and construction crews for the county, one who fishes for a living, one who has a regular but low-paying job with the Government, and one who drives a taxi—the taxis in Trinidad compete vigorously with bus transportation. Two women run small *parlours*, and are helped by their husbands when they are not engaged in estate labor. But although there are these differences in occupation, there are no large differences in the amount of money earned, and the occupational differences do not serve to mark off one worker from another. The only real exception is the shopkeeper, who has much larger earnings and land holdings than any other villager. But there is no group of villagers that keeps itself apart from the others; even the shopkeeper's children mingle freely with all of the villagers.

Aside from their regular, or I should say irregular, occupations, most village men and some women take on a variety of occasional jobs. Some men fish in the sea and in the nearby river for river lobsters, crayfish, and large crabs. One man hunts from time to time. Two others do logging work on occasion, buying trees on Crown lands, cutting them down, and preparing them for sale. For many, the idea is to "catch a day work here and a day work there," including carpentry, house-building, and planting and cutlassing on coconut, cocoa, or citrus estates.

When a villager does not have a cash job for the day, he will frequently work on his small plot of land. Many villagers, as they put it, "make garden"—they grow provisions such as yam, dasheen, tannia, plantain, banana, and cassava. Most of these crops are small and are grown for eating, although a small amount is sold. Some villagers also "mind" fowls and pigs, and one woman was raising a goat.

The above sketch gives a brief picture of village life, and of the houses and jobs of the villagers. Although on the surface life in the village seems placid, the villagers have a good idea of the disadvantaged position in island society that they occupy, and of the relative hardships they face. It is this position of the lower-class person in its social, economic, and political sense that we shall bear in mind in the following chapters when we describe some of Trinidad's lower-class Negro families.

NOTES

1. The ethnographic present of this description is 1956. Although the Village Council tried to complete the Center by voluntary village labor, it was unsuccessful. From 1956 to 1959 no progress was made, and by 1962 the partly built center was torn down to make room for a government self-help housing project. When I was first in Coconut Village, in 1956, there were 31 households and 100 residents. In 1968 there were 40 households and 137 residents. In addition to my observations I carried out extensive informal interviews with almost all adults in the village. I also carried out numerous informal interviews in many other areas of northern Trinidad.

2. The importance of peer group relationships for lower-status men has been documented by many investigators. A few examples are: Norman Dennis, Fernando Henriques, and Clifford Slaughter, *Coal Is Our Life* (London: Eyre & Spottiswoode, 1956); Elliot Liebow, *Tally's Corner: A Study of Negro Streetcorner Men* (Boston: Little, Brown, 1967); Gerald D. Suttles, *The Social Order of the Slum* (Chicago: University of Chicago Press, 1968).

3. By 1962 there were two *parlours* on the street; in 1968, one of these had closed and another had opened.

4. Morton Klass, *East Indians in Trinidad: A Study of Cultural Persistence* (New York: Columbia University Press, 1961).

PART TWO

FAMILY RELATIONSHIPS IN COCONUT VILLAGE

4. *The Husband-Wife Relationship*

Marié tini dents (*Marriage has teeth*)
PATOIS PROVERB, TRINIDAD

WHEN A MAN and woman engage in sexual intercourse and in economic cooperation with the approval of the community in which they live, we can speak about a relationship between a "husband" and a "wife." [1] Another way of saying that a husband-wife relationship exists is to say that the man and woman are "married," provided that we make community approval our criterion of marriage, and not the approval of a specific church or national state.[2] The approval of the community would ordinarily be symbolized by certain wedding rituals, but in some instances the community's approval may be tacit, and marriage may not be marked by any specific rituals. For these reasons, a marital relationship may be established in a variety of ways, and there may actually be several types of marital relationships within the same community.[3]

In Trinidad there are three types of marital or quasi-marital relationships—*friending, living,* and married.[4] When *friending,* the marital pair do not live together in the same household; when *living* they do live together, but are not legally married. ("Common law" is the census term equivalent to *living.*) It is important to detail the nature of each type of relationship, its frequency, and the attitudes associated with it in order to see how these relationships are part of the larger web of lower-class life.

Within Coconut Village, in September 1956, there were eight couples *living* and seven couples married; in June 1968, there were eleven couples *living* and eleven married. Data on marital unions for different populations in Trinidad and Tobago are presented in Tables 3 through 6. These indicate that the Coconut Village distribution (Table 3) is most nearly representative of the Negro group in the Eastern

Table 3

POPULATION, AGE 15 TO 64, BY SEX AND TYPE OF
MARITAL UNION: COCONUT VILLAGE, 1968

MALES			FEMALES		
Married	Common Law	Single	Married	Common Law	Single
9	10	11	10	11	10

Source: Author's survey. Type of marital union was recorded as of
July 1968. Only villagers aged 15 to 64 are included in the table,
to make the data more comparable to the census data in Tables 4,
5, and 6.

Table 4

WOMEN BY TYPE OF MARITAL UNION AND AGE:
TRINIDAD AND TOBAGO, 1960 [a]

AGE	MARRIED	COMMON LAW	SINGLE [b]	NOT STATED	TOTAL
15–44	71,277	27,993	71,145	397	170,812
	41.7%	16.4%	41.7%	.2%	100.0%
45–64 [c]	25,600	8,559	17,025	362	51,546
	49.7%	16.6%	33.0%	.7%	100.0%

Source: *Population Census 1960,* Vol. II, Part A, Central Statistical Office, Government of Trinidad and Tobago, 1963, Table 11C.

[a] In 1960 data on type of union were not collected for men and
were not made available by racial or ethnic background.

[b] Includes the census categories "Visiting," "None," and "Other"
as well as "Single." In all of these categories the woman is not living with a common law or a married husband. This simplification
makes the 1960 data somewhat more comparable to the 1946 data.
It also involves little loss of important information because the
enumerators gathered data on the more specific categories inferen-
tially and incompletely.

[c] For women aged 45 to 64, the union type is the one that was in
effect when she was 45, and not necessarily the one in effect at the
time of the census interview.

Table 5
NEGRO POPULATION BY AGE, SEX, AND TYPE
OF MARITAL UNION: TRINIDAD AND TOBAGO, 1946

AGE	MARRIED	COMMON LAW	SINGLE [a]	NOT STATED	TOTAL
		Males			
15–44	18,236	11,477	33,329	338	63,380
	28.8%	18.1%	52.6%	.5%	100.0%
45–64	10,090	3,374	4,481	139	18,084
	55.8%	18.7%	24.8%	.8%	100.1%
		Females			
15–44	21,998	13,408	29,208	105	64,719
	34.0%	20.7%	45.1%	.2%	100.0%
45–64	8,068	2,258	8,106	67	18,499
	43.6%	12.2%	43.8%	.4%	100.0%

Source: *West Indian Census 1946*, Vol. II, Part G, Table 32, p. 33.
[a] Includes the census categories "Widowed" and "Divorced," in order to make the data comparable to the 1960 data. The "Single" category includes all women who were neither married nor in a common-law relationship.

counties (Table 6)—the poorest region of Trinidad. The village is itself in one of these counties. In the rest of Trinidad, which is in a better economic position, marriage is distinctly more common than *living*.

Table 4 on the total population and Table 5 on the Negro population of Trinidad and Tobago show that there are at least twice as many people in the married as in the *living* state. The census material is not altogether accurate on this point, however, because many people who are listed as single or as married are undoubtedly *living*. Moreover, the census listing does not take note of the *living* arrangements that are formed and broken through time. In fact, in all of lower-class Trinidad the total number of *living* arrangements exceeds the total number of marriages to a considerable extent. It can also be seen in Table 6, which contains a more detailed breakdown, that many of the marriages that do take

Table 6

NEGRO POPULATION BY AGE, SEX, AND TYPE OF
MARITAL UNION: EASTERN COUNTIES, TRINIDAD, 1946

AGE	TOTAL	SINGLE	COMMON LAW	MARRIED	WIDOWED	DIVORCED	NOT STATED
			Males				
15 & over	15,023	6,118	4,257	4,185	418	18	27
15–19	1,807	1,756	36	12	1	—	2
20–24	1,750	1,248	350	148	1	1	2
25–29	1,593	662	588	331	8	2	2
30–34	1,560	435	657	456	8	2	2
35–39	1,654	374	685	575	14	2	4
40–44	1,460	333	579	516	27	2	3
45–49	1,311	314	447	527	20	2	1
50–54	982	239	297	406	33	7	—
55–59	861	225	228	360	46	—	2
60–64	664	159	146	307	51	—	1
65–74	1,079	294	206	438	138	—	3
75 Plus	283	76	32	102	71	—	2
Not Stated	19	3	6	7	—	—	3

Females

15 & over	13,015	3,493	4,588	3,948	954	16	16
15–19	1,837	1,265	395	170	3	2	2
20–24	1,764	570	768	417	6	1	2
25–29	1,531	294	755	465	15	1	1
30–34	1,496	211	733	526	22	3	1
35–39	1,317	191	609	484	32	1	1
40–44	1,180	173	456	480	70	—	1
45–49	977	159	321	407	85	3	2
50–54	790	139	220	317	113	—	1
55–59	624	114	131	250	127	2	—
60–64	388	83	76	138	87	3	1
65–74	876	232	112	249	279	—	4
75 Plus	234	62	12	44	115	—	1
Not Stated	1	—	—	1	—	—	—

Source: *West Indian Census 1946*, Vol. II, Part G, Table 32, p. 32.

47

place occur late in life. It is not until the 45 to 49 age group for males and the 40 to 44 age group for females that there are more individuals in the married than in the common-law (*living*) category.

Friending relationships are not listed in the census, but the fact that the percentage in the single group is so high in all of the age groups suggests the high frequency of the *friending* relationships.[5] In addition, *friending* is not confined to those who are single.

It is important to remember that these three marital relationships—*friending, living,* and married—are not mutually exclusive, either at one point in time, or through time. That is to say, a man could be *friending* with one woman, *living* with a second, and married to a third; and he may also be married to a woman with whom he was formerly *living* and *friending.*

FRIENDING

The *friending* relationship is one in which a man visits or meets a woman at intervals for sexual intercourse, and in which he has certain obligations to the woman and to any children of his that she may bear. In many cases the relationship is a casual and temporary affair. Information collected in 1962 on more than five hundred *friending* relationships that had ended,[6] indicates that 33 per cent endured for six months or less (and did not shift to *living* or marriage). The ties between the partners are not extensive:

> (*If you friendin', what does the woman expect?*) Accordin' to how you friendin', whenever you have anything you give her, but you is not responsible for her, you only jus' come and frequent her and what you have you give her. (*Do you give her something every time you go?*) Well, yes. (*And what if you have no money?*) Well, accordin' how you treat her she won' look at you so hard, she may still admit you en have, because is not all the time a man have.

Despite the statement that "you is not responsible for her," where the relationship is a continuing one, mutual obliga-

tions do exist. One encounter between a man and woman—
for example, sexual relationships after a dance—is not
friending. In *friending*, the woman is expected to be sexually available to the man at his leisure, while he is expected
to contribute to the support of the woman and to any children of his that she may bear. Although it is true that the
relationship is usually a casual and temporary one, this is
not always the case, and a *friending* relationship may en-
dure over a long period of time, with the man and woman
living in separate households. One relationship out of every
five reported in the 1962 survey endured at least two years.
The children born into such a relationship ordinarily live
with the mother, although, if it is more convenient, they
might live with the father; in either case, they spend a certain amount of time in the household of the parent with
whom they do not regularly live. As can be seen in the
following case, the *friending* relationship has become,
in effect, a marital relationship with a dual residential
base.[7]

> My brother, his girl come to stay here, she live for
> about a year and a half or two, and my mother got fed
> up, makin' her so have a hatred and grievance, livin'
> couldn't get along between her and her son. Once that,
> livin' goin' on quite better. He still livin' here, but she
> livin' elsewhere. (*Is he married?*) No, not married, jus'
> have a child with her. (*Where is the child?*) The first
> is dead, and the other one is be down here, sometimes
> is be up there. (*Where is the child sleeping now?*)
> Sleeping here now, most of the time here. (*Why is
> that?*) 'Cause the mother is workin' and we have more
> hands down here, but he stays there sometimes, too.

Before the man and woman establish a *friending* relationship, the man would be "gettin' in." This refers to the
period between meeting the girl and *friending* with her, and
is usually of short duration. To the villager it is practically
inconceivable that an unrelated man and woman would
continue to see each other for any length of time without
engaging in sexual relations:

(Before they friendin', what do you call it?) He gettin'
in. *(What does that mean?)* They gettin' to know each
other. *(How long does that take?)* A week or two
weeks. *(When they gettin' in, how often do they see
each other?)* He might want to see her every day or
every hour. *(When they gettin' in, are they sleepin'?)*
No. *(How about if they start to sleep right away, the
first night they get to know each other, what would
you say?)* He get in right away with her.

Once the man and woman are *friending*, since they are
not living together, they are faced with the problem of where
they can see each other and have sexual intercourse. If
either the man or woman is "livin' bachelor," that is, living
alone in a household, there is no problem. Otherwise, there
are a great variety of places where they may meet, including
the girl's own household especially vacated by the other
members so that the man and woman can have privacy. The
following examples illustrate the various places where the
friending couple could meet:

(Where would they be friendin'?) At no special place.
Often go in hotels, or I, the man, may have a man-
friend, and use his place; some may even take a
chance in the open air; very often, if get a little house,
can go there, call it a batchie, use it only for this particular purpose. *(Does the man stay at the batchie?)*
Not possible, might be a married man, or livin' with
somebody; that don' signify it will be only she alone
for this purpose.

*   *   *

*While living in town, in the late evening, I asked a
woman who was sitting on a chair outside her house
if I could interview her. She suggested that I return the
next day, that her niece was inside then entertaining
her boyfriend, and it would be easier if I came back the
next day, we could sit down inside in comfort.*[8]

*   *   *

*(When friendin', where would you meet the girl, where
would you be able to go to bed with her?)* You, the boy,

will have a place fix up for that purpose. (*Would it ever happen that the family would let them stay in the house, sleep there?*) You mean if the mother would allow; yes. (*Why is that?*) To satisfy the girl.

One factor which is important in considering the three types of husband-wife relationships, but particularly the *friending* relationship, is the emphasis upon the biological basis of parenthood. Regardless of anything else, the child's genitor always remains the parent of the child, and even if the child is not living with or being supported by his genitors, he still recognizes them as his mother and father. Since the father is expected to provide financial support for his child, he wants to be certain that he really is the father. The woman who has had sexual relationships with only one man would, of course, know who the father was. But she may be having sexual relationships with more than one man, and a man would be on the alert to discover whether this is so. When a man is *friending* with a woman he may visit her without prior notice to discover whether or not she is *friending* with him alone:

> (*When friendin' with a girl would you go to see her at any time, or only at certain times?*) Go any time; if she have somebody else and want to tell you to come some time, you en coming when she say, but you coming another time, to see if you can bounce up somebody. If she have husband is different, but if she is a single girl, you go any time.

*   *   *

> *Mr. Johnson told of a case where a man was on trial for stealing cocoa, and a girl he was friending with, from Matelot, went up for him and said that he was spending the night with her and so it could not be him.* They asked her, "He is from Toco and you're from Matelot, how does he get to see you?" "He comes, na." She wasn't backin' down at all, and the man was nervous at first, but when he see her speak so he get alright. "Were you expectin' him?" they asked, and she said, "No, but we is friendin', and I expec' him any time."

When a girl he is *friending* with becomes pregnant, the man's concern about the child's paternity is heightened. He feels that she might have been *friending* with someone else though he may not have discovered it:

> What some girls do, they knock around, and then they get in the family way, maybe it could be three or four different fellas, and she love one, well, probably it en he own, but she say is he own and sometimes he don' know, he really think is he own. Someone try that on me one time but you can' do that to me. Figure I is gettin' a steady salary, and the other fellas en workin' steady, she say I is father.

> * * *

> (*What happens when a couple is friendin', and the girl gets a child?*) In some cases a contradiction there then, and man saying I am waitin' till that child born, I don' know if that child mine, she could have been an intimate friend with someone else.

The reason a man wants to be certain the child is his is that he is expected to support his own child, and ordinarily does support it if he feels certain that it is his child. But a man is often doubtful and admits that he may "own what is not his own" or "disown what is his own." The man who supports a child that is not or may not be his own is ridiculed, and the appearance of the child is carefully checked to see whether or not he looks like the father:

> (*Do most people prefer a child to look like the mother or father?*) Always prefer it to look like the father, especially the father himself. Give another man jokes about his family where a lot of men working together: "You don' see the child en resemble you? You alright, man, you mindin' another man' child!"

> * * *

> (*Does a child resemble the mother or the father?*) Well, is a two-between, sometimes will resemble the mother and sometimes resemble the father. (*Which*

do you prefer it to resemble?) Well, you can' prefer, it come accordin' to nature. (*Well, which would you be more glad for it to resemble when is born?*) Dinah! Dinah! (*calling his keeper*) Oh, Dinah! You might be able to answer this question better. (*He repeats the question to her.*) *Dinah:* I'd like the child to resemble he. (*Why is that?*) When it resemble he, no fear. *Dinah's keeper:* So I can' doubt. *Dinah:* Fitz take me colour and resemble the father, and Millie take the father colour and resemble me. But I rather the child resemble the father, because you can' doubt. *Dinah's keeper:* I can doubt, but you would know you is the mother. Well, (*smiling*) that good, yes.

*   *   *

(*How would you know when the baby is yours or not?*) It's a hell of a thing (*laughing*), I really can' know. (*How would anybody know when the baby is their own?*) Well, the child should have some mark belongin' to the father. (*What kind of mark?*) You see I has a mole, my mother have that mole and I have it and my child have it.

Calypsonians have often dramatized the man's surprise at discovering that a child is not his own. Most of Trinidad's calypsonians are Negro men, and they have used the racially cosmopolitan composition of the island to comment on a woman's infidelity, and a man's need to be wary.[9] The child may turn out to have physical characteristics markedly different from the supposed father.

Once the woman does become pregnant, she usually hopes to be "put in a house," to live with the child's father, and to have him support her and the child. Those who know the couple may urge the boy to do this, but there is no strong social pressure in this direction, and the man who does not "put the girl in a house" will not be subjected to any severe sanctions. He will, however, be expected to contribute to the support of his child, insofar as he is able, provided that he "owns" the child. But if he "disowns" the child, and claims that he is not the father, the girl cannot bring any concerted social pressure to bear upon him:

(*If a man is friendin', and that girl has a baby, what is he supposed to do?*) That is belongin' to the man and the man have a right to min' the child. (*If that happened here, what would the people do?*) Well, it depends, they would give him advice to min' his child, not to allow his child to suffer. (*Would they expect him to live with the girl?*) They really can' expect that, that is to you, if is your mind to live with she; even if somebody give you advice and say is a good lady and it isn' your mind you en going to live with she.

* * *

If she get a baby and you is a right-thinkin' person and you is certain is your baby, you would put she in a house, the people in the village would tell you to put she in a house; it's a shame, look, she havin' children for you and you en puttin' them in a house, how you could do that to the girl? (*How would they tell you this?*) Well, in everyday talk, some people would get together and talk about this and say, I mus' give him some advice, and then when they meet you they would tell you. Sometimes, maybe you would wait until she have two children before you do it. (*And if you don't want to mind the child?*) Then you don' mind it, you disown the child. (*What would happen if you did that?*) Nothing happens. (*Would the people do anything to the fella?*) No, nothing. (*What if the boy says is his child and he won' mind it?*) He wouldn' do that, he would disown the child. (*Why?*) Well, if he say is his child then she can get maintenance (through the courts), but if he disown it maybe she can' prove is his child.

Social pressure would not usually be effective to get the father to support the child when he does not want to do so. The woman may try legal pressure, and bring the putative father to court, but this is not commonly done, and most women reject such a course of action:

(*What do most people think about a father, generally?*) Well, I don' know about somewhere else, but in West Indian culture (*sic*), a man he see a girl and love her,

as best he can, and when she in a family way he say,
I en mindin' the child, and he keep far. If the girl try
to make a row, well, he still en mindin' the child, and
the mother, well the mother is afraid of the courthouse.

*   *   *

(*When you friendin' and have a child, what would
happen then?*) *Mistress Dennis:* Well, this courthouse
business right away. *Mr. Dennis:* Some people put the
father in court for maintenance. *Mistress Dennis:*
That's a rotten thing. *Mr. Dennis:* That's a rotten thing.
Mistress Dennis: Is you both child, and both you mind
the child, and if you don' want to I mind it myself;
courthouse was never in that and it have no reason
for that, it cause father to hate the child.

Once a man feels certain that a child is his, he will own
it, and at least initially contribute to its support. He does so
regardless of whether he is in another marital relationship,
and we must recognize his economic, symbolic, and perhaps
social (for he may continue the *friending* relationship) significance for the mother and child. *Friending* may, at this
point, approximate marriage based upon dual residence,
and it may also be the jumping-off point for a *living* relationship. For all of these reasons we cannot ignore the
importance of *friending* for a full understanding of the
husband-wife relationship, and we must recognize that
friending itself may become, in effect, a marital relationship
marked by mutual sexual, economic, and social responsibilities.

LIVING

Most *friending* relationships are, sooner or later, broken off.
A substantial number, however, develop into a *living* relationship. Information collected on about six hundred *friending* relationships in 1962 shows that 12 per cent were current, 56 per cent had been broken off, and 27 per cent had
been transformed into *living* relationships (4 per cent were

transformed into marriage, and one per cent were ended by death). The amount of time that most couples spend *friending* before *living* together ranges from several days to several years:

> (*Do some people live right away, before friendin'?*)
> Always friendin' before livin' takin' place. (*For how
> long friendin' before livin'?*) Three-four months, up to
> a year, two years.

*   *   *

> (*Are most people friendly first and then livin'?*) Yes.
> (*Would any start to live first without friendin'?*) No,
> that can' work, in any case if you don' know each
> other, you can' do it. (*About how long would most
> people be friendin' before livin'?*) Some person take
> it quickly in just a few months, some person in per-
> haps a year or so.

Living refers to the fact that the man and woman live together under one roof. Although a common and widespread feeling of impermanence is expressed about the *living* rela-tionship—"People don' *live* forever, they *live* and they part" —it may nevertheless be of long duration, and terminate only at the death of one of the partners. It is a socially recog-nized, and to an extent positively evaluated, relationship. And it is widespread, being more common in the lower class than marriage and usually preceding marriage where mar-riage does take place.

There is no formal announcement or ceremony to mark a couple's shift from *friending* to *living,* although the man's efforts to obtain a house in the village, and his casual con-versation, will make the event generally known beforehand. Some, however, find out when they "wake today and find them together."

> (*When people decide to be livin', not to marry, do they
> have any fête?*) No. Eh-eh, no fête. (*Why is that?*)
> That en make no use, they jus' livin' together. (*Do you
> ever find a fête for that?*) No. (*If they had a fête, what*

would the people say?) Truth is, I never know nobody
give fête for that, only for wedding, christening.

Within a *living* relationship the woman is expected to
carry out the household chores of cleaning, washing, and
cooking, while the man is expected to contribute enough
money to keep the household going. This reciprocity is basic
to the *living* relationship, and any deviation from it endan-
gers the stability of the relationship. If the man cannot, or
does not, contribute enough money to run the household,
the woman may leave him for someone who will, or she may
seek work to help with the household expenses, or to get
extra money for herself that she cannot save from the
household money. A temporary job of a few weeks' time
would not have much impact upon the relationship, but a
permanent job would. For the woman would then be financially independent of her husband, even though a major
consideration in deciding to live with him initially was his
ability to support her. Indeed, a woman would not agree to
being "put in a house" and to living with a man, even if she
had a child by him, unless she felt that he could adequately
support the household. Added to this is the fact that the
woman who works is unable or unwilling to do the household chores thoroughly. In all of these ways, where the basic
reciprocity of the *living* relationship breaks down, the relationship is threatened and a separation is likely.

The following examples illustrate the role of the woman
in the *living* relationship:

> (*What does a fella expect from a girl he is livin' with?*)
> He expectin' the girl to do everything that is good.
> (*What kind of things?*) She have to provide his meals,
> his clothes washin', keep the house clean, and all kinds
> of things, take care of the man and be good to he and
> he be good to she.

> * * *

> (*For what reasons does a man live with a girl?*) From
> my opinion, most of the little domestic work at home,
> sew and feed, and the laundry is far, and she do all

this at home; instead of buying a lunch have someone at home to occupy that for you. In case sickness in the night, you take in sudden, she's a help to you.

* * *

(*For what reasons does a man take a wife?*) Only a companion. I don' know if you read the Bible, about how God made Adam and then Eve as a companion. (*What would the companion do?*) To keep your clothes clean, cook your food and meals, keep the house clean, all the little tidying and so forths, keep the children clean. You working far, come and meet the meals done, wouldn' have to do any cooking at all.

The role of the man as the financial supporter of the household can be gathered from the following examples:

The husband have to do all the workin' and supportin' to the home. That is why women usually take a husband, to work and mind them. Because they haven' got the instinc' as men do to the labouring side and gain a living.

* * *

(*Why is he vex with you?*) He does say something to the lady about me, something rude, and I tell him a word, not a insult, and he vex. (*What was it he said?*) The lady buy a fish and come with it and he say, "Don' spend all the money from the parlour (which she owns) on the fish or the parlour go bus' "; and she say, "I don' have to spend from the parlour, my husband works"; and he say, "Who you callin' a husband, that *brocko* man." Then I come and said, "Don' mind if I is *brocko* or no, as long as I en have to t'ief to gi' her." And he vex and say I tell everyone he t'ief. But I en say that, I said as long as *I* en have to t'ief to gi' her.

Interestingly enough, sexual privileges are not mentioned by the informants in response to a question on why they decided to live together. This is easily understandable when we remember that there is no strong taboo on premarital sexual activity, and that the *friending* relationship, which

includes sexual intercourse, usually precedes the *living* relationship. Though premarital sexual taboos are not strong,
they do exist, and a person who is extremely "wild" is talked
about. For instance, a single girl with a child is not seriously
hampered in entering into a marital relationship, but if she
is known to be free with her sexual favors, she would have
difficulty in establishing a permanent relationship.

The ideal is for sexual relationships to be confined to the
friending, living, or married relationship, but in actual fact,
particularly for the man, this is not the case. He would often
"behave as if he was livin' bachelor," and maintain a *friending* relationship with another woman:

> (*Why are some people friendin'?*) Some women like
> it that way; that is a Trinidad custom. Some men the
> same way, too. (*Why is that?*) A man like the irre-
> sponsibility, or a man may have his wife and he still
> friendin' with a girl outside.

* * *

> *Robert:* The wise man, he want a wife for a servant, a
> helper, every wife is a helper to her man. But that en
> mean co-habitation, is plenty of women for that, you
> can have the wife in Port of Spain and you take a taxi
> and is plenty of women. *Lloyd:* Yes, man, plenty.
> Sometime you can go one month, two month, and not
> co-habiting with wife; I know from experience, is come
> home and rest when with the wife.

I asked Dom and Septie how many of those *living* and
married were faithful:

> *Dom:* The old ones, those that are married, are faith-
> ful; but which young ones are married? *Septie:* Janey;
> Janey and Lloyd McCloud. *Dom:* Well, besides those,
> the rest is livin', and I would say hardly any does be
> faithful, they does go all about. Like myself, I feel that
> I can talk to this girl and then if I want I can talk to a
> nex' one, but those that are livin' they feel just the
> same as me, they feel as if they is single fellas, and
> can go and talk to anyone jus' as they please.

The woman in a *living* relationship, however, would not have as much freedom as the man, and would not often maintain a *friending* relationship outside of the *living* relationship. If she did, she would do so secretly, and risk breaking up the *living* relationship if the man found out about it:

> (*Would the man rely on the wife for sexual satisfaction?*) Don' rely on her at all; as soon as it's holiday time, well, have old friend, I'll be glad to see her for a day or so. Or if woman I livin' with go to spend a day away with her family, can use the house for dating somebody else. (*And how about the woman?*) Not to my knowledge, those who I know are more hold on to them. In most cases the man. (*For a man, would the people criticize that, say it was wrong, or not?*) They don' find anything so bad on his part as if it's a woman, when it's a woman, more shame. These fellas feel is not a shame, but a feather in their cap.

> *After the informant explained a list of slang terms, I asked him for other terms. He offered "sweet man," which he explained thus:*

> When she is married and husband is at work, he (sweet man) take over. (*Where would they meet?*) At his house or at her home. (*Would the husband know what was going on?*) He wouldn' know, if he find out they probably separate.

> * * *

> (*How come you part with she?*) Row again, some dispute, I get annoyed with she and left she, she en know where I gone. (*What kind of row?*) Some misunderstandin'. (*What do you mean, a misunderstandin'?*) Something happen would cause you or I to vex. (*She was seeing someone else?*) Yes, so I lef' she and go away and she en know where I go.

The "double standard" for extramarital sexual relations was nicely summed up by one informant who said that what was "fame for the man" was "shame for the woman." A palindrome that was used to express the same sentiment had it that: "When women are wild you call them *rats;* when a man is wild you call him a *star.*" The actual behavioral difference between men and women in this respect is not so marked, for the woman can leave the man if she is financially able to do so, perhaps by forming a new marital alliance, and in this way she can exert pressure upon her husband to confine his sexual activities to the marital relationship. Ordinarily, she is less concerned about his extramarital sexual activities than about the amount of money this might be costing. In addition, she herself could secretly "horn" [10] the man in an extramarital *friending* relationship, thereby getting some extra money for her own use.

A woman's infidelity is a very common subject of Trinidadian calypsos. Part of the reason for this may be that the calypsonians are practically all men, and therefore more concerned about a woman's infidelity than a man's. Another reason is the double sexual standard according to which women's extramarital relationships are not culturally sanctioned to the extent that the men's are. Nevertheless, there are pressures which do lead to a considerable amount of extramarital relationships by women. The double sexual standard can best be maintained where the significant group of women are revered while some other group of women are sexually available to the men. This was the case for the whites in the southern United States, especially during the days of slavery, where the Negro women were accessible and the white women revered by the men.[11] Lower-class Negro men in Trinidad, however, do not have easy sexual access to any group of women other than lower-class Negro women. The small group of prostitutes and the promiscuous women who might jokingly be referred to as "susu" or as "wahbeen" do absorb some of the premarital and extramarital sexual activity of the male. But to a considerable degree the other women also engage in extramarital relationships, and the calypsos which deal with a woman's infidelity reflect the gap between what is ideally expected of the woman and what is actually the case.

A man and woman in a *living* relationship may have some

common goals, but they also maintain a considerable degree of separateness. For example, in some cases they save their money jointly, and perhaps look forward to buying or building a house of their own. But in most cases, insofar as they can save any money, they do it separately. This behavior highlights their separate interests. Each may want money for his own parents, for *outside children,* or for himself, and would therefore keep the money apart from that spent on the household—the man by not giving all of the money to his wife in the first place, and the woman by putting aside household money for her own use.

There is no denying that a married relationship is said to confer greater prestige than a *living* relationship. Lower-class people say that it is the right way of doing things, that you "have more respec'" that way, and that, indeed, they themselves "are planning" to get married. In fact, however, there is little discernible difference in the village between the way those who are *living* and those who are married are treated. Villagers assume that middle-class visitors draw a distinction, and it is this distinction that they occasionally projected for me. In querying individuals on the "greater respect" involved in a marriage, I was told that this would be shown by a teacher or priest. In one case I was told that a physician inviting people to a party at his house would not invite individuals who were *living.* In another case I was told that marriage was more respectable "for society." When I asked what that meant I was informed that "in the Bar Society every man that enters must have a wife." These perceptions, or misperceptions, about middle-class professionals are far removed from the everyday life of the poor and are abstract and occasionally farfetched. In short, differences in treatment were always said to emanate from outsiders and not from members of the lower-class community.

Before my first field trip to Trinidad I had read that the popular term for the *living* relationship was "living in sin." I therefore expected to hear the term, and I listened carefully for it, but it was never used. *Living* was the popular term. I became impatient, and asked people whether they used any other terms. They were polite, and tried to oblige, and told me that they might say "jus' livin' " or "livin' as man and wife." But they still did not use "living in sin." I finally asked them outright about the term:

> (*"Livin' in sin," did you ever hear that expression?*) Used to be, a long time ago. It depends on the denominations. A Catholic would frown on that. But is now old-fashioned, not now considered as sinfulness. (*Who would use that expression?*) Only religious people, people who have a religion, young people would laugh at you. I know for one that is nonsense; some who are livin' live better than those married.

* * *

> (*Did you ever hear the expression "livin' in sin"?*) Yes, I heard it. (*Who would say that?*) Everybody, like if she take communion now (indicating unmarried daughter who had a child), will be a gossip. *Daughter:* Mostly the people who go around, the Jehovah, the Baptists, some people comin' down on a crusade. (*Would you yourself say that?*) No, 'cause sometimes you yourself will have to take it like that. Sometimes you jus' can' say things about other people, and you might get the same.

Individuals identify the Roman Catholic Church, or other religious organizations, as the source of the term "living in sin," but they do not use the term in everyday conversation.[12] How is it that Dom Basil Matthews reported that it was the term popularly used?[13] This report was evidently based upon his work as a priest in the Benedictine Abbey of Mount St. Benedict in Trinidad, where many people undoubtedly said to him, "Father, I am living in sin." Religious functionaries may not know what is appropriate in lower-class company, but lower-class people certainly know what is appropriate in a religious setting!

While I was in the house of one couple, a woman came to the door with a Bible in her hand, explained that she was a Bible Student, and asked if she could speak to them. They agreed, and she, in effect, delivered a memorized, five-minute sermon. The following was taken down verbatim:

If you love a woman, you must marry her. If she's good enough to live with, she's good enough to marry, because if you leave her it's only to take another woman and you're committing fornication, and the same thing for a woman.

The Bible Student then left some pamphlets for the couple and departed. When she did, the couple breathed an audible and visible sigh of relief. She made a complete tour of all the houses in the village, repeating her sermon to all couples who were *living*. Such religious visitors come by several times a year with their solemn message for fornicators. They are almost always politely tolerated in the village, and they sometimes get encouraging verbal agreement with their preachings. In truth, however, the villagers agree with them very little. One of my informants took pleasure in engaging such visitors in gentle debate and argument. But he did not tell them to their face that he considered them to be insincere hypocrites, and he had a fund of stories about ill-mannered religious functionaries.

"Better a good livin' than a bad marriage" is a very common saying throughout Trinidad. It is an expression that is also much used throughout the French, Spanish, and Dutch islands of the West Indies, as well as the British or English-speaking areas. It indicates that *living* is an extremely important type of marital relationship. We shall have more to say later about the reasons for its importance.

MARRIED

The married relationship differs little from the *living* relationship, and simply refers to the fact that a church marriage has been performed and that the union is a legal one. Of course, two people could be married and yet not living together, but when they are living together, almost all that has been said of the *living* relationship holds true for marriage. The major exception would be among those families that are moving out of the lower class and striving to maintain middle-class standards of behavior.

The median age of entry into marriage is considerably

higher than the median age for entering a *friending* or *living* relationship. We saw earlier, in Table 6, that *living* (common law) predominated in the younger age groups, while marriage predominated at older ages. The age distribution for all marriages recorded in 1966 in St. Andrew—one of the Eastern counties—is shown in Table 7. The median age category for bridegrooms is 25 to 29, and for brides it is 20 to 24. This compares to a median age for entering the first relationship (usually *friending*, occasionally *living*) of 15 to 19 for both men and women.[14]

Table 7
MARRIAGES BY AGE OF BRIDE AND BRIDEGROOM:
ST. ANDREW, 1966

AGE GROUP	BRIDEGROOM	BRIDE
Total	234	234
Under 15	—	—
15–19	10	73
20–24	67	62
25–29	54	24
30–34	24	16
35–39	17	13
40–44	8	13
45–49	13	8
50–54	13	11
55–59	8	5
60–64	14	4
65 plus	3	2
Not Stated	3	3

Source: Prepared by the Central Statistical Office, Trinidad and Tobago, 1968.

Women are more interested in getting married than men. As one informant put it, "When the man waver, the woman wouldn't. They call it 75–25—75 per cent of the woman is for it, but only 25 per cent of the man is for it." The reasons given by women for wanting to marry are the honor and respect that it brings, and its legal advantages. On questioning, however, the first reason turns out to have relatively little importance within the lower class.

Women refer to two major symbols of respect within marriage—the wedding ring and being addressed as Mistress (Name) rather than Miss (Name). The similarities between marriage and *living* are more prominent than the differences, and the differences that do exist are minimized within the village. For instance, whether married or *living,* husband and wife are used as terms of reference for the spouses, so that it was necessary, when I wanted to be certain, to ask, "a married husband?" or "a married wife?" Moreover, although a woman might be addressed as Mistress when she was married, she often continued to be addressed as Miss:

> It don' have Mistress in Trinidad. Trinidad is reckless place, everybody is Miss, Miss, Miss, it don' have many call you Mistress. You livin' and call she wife; you have to be married to own a wife in my country (Grenada).

*   *   *

Speaking heatedly, one informant told me: "Marriage is only a bilateral contrac'. . . . Two people under one roof are husband and wife."

Another informant told me that when you were not married you were Miss and when married you were Mistress, yet she used Miss Jerome several times in the conversation, knowing that Miss Jerome was married. I also asked her, "How come they use Miss Essie?" She replied, "They uses to call she Miss Essie before she married, and they accustom with that, and still call her that."

There is more substance to the legal advantages gained by a woman in marriage. With marriage she is entitled to financial support from her husband. In a *living* relationship, which has no legal status, only the man's children are entitled to such support. Typically, however, the man's poverty and the woman's reluctance to bring a paternity suit, mean that even this legal advantage of marriage is limited. The advantage of marriage for the purpose of inheritance is potentially more important. A woman who is *living* is not legally entitled to inherit. A house or a small piece of land—perhaps valued at no more than a few hundred dollars—represents a sizable property for a villager. Though a woman has been living harmoniously with a man for many years, it is legally possible for someone else to lay claim to the inheritance. Although this is frowned upon, the villagers recognize that it is possible, and women are concerned about safeguarding their rights through a legal marriage.

Men, on the other hand, are reluctant to marry. Some of the reasons they list are the inability to give an appropriate marriage fête due to poverty; the wish to test the woman before marrying her; and the fact that *living* is customary. But the major reason which comes up again and again is the legal bonds and responsibilities that marriage represents— if the woman secures such legal advantages, they fear that she will behave differently.

> (*Some persons here live together and are not married, why do you suppose that is so?*) You know, you are very technical (laughing). You got it in various ways. Finance in mos' cases. Understandin' in mos' cases. Some of them has not common good as far as marriage is concerned. Some feel woman is up to standard to live with, but not up to standard to marry. It make a man bound to a woman, she may fall back when you marry. Man believe in a good livin' and a bad marriage. Life is so peaceful if for ten years we livin', and then I can marry to she and from the time she get married she start to fall back. Better a good life in livin' than a bad life in marriage. But also, some live better when they are married.

*   *   *

> (*Why do you find people livin' and not married?*) I really can' say, na. The man jus' figure to live a life like that is easier, because a marriage life is not easy to break, the law intervenes, and suppose to pay maintenance fee, but if not married, jus' singles, only have to mind child.

*   *   *

> (*What advantages are there if you livin' instead of married?*) Sometimes a man don' have the confidence

in them, sometimes you with them good and thing, and marry them and they change, and do all kind of thing. The majority they want to live rather than marry, because the woman when they marry, they change. Well, like me, I can marry she, but you don' know if she gonna be faithful. But a man want to take them to cook and so on, but when it comes to puttin' a ring on the finger (*tone indicating reluctance*). . . .

*   *   *

(*What are the advantages of livin', not married?*) A man does be afraid to get married, and if anything happen, you have to be by yourself and you have to maintain the wife. But if you never marry, wouldn' have to maintain wife, only children. Well, I, of myself, I don' see why a man should really marry, na. I 'fraid that, it does bite, yes. You leave she and have to pay she and you en gettin' the uses of she, somebody else gettin' them, and you still pay.

The following apocryphal story, as told to me by one informant, gives a beautiful illustration of the concern about a woman changing once you marry her:

This friend of mine in Cumuto had eight children with a woman, and he was livin' with her for nineteen years, and it happened that one Sunday afternoon they were taking a little rest in bed and she began to talk about their children and what would happen to them when he died, and how he ought to get married with her to make sure that they would all be well cared for when he died. Well, he thought about it for the week, and decided that his wife was right; she spoke very well, almost as if she had been coached in what to say. And he never even gave a thought to how she might change, after all these years of being together, and being so old at that time.

So he decided to marry her, and everyone was glad because that meant a big fête, and they came and drank and danced, and then he went away with her for a little honeymoon on the next day, Sunday, and on Monday he had to go to work. Well, he woke up at five o'clock, and usually the wife was up and getting his breakfast ready, but this day she was there sleeping beside him. Well, he figured that she was tired out after the marriage and the fête and the honeymoon, so he let her be and got his own breakfast. When he came home from work in the evening his wife would have his supper for him, and his slippers ready, and this evening she hadn't done anything. Well, he figured perhaps she was still a little tired and he didn't say anything—he thought he would let her take things easy for that day, and that from the next day things would return to normal.

Well, he woke up the next morning, and there was his wife, still sleeping beside him, not making a move to get breakfast. Well, he had enough, so he nudged her to wake her, but she continued sleeping; so he nudged her harder, but she still remained asleep, and he nudged her harder still and told her, "It's time to get breakfast for me." Well, all she did was turn over on the other side and start singing, "Now My Daily Task Is Done." Well, he went off to work, and came back in the evening, very calmly, and started to pack his bags, and she came over to him and asked him what he was doing. But he didn't say a thing to her, he just marched out of the house singing, "Onward Christian Soldiers."

In another version of the story that I have heard, the final hymn sung by the man as he left was, "God Be With Thee Till We Meet Again."

Lower-class people, faced by the conditions of poverty, therefore seem to be more attuned to legal advantages and disadvantages of marriage than to moral considerations. Marriage is an ideal, but as a practical matter *living* has also become a normative relationship. The greater respect that marriage is said to bestow is clearly seen by villagers as stemming from middle-class outsiders. Within the village both marriage and *living* are normative relationships that are fully accepted.

An example neatly illustrates the distinction made between outsiders and villagers. I addressed a married woman who had recently moved into the village as Mistress King, and this was overheard by a man. He knew us both, and jokingly commented, "Oho! So you is *Mistress* King! I didn't know that was Mistress King!" She held up her hand and showed her ring, saying, "Yes, yes, and here's the proof right here!" My interpretation of this byplay, later confirmed by an informant, was that I had introduced a formal term into the conversation. It was the correct term for me to use, particularly since I had not previously met the woman, but among villagers it was an alien term and the occasion for joking remarks.

GENERAL COMMENTS

The inquiry we have made into husband-wife relationships reveals a reluctance to accept responsibility, especially on the part of the man. *Friending*, which involves the least responsibility, occurs most frequently. Legal marriage, which involves the most responsibility, occurs least frequently.[15] The *living* relationship, in a sense, combines the advantages of the common residence of marriage and the limited responsibility of *friending*, and is therefore of extreme importance in the village.

The reluctance to accept responsibility, which is reflected by the marital patterns I have discussed, is closely related to the general attitude of both sexes that trust and confidence cannot be placed in a spouse. They also share a feeling that any marital relationship is a temporary one, and are always ready to replace an unsuitable spouse. The following examples, in addition to examples given previously, illustrate these points:

> The mind of the girl is so funny and contrary that you can' make it out. The way they move and talk you cannot base confidence in them. The woman turn as the sea change; some of them, not all, but you jus' can' know which one.

> * * *

> (*If a couple en married, would each one save separately, or would they save their money together?*) For

self, 'cause you live with expectation any time he can
leave and marry another woman, same as you can
marry another man.

I was asking an informant the same series of questions
about each of the five women he had lived with. One question was on the reasons for separation. I was still asking the
same questions after he had told me about the first two
women, and he apparently felt that I was slow in getting
his message. When I asked him about the third woman he
changed his tone of voice in order to see whether he could
finally explain matters to me: "Look, na. A woman today,
jus' as a bus. Oh, the bus gone, man! Well, don' get frighten,
you catch the nex' one!"

This casual attitude between the sexes, which is held more
particularly by the man toward the woman, is closely bound
to the whole complex of husband-wife relationships as they
have been discussed in this chapter. Separations frequently
occur, and such an attitude cushions the effect of a separation. In the 1962 survey, the median number of *friending,
living,* and married relationships reported by men were, re-
spectively, 5.2, 1.0, and 0.5. For women these figures were
1.9, 0.8, and 0.3. Since few of the men or women had completed their marital life, these figures are low. Men aged 50
and over had medians of 6.0, 2.8, and 1.0; women 50 and
over had medians of 2.5, 2.5, and 0.5. These figures are
evidence of the formation and breaking of many relationships throughout a person's marital career. Such behavior
can aptly be called "marital-shifting." [16] Individuals may
shift from one relationship to another with the same partner,
or they may shift from one partner to another.

The basic patterns of lower-class marital relationships in
Coconut Village have been presented in this chapter. The
published material by such investigators as Lloyd Braithwaite, Raymond T. Smith, and Michael M. Horowitz contain
additional data that suggest a great deal of similarity in the
marital and kinship relationships to be found in the Caribbean area.[17] There are also data on non-Caribbean lower-
class patterns that are remarkably similar to those described

here. An important question that we will begin to explore in the final chapters is whether lower-class conditions, no matter where they may be found, tend to have similar consequences for lower-class family organization. Or, if lower-class conditions do not *always* have similar consequences, in what types of societies *do* they have similar consequences for family organization.

NOTES

1. George Peter Murdock, *Social Structure* (New York: Macmillan, 1949), pp. 4–8. Cf. E. Kathleen Gough, "The Nayars and the Definition of Marriage," *Journal of the Royal Anthropological Institute* 89 (1959): 23–34; E. R. Leach, "Polyandry, Inheritance, and the Definition of Marriage," *Man* 55 (December 1955): 182–86; E. Kathleen Gough, review of Peter of Greece and Denmark, *A Study of Polyandry* (New York: Humanities Press, 1963), in *Man*, 65 (1965): 30–31.

2. Edward Westermarck, *The History of Human Marriage*, 5th ed. (New York: Allerton Book Co., 1922), pp. 1, 26; Hyman Rodman, "Fidelity and Forms of Marriage: The Consensual Union in the Caribbean," in Gerhard Neubeck (ed.), *Extramarital Relations* (Englewood Cliffs, N.J.: Prentice-Hall, 1969), pp. 94–107.

3. For examples, see Laura Bohannan, "Dahomean Marriage: A Revaluation," *Africa* 19 (October 1949): 273–87; Meyer Fortes, "Analysis and Description in Social Anthropology," in British Association for the Advancement of Science, *Advancement of Science* 10 (September 1953): 190–201; Hyman Rodman, *op. cit.*; Jean La Fontaine, "Gisu Marriage and Affinal Relations," in Meyer Fortes (ed.), *Marriage in Tribal Societies* (Cambridge, Eng.: Cambridge University Press, 1962), pp. 113–19; Alan Howard and Irwin Howard, "Pre-Marital Sex and Social Control among the Rotumans," *American Anthropologist* 66, (April 1964): 266–83.

4. Hyman Rodman, "Marital Relationships in a Trinidad Village," *Marriage and Family Living* 23 (May 1961): 166–70.

5. The term "Visiting" is used in the 1960 census. Although it is equivalent to *friending*, such a relationship was only inferred for women who were in no other relationship and had had a child in the previous twelve months. This leads to such a serious underestimation of the number of women in a *friending* relationship that it is not worth reporting the figures here.

6. Information was collected on 603 *friending* relationships during an interview survey of 176 lower-class men and women in northern Trinidad. This survey included 47 respondents from Coconut Village, and will be reported in a separate publication. The few

references I make to 1962 data were obtained in this survey, and are occasionally used to provide additional documentation for this study, which is primarily based upon participant observation. Of the 603 *friending* relationships for which I have information, 534 had ended at the time of the survey.

7. Murdock (*op. cit.*) first distinguished only five alternative types of residence, and felt that a marital relationship required a common residence. Later, he changed his position in the light of additional data ("World Ethnographic Sample," *American Anthropologist* 59 [August 1957]: 664–87), and distinguished several other types of marital residence—among them duolocal (dual) residence, in which no common residence is established by the spouses (p. 670). He classified four societies in his new sample as having this type of residence pattern.

8. See also Chapter 8.

9. See calypsos in Appendix 1, pp. 219–21.

10. According to the *Oxford English Dictionary,* "horn" was used in England from the fifteenth to the nineteenth centuries and meant "to cuckold." This usage is now listed as obsolete; however, it has survived in Trinidad.

11. Kenneth Stampp, *The Peculiar Institution* (New York: Alfred A. Knopf, 1956), pp. 350–61.

12. The term is occasionally used in calypsos, but in a way that shows it is not the usual term.

13. Dom Basil Matthews, *Crisis of the West Indian Family* (Trinidad: Extra-Mural Department, University College of the West Indies, 1952), pp. 2, 6–7.

14. Based on my 1962 survey of 176 lower-class respondents. Cf. G. W. Roberts and Lloyd Braithwaite, "Fertility Differentials by Family Type in Trinidad," pp. 102–19, and "A Gross Mating Table for a West Indian Population," pp. 128–47, in *Trinidad and Tobago Research Papers* (Port of Spain, Trinidad: Central Statistical Office, December 1967); J. Mayone Stycos and Kurt W. Back, *The Control of Human Fertility in Jamaica* (Ithaca: Cornell University Press, 1964), pp. 125–26.

15. For comparable Jamaican data on the three types of marital unions, see J. Mayone Stycos and Kurt W. Back, *op. cit.*, pp. 125–44.

16. This usage is similar to Sorokin's use of interfamily shifting. See Pitirim A. Sorokin, *Social and Cultural Mobility* (New York: Free Press, 1959), pp. 397–99.

17. Lloyd Braithwaite, "Social Stratification in Trinidad," *Social and Economic Studies* 2 (October 1953): 5–175; Raymond T. Smith, *The Negro Family in British Guiana* (London: Routledge & Kegan Paul, 1956); Michael M. Horowitz, *Morne-Paysan: A Peasant Village in Martinique* (New York: Holt, Rinehart and Winston, 1967). For other comparative material on the Caribbean, see George

74 FAMILY RELATIONSHIPS IN COCONUT VILLAGE

E. Simpson, "Sexual and Familial Institutions in Northern Haiti," *American Anthropologist* 44 (October–December 1942): 655–74; T. S. Simey, *Welfare and Planning in the West Indies* (London: Oxford University Press, 1946); Melville J. Herskovits and Frances S. Herskovits, *Trinidad Village* (New York: Alfred A. Knopf, 1947); Dom Basil Matthews, *op. cit.;* Fernando Henriques, *Family and Colour in Jamaica* (London: Eyre & Spottiswoode, 1953); J. Mayone Stycos, *Family and Fertility in Puerto Rico* (New York: Columbia University Press, 1955); Yehudi A. Cohen, "Structure and Function: Family Organization and Socialization in a Jamaican Community," *American Anthropologist* 58 (August 1956): 664–86; Julian H. Steward et al. (eds.), *The People of Puerto Rico* (Urbana: University of Illinois Press, 1956); Edith Clarke, *My Mother Who Fathered Me* (London: George Allen and Unwin, 1957); Raymond T. Smith, "The Family in the Caribbean," in Vera Rubin (ed.), *Caribbean Studies: A Symposium* (Seattle: University of Washington Press, 1957); Suzanne Comhaire-Sylvain, "Courtship, Marriage and *Plasaj* at Kenscoff, Haiti," *Social and Economic Studies* 7 (December 1958): 210–33; Mariam J. Kreiselman, "The Caribbean Family: A Case Study in Martinique" (Ph.D. dissertation, Columbia University, 1958); David Landy, *Tropical Childhood* (Chapel Hill: University of North Carolina Press, 1959); Celia S. Rosenthal, "Lower Class Family Organization on the Caribbean Coast of Colombia," *Pacific Sociological Review* 3 (Spring 1960): 12–17; Judith Blake, *Family Structure in Jamaica* (New York: Free Press, 1961); Morris Freilich, "Serial Polygyny, Negro Peasants, and Model Analysis," *American Anthropologist* 63 (October 1961): 955–75; M. G. Smith, *West Indian Family Structure* (Seattle: University of Washington Press, 1962); M. G. Smith, *Kinship and Community in Carriacou* (New Haven: Yale University Press, 1962); Raymond T. Smith, "Culture and Social Structure in the Caribbean: Some Recent Work on Family and Kinship Studies," *Comparative Studies in Society and History* 6 (October 1963): 24–46; Helen Icken Safa, "From Shantytown to Public Housing: A Comparison of Family Structure in Two Urban Neighborhoods in Puerto Rico," *Caribbean Studies* 4 (1964): 3–12; J. Mayone Stycos and Kurt W. Back, *The Control of Human Fertility in Jamaica* (Ithaca: Cornell University Press, 1964); Oscar Lewis, *La Vida* (New York: Random House, 1965); Keith F. Otterbein, "Caribbean Family Organization: A Comparative Analysis," *American Anthropologist* 67 (February 1965): 66–79; Sidney M. Greenfield, *English Rustics in Black Skin* (New Haven, Conn.: College & University Press, 1966); Keith F. Otterbein, *The Andros Islanders* (Lawrence: University of Kansas Press, 1966).

5.   *The Parent-Child Relationship*

You don' give your parents if you don' get.
COCONUT VILLAGER

IT IS a biological fact that a mother is always certain a child is hers while a father is never absolutely certain. Of course, if a man becomes a father through a social rather than a biological act, as in the case of adoption or artificial insemination, there need be no problem of identifying the biological father. But since biological and social paternity ordinarily coincide, or at least are expected to coincide, the element of doubt about the biological father may become important. Perhaps the double sexual standard, by putting more emphasis upon a woman's fidelity, is a common way of minimizing the father's doubt. Another common solution is that of repressing whatever doubt exists, and this may be buttressed by a patronymic tradition and by identifying the child's resemblances to the parents, so that, at the very least, the child is said to have the father's eyes or mouth or nose or sheepish look.

FATHER'S ROLE

In Trinidad, as in most contemporary societies, the biological tie is of crucial importance in establishing parenthood. However, unlike many societies, there is ordinarily a greater element of doubt about the identity of the biological father. Since the obligations of the father are onerous for a lower-class man, he is cautious about assuming the father's role.

The role of the father who acknowledges his child is to *mind* the child. This is the essence of the father's responsibility, and he will be praised or blamed according to how well he discharges this duty. Put simply, to *mind* means to

75

provide the money needed to bring up the child—money for food, clothing, school, etc. The following statements provide evidence of the extreme importance attached to this aspect of the father's role:

> (*What is expected of a father?*) Most essential fact is as far as finance is concerned, for clothing, and see is well fed, hardly he'd bathe the child or put on the clothes. He is what is called the breadwinner. The mother would rather you bring the money and she do the shopping, she would go to maybe twenty stores and find something jus' as good, maybe even better, and get it cheaper.

*   *   *

> (*What is the father expected to do?*) The father will be expected to working, to bring in money to upkeep the house and the children and thing.

This duty of *minding* the children falls upon the father regardless of where he is living or what marital relationship he is in. An *outside child* counts as much as a child born within a *living* or married relationship and is ideally expected to receive the same amount of support. In actual fact, however, where the father is living away from the mother and child, he usually provides financial assistance in a very irregular fashion, and contributes only a portion of what is needed to support the child:

> (*How often do you see your two outside children?*) I doesn' see them regular, they far from me. (*Do you give anything to support them, or not?*) Yes. (*About how much do you give?*) Is accordin' as how I could make, not a regular amount.

*   *   *

> (*Do you hear from your husband?*) He does send maintenance for the children. (*How much does he send?*) He does send a certain amount of money. (*Does he send money regularly, or not regularly?*) At first regular, now every two months, three months, four months.

Listen, he haven' a regular job, and now sometime he
doesn' send, understand.

* * *

We have a little baby here, me grandchild, Andrew
Stewart. He have four months. Is Nella's child, and
the father is Mr. Thompson's son, Joseph Stewart.
(*Where does the father live?*) The father live at his
father, and Nella live here. And the baby is living here.
(*Who minds the baby?*) I mindin' it. (*Does the father
help?*) He en mindin' it, he stopped mindin' it. He
mind the child about three months, and just at once
he stop. Nella does go to him for a thing, but he en
give. (*How is it that he suddenly stopped mindin' the
child?*) I can' say. He en workin', he en have money.
She does go to him all the time, he say he en have
money. (*Does she still see him?*) They was talkin'
last night, they en vex, but he does take bad advice.
(*What kind of advice?*) His friends, they does say the
child en his. When you does like a girl you does make
a child, but some they en think about that then. Perhaps he studyin' someone else.

A man may also be *minding* children who are not his own
—his wife's children. For example, if the child's biological
father is not *minding* it, and if the child is living with its
mother and stepfather, the stepfather will, in effect, be
minding the child. This can be a touchy situation, however;
for if the man does not wish to *mind* the child, he may force
his wife to leave the child elsewhere. Moreover, when the
child does live with its stepfather, it may be the cause of difficulty between the husband and wife, and perhaps the cause
of their separation:

(*Were you married to her or livin'?*) Jus' livin'. (*How
did you happen to break up?*) Through a child, when
I took with her she had a child of four, and this girl
grew with me, I mind she. Later, she got in fault with
a boy. I spoke to her and said, don' let it happen a
second time or you'll have to get own place. When first
baby was a year and a half she got pregnant, and I

got annoyed and told her mother, "The father of the
first child never mind it, attend to it, and here she is
get another one, and if you don' get a place for her I
cannot stick it." She said she tried and tried and
couldn' get, and I didn' think she tried, and I got annoyed and when she went out one day I picked up bag
and baggage and went to my mother.

* * *

(*How long were you livin' with her?*) We live a year
and eight months and we part. (*Why did you part?*)
Jus' a little misunderstandin' between us, not anything,
jus' a slight. When I take up with she, she had a little
girl eight years, and when she come and have a child
with me, and one night we talkin' and the baby cry,
and her little girl said, "Boy, you bad," and I tell she,
"How you could say that, he en bad more than you,"
and that brings words, words. She say now I have my
own child I want ill-treat she own, and she leave and
tell me she en comin' again.

Since the obligations of a father may be difficult for the
lower-class man to fulfill, a complex of attitudes and activities has developed around establishing paternity. A man is
concerned about whether he is being *horned* by his wife (in
a *friending, living,* or married relationship). When a child
is born, he wants to be sure it is his own child. He therefore
pays attention to his wife's behavior and to the child's physical features. Since the man's esteem would be lowered for
minding a child that he mistakenly thought was his own, he
is wary about acknowledging and supporting the child in the
first place. In addition, he might later change his mind and
stop supporting a child as a result of further information
about his wife, and perhaps as a result of jibes from his
friends. The following account of a conversation elicited
from two informants in a discussion about the name that a
child will carry illustrates the importance placed upon the
biological tie, and also throws further light upon the reluctance men have to marry:

Woman: When you didn' marry, the child is the mother's own, she have more clue on it, but if you married, the man have to own it, even if not his own. *Man:* So the government is doing wrong. *Woman:* When you married, yes or no, it have to carry the man's name. When you go register child and you know well is somebody else child, if we livin' together, still on your name. Not to say friendin', I don' know about friendin'. And if you married, and you live with another man, christen the child on married husband's name. *Man:* The government upholding wrong things. *Woman:* That is right, not wrong thing. *Man:* Should put on nex' man's name, because nex' man's own.

One way a mother has of signifying paternity is through the assignment of the father's *title*, or surname, to the child. Although in registering the child the mother's name must be used unless she is married, for everyday purposes, and often for school purposes, the father's name will be used. This serves as a public expression of paternity, in the hope that support will be forthcoming from the father.

The reaction of the reputed father, however, is the most important factor, for, in effect, he holds the power of veto. If he is *living* or married he has come to know his wife well and is probably convinced of her fidelity. If he is *friending* with the girl, he has visited her at irregular intervals to see whether he could "bounce up" somebody else that she was seeing. If he is satisfied that the woman has not been *friending* with anyone else, and that the child is his own, he will ordinarily acknowledge the child and contribute to its support, for "who disown it, and know the child is yours, is wrong, is bad."

There will also be some social pressure upon the man to support the child, particularly if the girl is known as a quiet, respectable girl who does not run around. But if there is any element of doubt in the man's mind, he can disown the child and not contribute to its support, and these social pressures will not usually be able to force him to own the child. Moreover, even if he believes that the child is his own, if he does not want to support the child he will disown it, and usually with impunity, unless the girl should bring him to court for the maintenance of the child. Of course, there are cases where the problems discussed above are not crucial, and where the man has no doubt about his paternity, owns the child, and supports it. But the general attitude is one of wariness, and the general problems discussed above are known to all adult members of Coconut Village and probably to most of the lower-class Trinidad population. Certainly the number of calypsos which deal with the questions of infidelity, mistaken paternity, and a father's financial responsibility is extremely significant.[1]

MOTHER'S ROLE

The role of the mother is to *care* her child—she feeds, clothes, and generally takes care of the child, almost to the exclusion of the father. The role of the father is to funnel money into the household so that the wife can run the household and *care* the children. As a villager said, "He work the money and bring it to the mother to care the child." The father is usually away working, talking with his friends at the shop, or perhaps playing draughts at the roughly built Community Center. In the meantime, the mother is completely responsible for taking care of the child:

> (*What would be expected of the mother?*) First is the care of the child, to see that it's well fed, keep clean, clothe it, send it to school, see that it get a good learnin', whenever it come from school overhaul the work, after school is finish, see he keep in line and be decent and get responsible job.

> * * *

> (*Which is more important between the man and woman in making a child?*) Well, both of them are important. You see, without the man the woman wouldn' be able to conceive with the children and when the child is born she is more important, she have to care it,

nurse it, feed it, grow it up. (*What would a good mother do?*) She would try to do everything good, grow children in the right way, to be obedient, send them to school, to church to confirm them, and to learn them something.

The mother is by far the most significant person in the child's life. But even so, as soon as the child is able to walk, he spends much of his time outside the house with other children, and away from the influence of the mother. The child is given a great deal of freedom in this respect, but within the household he is subject to severe discipline, and will be punished physically if he interferes with the activities of his parents.[2] Although a child has much less interaction with his father, from a psychological point of view the presence of the father is of great importance, for his behavior is closely observed by the child and has a good deal of influence. In addition, the father's contribution to the upkeep of the house might have profound consequences for the child in terms of who *cares* him.

The division of labor between mother and father is ideally sharp and clean—the father *minds* and the mother *cares* the child. What does the mother do, however, if the father does not *mind* the child? Then, as an informant said, "The *mother* work hard and mind the child." If the child is old enough, she might leave the child with someone during the day while she worked, and take the child back in the evening. In this way she would *mind* the child herself, and also play a big part in the *care* of the child.

However, where the father stops supporting a young child, or disowns the child from the start, the mother's solution will differ. The baby needs more attention, and the mother usually leaves the baby completely in the care of another person, and goes out to work so that she can *mind* the child. Since the mother is often living with her own mother, she usually leaves the child in the care of its grandmother while she works. But, in decreasing order of frequency, she might also leave the child with her sister, with some other female relative on her side (e.g., her mother's sister), with a female relative on the father's side (usually father's mother or father's sister), or with a friend. One important point to note here is that the mother will be taking over the father's role of *minding* the child, while she would pass along the job of *caring* the child to another woman.

This practice of turning the child over to someone else's care is a common one, and I shall refer to it as "child-shifting." These child-shifting arrangements operate by custom and not by law, and they frequently benefit from the flexibility of Trinidad's customs. When the child's biological mother *minds* him, while he is *cared* by another woman, the child knows his mother and shows affection to her as well as to the woman with whom he is living. If financial support from the mother decreases, the slack may be taken up by those in the household where he is *cared*, until he may actually be completely *cared* and *minded* within the home of his foster parents. In such a case it is likely that the child's affection will be primarily for his foster parents, even though he still knows his biological parents. However, regardless of where the child's affection lies, once he is given over to the care of another woman by his mother, and "grows" with this woman, he would ordinarily not be taken back by the mother at some future time, even when she may be in a position to do so:

> (*How come Louis is not with you?*) *Wife:* When I make him I got spasm, was in hospital twenty-five days, and the father's sister took the baby. (*And you didn't take him back?*) I didn' nurse him, I was still sick, so she take care of him. *Husband:* (*smiling*) And from then to now, wouldn' get him again.

*   *   *

> My son was with my mother, she said she was not giving him up at all. I was home that time, and when I married and lef' there, I lef' him home. You can' leave with them; the second one you're in hopes, but not the first.

CHILD'S ROLE

A child is expected to help with a variety of household tasks from a very early age. As the informants put it, as soon as the child "has sense," or as soon as he "can walk and talk," he will be expected to help. I have seen young children engaged in many useful tasks: a four-year-old boy bringing a small can of water from the river, and tidying up the house; an eight-year-old girl cutting out the center strip of coconut leaves to make a *cocoyea* broom; a nine-year-old girl cooking; and a six-year-old boy and an eleven-year-old boy carrying tins of water from the river.

> During my conversation with the mother she was giving orders to her children. She sent Rol, nine years old, for water, and told him to scrub the steps. When he grimaced she added, "Don' make a face like that, you must be willing to do work for your mummy, boy." And she later said to her four-year-old son, "What are you doing, nothing? Then put the shoes away, two by two." And the youngster quietly obeyed.
>
> As I was talking to her she sent her three-year-old son, wearing only his undershirt, to the parlour to buy a sweet drink and bread.

Girls are expected to run errands and to do various tasks within the household, and when a bit older they are expected to cook, wash, and care for younger siblings:

> (*What kinds of things would a small girl be expected to do?*) Teach them cleaning the house and little housework and keep the yard clean. (*And later, when they're growing bigger?*) Start teachin' them to wash, and cookin'.

*   *   *

> (*What kind of work would be expected of a little girl?*) Teach her to wash wares, keep goin' in the shop, sweep the house, you have to be more pressin' with a little

girl. When she start to grow up, teach her to make the
bed, clean the home, empty out the utensil, wash it, put
it inside. That is girl's work.

A boy, as soon as he is able, is also expected to help out
around the house and to run errands; in addition, more
work outside the house is assigned to him. He is expected
to sweep the yard, buy things at the *parlour,* get water from
the river, and feed the fowls or pigs:

> (*When would you expect a small boy to help out around
> the house?*) Since he have real understandin' and have
> body, can talk and move around, at five, six years.
> (*What would he be expected to do?*) Sweep, like the
> yard, or if he have to take water in some little, small
> pan, or he could run in the parlour, if have animals,
> can see about them.

*   *   *

> (*What tasks would a small boy do?*) Bringing water,
> looking for wood, help sweep the yard. (*From what age
> would you expect him to help out?*) From about eight,
> and even when smaller ask them to do little things like
> bringing wood from yard to the house.

When a boy does not have a sister to do the girl's tasks of
cleaning, cooking, and washing, he is expected to help out
in these tasks as well:

> (*What work would a boy do when young?*) Little odds
> and ends, sweep, messages in shop. (*From what age?*)
> From time he have sense as long as have sense, start to
> work you. Son-son here (*three years old*) gets matches
> and papers. As soon as a child can walk, talk, expect to
> help. (*What would a girl do?*) They teaches girl to keep
> house clean, and even cook, wash—domestic home
> work. (*Would a boy ever have to do such work?*) Yes,
> let's say parents have only one boy, he have to assist in
> everything. I, was only one, had to do everything.

*   *   *

> (*Would anybody give a boy wares to wash?*) Yes, some

boys wash wares, they cook, too. (*Who would do that?*)
If you haven' got a girl you have your boy you teach
him to do that. (*And would he do it?*) Yes, I used to
teach Boysie to do that, and I busy, make him do that.

FAVORITISM TOWARD CHILDREN

There is no strong feeling in the village about treating all
children equally well, and parents frequently have a favorite
child.[3] Favoritism is explained by informants as resulting
from the way the child behaves toward his parents. A child
who is more obedient, loving, or respectful would be favored:

> (*Would all children be treated the same, or would most
> people have a favorite?*) Accordin' to the love of the
> children, you might like one more, like his doings to
> you most, the respec' he have for you, some might be
> in a nicer way to you.

*   *   *

> (*Would parents have a favorite child or treat them all
> the same?*) Sometimes beating two and nex' one not
> beating at all, that is favorite. (*Which one would be the
> favorite?*) Well, they like all but they like one the most.
> (*Why is that?*) Accordin' to the child's behavior.

*   *   *

> (*Would parents treat all children the same way, or
> would they have a favorite?*) Most have a favorite;
> mother would have one, father would have one. (*Why
> is that?*) Through the child, the affection it show to
> parents, and might have a different favorite one for
> each parent.

*   *   *

> (*Would all children be treated the same, or would par-
> ents have some as a favorite?*) Accordin' to the love of
> the child, the obedient of the child, you know some chil-
> dren rude, some disobliging.

*   *   *

Some parents love a child more than a next; that goes
when you have plenty of children. One might be a good

one, more obedient, and you may love him more. And a next one might be a "slowtish," you tell him to do a thing and he do as if he not feeling well.

*   *   *

(*Would parents sometimes have a favorite child?*) *Wife:* Yes, that is love, to have a favorite. Yes. (*Which one would the parents have as the favorite?*) *Wife:* One that is more honest and meek and mild to them. *Husband:* The one that is more obeysive to the father and mother. You must make he or she a favorite.

The following selection from *Mamam Moi* (*My Mother*), a Trinidad folk song in French patois, illustrates the theme of favoritism:

> Mamam moi ebouille di riz doux,
> Y fait la cocotte,
> Y pas bas moi piesse
> Comment diable on vlay moin garde bien,
> A verité de Bon Dieu, si mieux moi pate ne?

> (My Mother she make sweet rice,
> She give her favorite,
> She does not give me any.
> How in the devil does she expect me to grow fat,
> By the will of God, if I don't get any?)

In addition to the child's behavior, the child's skin color is sometimes used as a basis for favoritism. A lighter skin color has historically been preferred; but the contemporary emphasis upon black dignity and pride have mitigated color preferences.

There is a slight preference for girls over boys in the village,[4] especially on the part of the mother, for girls are recognized as being more closely tied to their parents, and as having a greater amount of concern for their parents' welfare:

(*Do you prefer a boy or a girl?*) I glad to have a girl child more. (*Why is that?*) Plenty helpful to the mother more than the boy, though it depends on their mind. (*What would the girl do that the boy wouldn't do?*) A girl, even if she leave home, will come back and help, if she have a good mind, don' mind the husband is vex.

* * *

(*Which do most people prefer, a girl or a boy?*) Indians say boy is most useful, we say love a girl child, she is less touchous with salary, study less for herself and more for the home, more attached to parents.

Black Fauns, a perceptive novel by Alfred Mendes of lower-class life in Trinidad,[5] also reveals the preference for girls over boys. The novel begins:

Ma Christine came out of her room into the yard and called out loudly. "Miss Miriam, ho! Miss Miriam, ho! Look, I receive a letter from Snakey. Come an' read it for me, doodoo."

A stout black woman appeared at a neighboring door and looked out into the yard. "Snakey!" she said, her arms akimbo. "It's a long time he didn' write you, Ma Christine."

The old woman shambled up to Miriam. "All boy-piccany is the same, Miss Miriam," she said. "Their hearts is black an' bitter. If you'se ever makin' a baby, ask God to breed a girl-child in you. Girls you can manage, an' when they grow up they show you more respec' an' gratitude than boy-child. But I can't complain so much about Snakey. Look Mistress Jeremiah's son. It is now ten years since the bit o' black boy leave his mother for America an' he never write her yet. An' he never send her a cent. . . .

A son has a greater amount of freedom and ordinarily severs his ties to his mother and father more readily than a girl. He is more likely to be "living bachelor" than a girl, and he is less likely to contribute money to the household if he is working. When a man "takes manship on his account" he means he has left his parents' household and has become completely responsible for his own affairs. Parents also use the phrase "to take manship on his account" about their son, which they may use sarcastically about a son who is still living with them but who is "behavin' disorderly, disobedient to parents, playin' big man." Although there is no strong expectation for the boy either to stay at home or to leave it, he is expected to show obedience to his parent if he is living with them, and also to contribute to the support of the household if he is working. This leads to difficulties that result in the boy's leaving home. In addition, his peers may urge him to leave his parents' home: "How you mean, man, you thirty and still in your mother's house?"

AFFECTION TOWARD PARENTS

A child's relationship to his mother may be extremely warm and affectionate, but this is not often the case between father and child. The core of the father's role is to support the child financially and not to be close to him emotionally. Furthermore, the father often cannot or does not fully carry out his obligations, and there is widespread acknowledgment in the village of the inadequacy of the father's performance. This recalls the diary entry by Carolina Maria de Jesus: "Father's Day. What a ridiculous day!" [6]

> (*How did you get along with your father?*) *Husband:* Well, when I was young I didn' know any better, I had to respec' him, but later on when I find out, well, I had no particular affection for my father. (*I noticed you were laughing a while ago when we were talking about what he called his father?*) *Wife:* Yes, well I was only thinking of my own case. I laugh because my own father, he's go down the road and we never see him. *Husband:* It's all their fault, they didn' care for their children, and we can' have no love for them.
>
> * * *
>
> My father wanted my mother to go with him to the country, to Coryal, but she didn't want to go because she wanted me to go to school. She told me that's why

she didn't go, on account of me. So he leave my mother and clear out, and he never help out. I went to him for help when I was 16. I was sick, but I didn't get a thing. He was making garden in Coryal, and took the money and lavish it, and he never say, here, a shilling for your son, he never turn back and help me and my mother. My mother wash and starch and iron to help me.

It is the mother's role to *care* the child, so that the mother-child bond may be very close. Even here, however, there are several factors which interfere with a harmonious relationship. In the first place, if the father is not *minding* his child, the mother may give the child's care over to someone else while she works. The child would then have a foster mother as well as a biological mother (and he may also have both foster and biological fathers), and his affection toward them would depend upon their behavior toward him. Does his biological mother continue to provide for him financially? Does she visit him and take him places? Does she buy him clothes or gifts? As an informant says, "It depends on how the mother or father show appreciation."

> (*Which of the relatives would it be easiest to get along with?*) Accordin' to what the person is like, it would be easier. (*Well, with which one would it be easier to get along for most people?*) It should be with the mother and father. But sometimes you find that even that is not easiest, if they en treat you right. (*Who else would be easier to get along with than some of the others?*) It depend on the type of person. Sometime auntie easier than mother, depending on the type of person should be the one you'd like to get along with.

Similarly, if a child is well treated by his foster parents, he will show them more affection. On the other hand, if the parents "chase us in work . . . get you up early, hustle you on," then the child's affection would be less.

Secondly, where the father is playing a marginal role in the family, and contributing irregularly to the upkeep of the household, the complete care of the children falls more and more into the mother's hands. She then takes over as the main source of authority and punishment. In this way a good deal of hostility toward the mother, which may be repressed, is built up. The following episode, only briefly reported, is an indication of how this hostility emerges. Del was in his mid-twenties.

> I was walking into the village, and at the first intersection, in front of Roger's place, Del was sitting on the ground with a small knot of men about him. Roger was pulling Del's foot up and down, manipulating it, and Del was shouting, "Pull it, pull it, it's out of compliance." I learned that Del was dead drunk, and had jumped off the concrete wall around Roger's house and injured his foot. Del continued his shouting all the while, and refused to lie down and keep his foot still.
>
> Earlier, he was at his mother's house, already drunk. She said, "I told him to rest and he cursed me, and so I has nothing to do with he, I has nothing to do with a drunk."
>
> Someone suggested Del use hibiscus on his foot, and someone else suggested saffron. He was too drunk to listen to anyone and continued shouting. He approached his mother's house, cursing all the while, and shouting that someone had taken his two dollars. On three separate occasions he had someone flash a torchlight on his wallet, to show that it was empty. This dramatic flourish was accompanied with shouts in which he roundly cursed his mother, and wondered who could have gotten into his wallet. "I'm going to fuck my mother's ass," he repeated several times; and also, "How am I going to pay Mistress Palmore (his mother) for the susu." Finally, he said, "When you see tears in Del, I is hurt. I en accusin' nobody, I en accusin' Dick, I en accusin' Harry. I just sayin' the money gone." He then turned his back to everyone: "People say Del apoplexive, but I gonna read my ass off till I get the two dollars. Who took the two dollars will be sorry when I find them."

Del is, of course, implying that his mother took the money.

GENERAL COMMENTS

Quid pro quo elements affect the parent-child relationship. The affection and obligations between parent and child are openly acknowledged to depend upon reciprocal behavior.[7] Children's affection for their biological or foster parents rests upon the treatment they have received from them. Parents frequently show favoritism to a child, and explain it in terms of love, obedience, and respect shown by the child. Since fathers are often unable to carry out their obligations as breadwinners, they are held in low esteem. Mothers may have to take over the dual role of *minding* and *caring* the child, or they have to shift their children to someone else's care. To the extent that mothers take over the punishment as well as the nurture of the children, ambivalent feelings are held toward them, and hostility occasionally breaks through.

In short, even the relationship between parent and child is affected by life's hardships. In a sense, love and care become scarce commodities which are granted only on the promise of some return. The relationship between parent and child, and especially between mother and child, is the last and the least affected by this *quid pro quo* exchange. But there can be no doubt that it is so affected. This is an extremely important topic, and since I feel that here, too, we are touching upon something that may be characteristic of lower-class families in many societies, I shall deal with it again in the theoretical chapters.

NOTES

1. See Appendix 1, pp. 215–23.
2. See David Landy, *Tropical Childhood* (New York: Harper, 1965), pp. 106, 134–35; Melvin L. Kohn, "Social Class and Parent-Child Relationships: An Interpretation," *American Journal of Sociology* 68 (January 1963): 471–80.
3. See Fernando Henriques, *Family and Colour in Jamaica* (London: Eyre & Spottiswoode, 1953), p. 127; Yehudi Cohen, "Structure and Function: Family Organization and Socialization in a Jamaican Community," *American Anthropologist* 58 (August 1956): 673.

4. See Judith Blake, *Family Structure in Jamaica* (New York: Free Press, 1961), pp. 65–66; Keith F. Otterbein, *The Andros Islanders* (Lawrence: University of Kansas Press, 1966), pp. 118–19.

5. Alfred Mendes, *Black Fauns* (London: Duckworth, 1937), p. 7.

6. Carolina Maria de Jesus, *Child of the Dark: The Diary of Carolina Maria de Jesus*, trans. David St. Clair (New York: E. P. Dutton, 1962), p. 113.

7. See Lloyd H. Rogler and August B. Hollingshead, *Trapped: Families and Schizophrenia* (New York: John Wiley, 1965), pp. 91–95.

6. *The Sibling Relationship*

Mother dead, father dead, family done.
COCONUT VILLAGER

THROUGH LIVING TOGETHER and playing together as children, siblings develop affection for each other and learn to cooperate; and the affection and cooperation frequently continue throughout their lives. However, there are a number of conditions in Coconut Village that strain the relationship between siblings and make affection and cooperation difficult.

In the first place, because of the marital-shifting and child-shifting patterns, siblings frequently do not grow up together in the same household. For example, if a couple enters a *living* relationship after having had one or two children, these children may remain in the household of the mother's mother, or another foster mother, while their later-born siblings will grow up in the household of the biological parents. For another example, let us think of a child that is born to a man and woman who are in a temporary *friending* or *living* relationship. He may acquire half-siblings through each of his parents after they have shifted into new marital alliances, and these half-siblings will usually be brought up in separate households.

Even for those siblings or half-siblings who grow up together in the same household, there are a number of obstacles to a lasting relationship. One of these is the favoritism that a parent often shows to one of his children. I have already pointed out that certain tasks are expected of children within the household on the basis of age and sex. A child is expected to make himself useful from the time that he is able, and a greater amount of work will be assigned to him as he grows older. In the assignment of these tasks, the practice on the part of parents of playing favorites among their children can lead to a great deal of sibling rivalry and hostility:

Recently I see a need of leavin' home and startin' another one. I am now seeing jealousy between brother and me-self. I will be earning a better salary than he, and have a strife; or I accustom' to doing more in house, some say he only do one piece of work and I have to do six or seven and enjoy the same life, so finally I pull away and start the same thing by myself.

*   *   *

I have a sister, she live in Treat Place (*about fifteen minutes' walking distance*). Long time I haven' seen her, since I sick, nine years, she hasn' come up here. When we was small we didn' agree, 'cause my mother didn' love she like me. I was a boy and girl to my mother, so she always hold that grudge agains' me, I used to help out my mother like a boy and girl.

A condition that aggravates the consequences of the parents' favoritism is their lack of resources. They have a limited supply of power, prestige, or money with which to reward their children. The competition between siblings may therefore become marked, a situation that Kardiner and Ovesey have noted in discussing lower-class Negroes in the United States:

> The deteriorated quality of sibling relationships is easily explained. The opportunities for affection and material necessities in the lower-class home are severely limited. In the struggle to obtain a share of these scarcities, the ensuing rivalry is bitter and enormously exaggerated. . . .[1]

When compared to the mutual obligations of parent and child, the obligations between siblings are vague in nature, and involve little more than a general expectation to help each other in time of need. Thus, we often find a girl *caring* for a younger sibling, or one sibling providing a place to stay for another, especially common when a person migrates to an area in which a sibling lives. But, in addition, many relatives other than siblings will also share a household.[2] We often find one sister *caring* the children of another sister, and occasionally of a brother:

(*How many children would you say a woman should have?*) I find the most a person should have is four. But here, they has thirteen, eight, ten, sixteen, twenty. (*How many children should a man have?*) I find a man should have the same amount. He can' maintain them if he's knocking up and down. But in some cases parents see about self, and don' take care of children, children go about half-naked. (*Are there any you know who do that?*) The people nex' door, the children go in rags. Finally the mother lef' and gone and the older children take care of the smaller ones.

* * *

I livin' here with my sister for two years. I was sick in hospital a few month, and then I get over, and my sister mindin' me and the government givin' me a little three dollars a month.

* * *

I was born in Carriacou, Grenada, and come to Trinidad around twenty-two year old, I was livin' with my brother on St. Joseph Street, stopped there for three-four year. He was rentin', he had his wife with him, and he never worry with me, bein' as brother and all.

When we come to consider the content of the sibling relationship from an everyday point of view, we find that there is little upon which to build strong ties. All households must rely upon cash wages, and the land a household head might possess does not provide work for a group of siblings. Neither the land nor household provides a stable focus about which the sibling relationship can be shaped. With the death of the parents, and usually before that time, each sibling will move into a separate household, and some of them may move away from the village completely. Distance separates the sibling group, for a sibling living twenty or thirty miles away is "living far" and may seldom be seen. It is therefore not surprising to find that more importance may be placed upon one's relationship to a friend or neighbor than to a sibling. In the following conversations a question comparing friends and relatives was partially transformed into a response comparing friends and siblings:

> (*Which is more important for a person, a friend or a relative?*) A relative is more important than a friend, but some friends that stay closer than a brother; some relatives in time of trouble, wouldn' come, but a friend would run right away. Some friends can be trusted more than a relative. I can' answer that direc', it depends.

*　*　*

> (*Which is more important, a relative or a friend?*) Well, a friend is better to me than family, and sometimes my family is better than a friend. Because if I have a friend right here is better than a brother that is far, because he can see to do for me and my brother can' see to do for me, neither can I do for he. So a near friend is always good to have.

Bearing in mind what has been said above, it is understandable that there is a large element of self-interest involved in the relationship between siblings:

> You have four sisters and one brother and one don' like the others to have more than they; now my bigges' sister have that very mind, she like to be up and the rest must be down, but the Bible didn' tell you so, says the eldest must serve the younger; some feel you the little one, you mus' always down.

*　*　*

> (*What would a person do when he in trouble and needing money, where would he get help?*) To depend on the family or anyone else is hard. If poor, apply to government for help, government will help you, either give you poor relief, if old give you pension. Or if sickly and can' help themself put them in the poor house, so it shows you that family is no use, I don' know about these people in position, maybe help if a poorer relative come to them. For we now, we can' depend on family or on anybody else. (*Why is that?*) Because not willing to

help you. Especially in Trinidad, everyone have to try to work and support their-self. (*If you would really need help, to who would you go?*) If have father and mother go to your father and mother and relate to them and may get it. Or may get it from brothers, but that does be hard.

In some societies weak or flexible marital bonds are related to strong sibling bonds. A lineage, consisting of all kinsmen related through either the paternal or maternal line, carries out certain tasks or rituals as a group, and may jointly own land or other property. Since individuals marry across lineage lines, marriage partners do not belong to the same lineage, but siblings do. The weakness of the marriage bond thus makes it easier for siblings and other lineage members to maintain their group loyalties. In Trinidad, however, there are no lineage ties,[3] and a strong sibling bond is not associated with the weak marital relationship. A sister seldom *cares* a brother's child—if the mother does not do so, then it is a female relative on the mother's side that ordinarily *cares* the child. Similarly, a brother seldom *minds* his sister's children—if the father does not do so, then the mother herself is expected to *mind* them. The care of the children may then be given over to the mother's mother, or her sister, but it must be remembered that the children will still be *minded* by their mother—she is expected to contribute money to the household of her own mother or sister for their support.

The emphasis upon the biological basis of paternity reinforces the ties between mother and daughter:

> I *was talking to a woman whose daughter and daughter's daughter live with her. (What do people call a mother's sister?)* Some say auntie, some say tantie. (*And a father's sister?*) The same thing. But some people say they has more love for a sister child than for a brother child. (*Why is that?*) Because you certain your sister child is she own, but when is your brother is not the same, you not sure is he own. For instance I can say this child is my daughter's, the boy's mother she can' be certain, it may be another boy's.

The biological tie, however, does not reinforce the tie between a brother and his sister's child. The man is expected to *mind* his own children, and the avuncular bond does not call forth any financial responsibility.

There are some differences in the literature about the nature of sibling ties in lower-class families. Writing about Jamaica, Davenport has pointed to solidary ties and affection; [4] most Caribbean researchers studying the family have said little about sibling relationships, perhaps reflecting that they have no special importance. In the United States, Kardiner and Ovesey have stressed rivalry and competition; [5] Riessman refers to "far less jealousy and competitiveness" among lower-class siblings.[6] It is evident that more attention must be paid to describing the sibling relationship in various societies. Care must also be taken in specifying the social classes that are being described, because some of the difficulties stem from a loose use of terms such as "lower class." It is not until additional data are collected that we can go very far in integrating the material on sibling relationships with a theoretical explanation of lower-class family patterns.

To sum up the Trinidad findings, although siblings do help one another, there is no common lineage or other strong kinship tie to bind them together tightly. They work as individuals, not as a group. As adults, and frequently as children, they live in separate households, and not in a common household. These things, along with the rivalry that may result from scarce parental resources and from overt parental favoritism, do not permit the development of a strong sibling bond or a stable sibling relationship.

An outstanding characteristic, and what is perhaps theoretically of greatest importance, is the situational difference between sibling ties. The strength of the tie depends upon early circumstances (were they reared together? were they driven apart or together by parental favoritism?), and upon their later personal relationship. In this sense the formal ties between siblings are of less importance than the personal ties that have grown out of the sibling bond. We shall have more to say at a later point on the possible relevance of "circumstances" and "personal ties" for understanding lower-class families.

NOTES

1. Abram Kardiner and Lionel Ovesey, *The Mark of Oppression* (Cleveland, World Publishing Co., 1962), p. 68; cf. Yehudi Cohen, "Structure and Function: Family Organization and Socialization in a Jamaican community," *American Anthropologist* 58 (August 1956): 672.

2. See Norman E. Whitten, Jr., "Strategies of Adaptive Mobility in the Colombian-Ecuadorian Littoral," in Norman E. Whitten, Jr., and John F. Szwed (eds.), *Afro-American Anthropology: Contemporary Perspectives* (New York: Free Press, 1970), pp. 329–44.

3. See Chapter 10 for a discussion of rules of descent.

4. William Davenport, "The Family System of Jamaica," *Social and Economic Studies* 10 (1961): 422–24.

5. Kardiner and Ovesey, *op. cit.;* cf. David A. Schulz, *Coming Up Black: Patterns of Ghetto Socialization* (Englewood Cliffs, N.J.: Prentice-Hall, 1969).

6. Frank Riessman, *The Culturally Deprived Child* (New York: Harper, 1962), p. 37.

7. Family, Kinship, and Community Relationships

When on your home falls unforeseen distress
Half-clothed come neighbors, kinsmen stay to
dress.

HESIOD

Up to this point I have dealt mainly with relationships within the nuclear family of husband, wife, and children. But in discussing the husband-wife, parent-child, and sibling relationships, it has also been necessary to refer to kinsmen such as mother's mother as well as to non-kinsmen such as friends and neighbors. This suggests that in some ways the relationships between nuclear family members may not be unique. For example, to what extent may a grandmother or a neighbor take the part of a mother?

It is informative, in any society, to examine the dividing lines between nuclear family, kin, and community. Are there sharp breaks between them, or do nuclear family relationships merge into kin relationships, and kin relationships into relationships with non-kin? It is only in describing the relationships in detail that we can answer the question. This is a problem in group organization, and the extent to which the nuclear family is strongly organized as distinct from other kin groups or community is influenced by the extent to which it is separated by such factors as group membership, residence, and activities.

These considerations are of crucial significance when exploring the universality of the nuclear family.[1] When we ask, "Is the nuclear family universal?," are we asking whether the nuclear family always resides together as a group? Whether the members of the nuclear family are conscious of belonging to a separate group? Whether the patterns of interaction and exchange demonstrate the existence of the nuclear family regardless of group consciousness or residence? When viewed in this way, the question of the universality of the nuclear family is replaced by a concern for the varying forms and functions of nuclear family, kinship, and community organization.

The central structural fact in Coconut Village is the extreme degree to which the kinship system is "open"— nuclear family relationships flow readily into kinship relationships and community relationships without any sharp breaks. There is no doubt that the fluidity here is exceptional, and it relates to the patterns of marital-shifting and child-shifting. If a man enters into a new marital relationship, he may contribute to the support of his wife's children by another man. A woman may turn her children's care over to her mother, sister, or another female relative or friend. The resulting household composition, with the addition of kinsmen and occasionally non-kin members around a nuclear family core, is a sign of this open structure. For this reason, the household or domestic group has been singled out as a distinctive object of study by many students of the Caribbean.[2] Another sign of the open organization is the ease with which changes in household composition take place, whether for a few weeks, months, or years. For example, while I was in the village in 1956 there was one month of school vacation in Trinidad, and the following household shifts were observed:

> Two schoolboys spent three weeks with their mother's sister in the village and then one week with their mother's friend in a household about two miles away from the village;
>
> A schoolgirl who was living with her sister in Port of Spain came to spend the vacation with her parents in the village;
>
> A schoolboy who was living with his mother's sister and attending school in a distant village came to spend the vacation with his mother;
>
> Another schoolboy who lived in a distant village with his father's sister came to spend his vacation with his parents.

Aside from these household changes which were related to the fact that there had been no village school until one year before the field work began, and only a private one after that, the following household changes were also observed:

> One woman left her husband "to see a doctor" in Port of Spain; she did not tell her husband when she would return and had not returned when the field work was completed two weeks later;
>
> A man came from his daughter's household in another village to stay in his son's household;
>
> A woman left her sister's daughter's household in Port of Spain to return to her husband after obtaining part-time work in the village;
>
> A woman, her husband, and two of their children moved in with the woman's great-grandparents, helped them complete their tapia house, and stayed on in the household.

All of these changes were recorded during a four-month period when the village had only thirty-one households, or twenty-four households if we exclude those with only a single member, where no changes took place. It is clear that there was a great deal of turnover in household composition of a temporary, or perhaps permanent, nature.

The tie between two kinsmen is personal and reciprocal. If the kinsmen have maintained amicable contact through the years, then they will attend each other's weddings and wakes and they may be of assistance to each other in times of difficulty. But there are few formal obligations that bind kinsmen together unless they happen to be living in the same household. There are, of course, formal kinship obligations which bind together members of the same nuclear family, but there is a strong personal and reciprocal undercurrent in these relationships as well. Bearing in mind the marital-shifting and child-shifting patterns and the resulting changes in household composition, it is clear that nuclear kin and other kin bonds intersect at many points, and are not altogether different from one another.

When we explore the line of separation between kin and

non-kin in other cultures, we may find a very clear differentiation of behavior and attitude toward the two, particularly in a unilinear system where one's kinsmen form a corporate group. But in Coconut Village, where there is a bilateral descent system,[3] we find that there is no sharp distinction between the two. The lack of a fixed kinship group engaged in corporate activity, the lack of formal kinship bonds with extended kinsmen, the mobility of the population which may lead a person to live at a distance from kin and in close contact with friend and neighbor— all contribute to the open community-kin boundary. The boundary, in fact, is often blurred, and the relative importance of a kinsman and a friend may be judged in universalistic [4] terms. It is as though the kinship relationship has become diluted to the point where blood is no longer thicker than water:

> (*Which would you say is more important to you, a relative or a friend?*) Depends on how the person is to you, have to draw up references on both sides. Friends so dear to you that they can more fill in for you than a relative. Better a devoted friend than a worthless relative, and better a devoted relative than a worthless friend. That is as far as it reach.

*   *   *

> (*Is a relative or a friend more important?*) A relative is more important to you, but at times you find a friend would be more important to you than a relative. Accordin' to how relative is coped, if you wouldn' have any good coping, if friend and I cope better, discussing things better, in case of needness; with family, may not look at you, whereas friend would always assist you.

*   *   *

> (*What is the difference between friends and relatives?*) Yes, a lot of difference in various ways. Very often what you can get from a friend you can' get from a relative, or what you can get from a relative, you can' get from a friend. Or what you tell a friend you can' tell a relative, or what you tell a relative you can' tell a friend. Some

friends you can take in confidence, some don' tell and
some do. Some friends will assist you, some relatives
won' assist you. When sick a relative may scorn you,
but not a friend. Very often when you come to die, you
leave it to a friend.

In short, there is a great deal of interpenetration of
nuclear family, kin, and community relationships. The
boundaries between these groups are not sharply defined
residentially or behaviorally, and are often completely
ignored in particular circumstances. For example, disputes
among kinsmen often take place publicly. The participants
quarrel loudly and do not ordinarily attempt to keep the
discord within the nuclear family or household. As a matter
of fact, a participant often takes up the dispute in public
with some of the villagers, trying to gain their sympathy.
I have been appealed to by villagers several times in this
way. Such behavior, however, is only in part an attempt
to mobilize community pressure to enforce conformity with
certain expectations. It is also evidence of the blurred
boundaries between family and community relationships,
indicating that family disputes take place in a wider community context. In many places the family's affairs are
the family's own business, and angry words in the private
world of the family are masked by smiling faces in the
public world of the community. This does not happen in
Coconut Village.

There are also no strongly divergent attitudes toward
sexual and marital behavior between kin and community
members. Kinsmen do not take special actions to control
or supervise each other's sexual behavior. The following
example illustrates the relative freedom a man has to approach a girl and make sexual jokes about her in front of a
kinsman:

*Pap was visiting from a nearby village, and standing in
front of the shop with John and Miss Mary. John had
stoned and killed an iguana, and Pap was joking with
him and Miss Mary about how nice the iguana would
taste. Finally Pap agreed to buy the iguana for 30 cents,*

commenting all the while on how nice it would taste with rice. He sang a few lines of an impromptu calypso, moving in rhythm, and rhyming nice, rice, and sacrifice. A girl of about twenty passed and went into the shop.

Pap (joking all the while): That is your family, Miss Mary?

Miss Mary: That's my niece.

Pap: How you would like to have me in your family?

Miss Mary ignored the question. After a pause Pap repeated it.

Miss Mary (sarcastically): You!

Pap: But why you en answerin' me? How you like to have me in your family?

Miss Mary: "You" should be answer enough for you. That is my answer.

Pap (looking at the girl in the shop): Mmmm, but that is nice. Let me go see.

He goes into the shop and talks to the girl. In a few minutes he comes out of the shop and returns part way toward John and Miss Mary.

Pap: But I must be in your family, Miss Mary. She is too nice. Come see, my heart pounding for so.

The girl comes out of the shop and he follows her for about twenty-five yards, talking to her, before returning. He then continues the same line of conversation with Miss Mary, who is in her fifties.

Miss Mary: The trouble is that you all gi' them belly and then you run away.

Pap: Well, yes, you mus' expec' that I will gi' them belly. They must get belly, yes. How you mean, I mus' gi' them belly. A man such as me, they mus' get belly, yes.

It is evident that the kinship tie between Miss Mary and her niece does not insulate the girl from a sexual approach.[5] Providing such insulation is not part of the kinship role; and in this area, too, the kinship bond is not sharply differentiated from other relationships.

The nature of the relationship between social class and the strength of kinship ties has general relevance. As with sibling ties, there are rather contradictory popular ideas—

that the bonds are stronger in the lower class because individuals have only kinsmen to fall back upon; and that the bonds are weaker because lower-class kinsmen have so little to offer each other. It is, however, necessary to go beyond the weak-strong dichotomy and carefully examine the content of kinship ties.[6] Are kinship ties to be defined as stronger if kinsmen live together, or engage in economic activities together, or engage in ritual activities together, or interact more frequently, or identify with each other, or help each other? These factors may vary independently, and as a result the question is complicated. For example, kinsmen who interact infrequently may provide crucial economic assistance, or may have strong affective ties.[7] The research literature provides only fragmentary information about the full range of kinship bonds; moreover, information on lower-class families in this regard is only very occasionally obtained.[8]

To summarize and oversimplify, the evidence indicates that kinship ties foster success in the middle class, security in the working class, and survival in the lower class. Within the middle class (and the upper class) most of the assistance is provided by the older to the younger generation.[9] This assistance is often crucial in aiding individuals to achieve educational, occupational, or economic success.[10] In the working class there is less concern for success and more concern for security and family interaction.[11] Kinsmen are therefore likelier to live closer together and to provide each other with the support needed to maintain a secure and family-based existence. Within the lower class there are insufficient resources to aid new members to achieve success or even security. Thus, *if achievement is the goal,* kinship bonds are not especially helpful.[12]

Lower-class kinship ties, in Trinidad as in many other societies, are activated for emergency help such as food and shelter—in short, for survival rather than for success or security.[13] This is especially the case where the kinsmen are homogeneously of lower-class background, and where little or no help for achievement can be expected from a kinsman.

NOTES

1. See George P. Murdock, *Social Structure* (New York: Macmillan, 1949), pp. 2–12; Melford E. Spiro, "Is the Family Universal?," *American Anthropologist* 56 (October 1954): 839–46; M. J. Levy and L. A. Fallers, "The Family: Some Comparative Considerations," *American Anthropologist* 61 (August 1959): 647–51; and Ira L. Reiss, "The Universality of the Family: A Conceptual Analysis," *Journal of Marriage and the Family* 27 (November 1965): 443–53.

2. Nancie Solien, "Household and Family in the Caribbean: Some Definitions and Concepts," *Social and Economic Studies* 9 (March 1960): 101–6; M. G. Smith, *Kinship and Community in Cariacou* (New Haven: Yale University Press, 1962); M. G. Smith, *West Indian Family Structure* (Seattle: University of Washington Press, 1962); Norman Ashcroft, "The Domestic Group in Mahogany, British Honduras," *Social and Economic Studies* 15 (September 1966): 266–74; and Keith F. Otterbein, *The Andros Islanders* (Lawrence: University of Kansas Press, 1966). Cf. Donald R. Bender, "A Refinement of the Concept of Household: Families, Co-residence, and Domestic Functions," *American Anthropologist* 69 (October 1967): 493–504.

3. For additional details on unilineal and bilateral descent systems, see Chapter 10.

4. Talcott Parsons and Edward A. Shils (eds.), *Toward a General Theory of Action* (Cambridge, Mass.: Harvard University Press, 1951), pp. 81–82 *et passim.*

5. A girl therefore has less bargaining power, as Goode suggests. But the kinship role, and sexual and marital patterns, are part of an organized system of lower-class responses, and are not necessarily a reflection of disorganization. See William J. Goode, "Illegitimacy in the Caribbean Social Structure," *American Sociological Review* 25 (February 1960): 21–30; and Hyman Rodman, "Illegitimacy in the Caribbean Social Structure: A Reconsideration," *American Sociological Review* 31 (October 1966): 673–83.

6. Robert P. Stuckert, "Occupational Mobility and Family Relationships," *Social Forces* 41 (March 1963): 301–7; and Bert N. Adams, "Kinship System and Adaptation to Modernization," *Studies in Comparative International Development* 4 (1968–69): 47–58.

7. Jane Hubert, "Kinship and Geographical Mobility in a Sample from a London Middle-Class Area," *International Journal of Comparative Sociology* 6 (March 1965): 61–80.

8. Leonard Blumberg and Robert R. Bell, "Urban Migration and Kinship Ties," *Social Problems* 6 (Spring 1959): 328–33.

9. Ethel Shanas, "Family Help Patterns and Social Class in Three Countries," *Journal of Marriage and the Family* 29 (May 1967): 257–66.

10. Eugene Litwak, "Occupational Mobility and Extended Family Cohesion," *American Sociological Review* 25 (February 1960): 9–21; Eugene Litwak, "Geographic Mobility and Extended Family Cohesion," *American Sociological Review* 25 (June 1960): 385–94; Marvin B. Sussman and Lee Burchinal, "Parental Aid to Married Children: Implications for Family Functioning," *Marriage and Family Living* 24 (November 1962): 320–32; and Paul J. Reiss, "Extended Kinship Relationships in American Society," in Hyman Rodman (ed.), *Marriage, Family, and Society: A Reader* (New York: Random House, 1965), pp. 204–10. Cf. Ernestine Friedl, "The Role of Kinship in the Transmission of National Culture to Rural Villages in Mainland Greece," *American Anthropologist* 61 (February 1959): 30–38; Milton L. Barnett, "Kinship as a Factor Affecting Cantonese Economic Adaptation in the United States," *Human Organization* 19 (Spring 1960): 40–46; Carmel Camilleri, "Modernity and the Family in Tunisia," *Journal of Marriage and the Family* 29 (August 1967): 590–95; and Peter Marris, "Individual Achievement and Family Ties: Some International Comparisons," *Journal of Marriage and the Family* 29 (November 1967): 763–71.

11. Raymond Firth (ed.), *Two Studies of Kinship in London* (London: Athlone Press, University of London, 1956); Joseph A. Kahl, *The American Class Structure* (New York: Rinehart, 1957); Michael Young and Peter Willmott, *Family and Kinship in East London* (Glencoe, Ill.: Free Press, 1957); S. M. Miller and Frank Riessman, "The Working Class Subculture: A New View," *Social Problems* 9 (Summer 1961); 86–97; Joan Aldous, "Urbanization, the Extended Family, and Kinship Ties in West Africa," *Social Forces* 41 (October 1962): 6–12; Herbert Gans, *The Urban Villagers: Group and Class in the Life of Italian-Americans* (New York: Free Press, 1962); and Marris, *op. cit.*

12. William J. Goode, "Industrialization and Family Change," in Bert F. Hoselitz and Wilbert E. Moore (eds.), *Industrialization and Society* (Paris: UNESCO—Mouton, 1963), pp. 237–55.

13. Camille Jeffers, *Living Poor* (Ann Arbor: Ann Arbor Publishers, 1967); Hylan Lewis, "Introduction," in Camille Jeffers, *Living Poor;* and Harry K. Schwarzweller and James S. Brown, "Social Class Origins, Rural-Urban Migration, and Economic Life Chances: A Case Study," *Rural Sociology* 32 (March 1967): 5–19.

PART THREE

RULES AND REFLECTIONS
OF FAMILY LIFE

8. *The Engagement Letter:*
Normative Versus Preferential Patterns

You may grease you' heel
And pare you' toe,
But married you never go get.
You' Toco bad lumber,
You' Toco bad lumber,
Married you never go get.
              TRINIDAD FOLK SONG

THE RELATIONSHIP between a boy and girl is ideally medi-
ated through the girl's parents or guardians. The boy is
supposed to write an "engagement letter" [1] in order to signify his intention to marry the girl and the girl's parents
either accept or reject the boy. Informants point out that
the engagement letter is still used throughout Trinidad,[2]
although the frequency of its use has declined in recent
years. It is more frequently used in rural than urban areas
and is fairly common in Coconut Village.

Ideally, the boy writes to the girl's father, asks to be more
closely associated with the girl, and promises to marry
the girl within a specified period of time. If the girl is not
living with her father, the boy writes to her mother or her
guardian. If the girl's guardian signifies his acceptance of
the boy, the guardian is later expected to stand the expense
of the marriage fête.

The engagement letter itself is a highly formalized document. Typically, the marriage is to take place between
twelve and eighteen months after the date of the letter.
In the following two letters, only the headings and names
have been omitted:

Sir,
    This is to inform you, that I feel very proud in claiming
this special previllege (*sic*) to ask Sir, for your daughter's
hand in the Holy Bond of Matrimony.

I am indeed very happy to state Sir, that for the short time I have known her, I have been paying my closest attention; and found her to be Charming, Loyal, Adorable and above all of Good Character and Upright Standing; the Qualification of which, in my opinion has made her the fit and proper person to join with me in the Sacrament now applied for.

If this my application meets with your kind Approval Sir, I shall be very much obliged for your permission to be more closely acquainted with her for a period of twelve (12) months as from the date of this letter, and at the expiration a further six (6) months within which time we shall make preparations for this Blessed Sacrament of Holy Matrimony.

Hoping to receive an early and favourable reply.

I have the honor to be,

Sir

Yours fraternally,

R——— P———

Dear Miss L,

I most respectfully beg to inform you that my acquaintance with your daughter (Name) for the Past Two years has waxed into a very deep affection which compels me to demand her hand in Marriage and to make her my Lawful wife at the Earliest date possible, although my calling in life is a humble one yet I shall do my utmost to support her to the station of life she wish to achieve, and should I find her Loyal, Industrious and obedient within fifteen (15) months from date to expiration I shall join her in Holy Matrimony.

I do hope you find me a suitable companion to your daughter as I shall do my best to bring no regret.

I remain

Yours respectfully,

J——— R———

The engagement letter is signed by the boy, who also affixes a postage stamp to the letter. A postage stamp is required by law to establish a legal contract between two parties. The engagement letter is not a contract, and although the stamp has no legal significance for the letter it is widely believed to be necessary by lower-class individuals.

Parental permission and involvement are at the core of the procedures surrounding the engagement letter. These procedures, by middle-class standards, would make it possible for a girl to have the protection and advice of her family. Her parents would exercise some control over the relationship. They could minimize sexual relationships prior to marriage and help the girl to strike a bargain with her prospective mate that assures her of the promised marriage. But the practice is actually quite different, and the promise often fades away.

The major attitude that mitigates the potential control of the girl's family is the expectation that sexual relations will take place prior to marriage. It is believed that only through experiences involving sexual relations can the boy and girl learn whether they can get along—if they cannot, it is "better for them not to married." Another reason given for premarital sexual relations is that "human nature" and "desire" demand it. Yet another reason is the pragmatic one of ascertaining the correct sex of one's potential mate. Stories about hermaphrodites are widely circulated within the lower-class population, and people want to be sure that they are not being taken in by a "morphadite."

> They might meet up with a girl that isn' no good. They does call it in Trinidad a morphadite. Since I go to school I always hear bigger fella talk, a fella one time marry a girl, he went on honeymoon and he met a girl and she was no good. I en mean a bad woman, because you go for honeymoon and you have to leave the next day. The woman is someone you call a morphadite.

> * * *

> (*Why do you say there should be* friending *before marriage?*) *Man:* I go to marry you and when I marry you you's a man as me. (*laughter*)

> * * *

> You mus' know if is a human, or an animal, or a dog,

or a man like you'self. You would like to know where you putting you'self.

* * *

Man: You mus' know who you marry, you may be married to a man, you can never tell how the coin may spin.

Sexual relations with a prospective marriage partner take place within a *friending* or *living* arrangement. In some cases the girl lives with the boy after he has written the engagement letter and been accepted by the girl's parents. If the girl's parents do not permit them to live together, the girl may leave her home against her parents' wishes and live with the boy. If the girl is living at home, it is expected that she will be *friending* with the boy. According to some informants, the girl's parents do not approve of such *friending*. According to most informants, however, the parents give tacit approval to it, and they might even encourage it by giving the couple the run of the house:

> (*After the engagement letter, if the parents accept the boy, would the parents know the couple is friendly?*) Yes, the parents would know that. (*Could you have sexual relations in the house?*) You steal a chance in the house. (*Would the parents of the girl turn the house over to the couple for them to use?*) Some willing to turn house over; some not. (*Why are some willing and some not?*) Some have love for a son-in-law, and do things to please him. Some seem to feel if they could hold you away it will quicken the marriage while others seem to feel if you know what you' buying you buy quicker. (*Did the parents of the girl you were engaged to make the house available to you?*) Yes. (*Would they say so, that they're turning the house over to you?*) No, they wouldn' say exactly, they would just leave to go somewhere for the evening. (*And it would be understood that you could sleep there with the girl?*) Yes. (*Did they turn the house over to you often?*) Yes.

* * *

> (*After an engagement letter, if the parents accept it, can the fella stay over at the girl's house?*) You can

spend a night or two. (*Would the parents know there would be sexual intimacy?*) They expect that.

The engagement letter and the *friending* relationship are a step toward marriage, but marriage is not a necessary outcome of the process. The testing that takes place in a *friending* or *living* relationship, prior to marriage, is customary. A decision about marriage—often negative—is made as a result of this testing. The girl or her parents may reject the boy because of his inability to support her, or because of his violence, drunkenness, or other undesirable behavior. The boy may reject the girl if she is unfaithful to him, or if he suspects her of being unfaithful. The boy who does not carry out the engagement letter's promise to marry can be brought to court for breach of promise, but such court cases are rare. So many community-sanctioned reasons for not marrying exist that the engagement would be of little use in a breach of promise suit. The engagement letter is, however, more likely to be used in a paternity suit. It is widely known that the privilege of visiting the girl, established by the engagement letter, frequently includes sexual intercourse within a *friending* relationship. The letter is therefore sometimes used as material evidence to support a paternity suit.

Another reason for the breakdown of the process leading toward marriage is the low degree of trust between males and females which pervades all stages of the marital relationship in lower-class Trinidad. It is widely recognized that the man may have no intention of getting married, despite the letter he has sent:

> Some new girl will come into the district and the boys will get together and one of them will say, you see that girl, that looks like a nice girl, you can never get in there, and another will say, le' we take a bet, in a month I will be in there, and then he start to be nice to the girl and to give her some sweet talk and some presents, and you might soon find the fella is writing a letter for the girl, and from the time the parents approve, well he win the bet. Well, say after five-six months go by, he

said he was going to marry she in a year, or eighteen months, one day he get drunk and he come into the house and start cursin' and t'ing or he start runnin' around wild, and the parents will see that, they will throw the letter back in his face, they glad to find out before it's too late, and so he don' have to marry she again—and all the time that was his plan, he mama-guyin' she.

Marriage plans are therefore highly vulnerable, and there is a suspicion that even those who say they are going to get married will not do so. For instance, one woman told a group of women about the postponement of a girl's marriage as follows:

"You know Jean's marriage due in August scratch off and put it September twenty-third." *Another woman added, to the accompaniment of laughter by all the women,* "All you see, scratch it off and put it December."

Sexual relations prior to marriage are not regarded as deviant; the strength of the favorable attitude toward them is well established. It is only through sexual relations that a boy and girl can really "get to know" each other. As a result parental involvement should not be viewed in the context of protecting a girl against premarital sexual relationships. Rather, parents are involved in a normative process that leads to *friending* and *living* relationships as well as to marriage.

The full range of attitudes of the villagers toward alternate marital forms is difficult to ascertain. Comparing marriage and *living*, it is clear that marriage is preferred, in the abstract, by almost all of them, including the majority who are *living*. But it is difficult to know to what extent their attitudes and their marriage plans are conditioned by outsiders—including an outside researcher, and outside religious functionaries who periodically invade the village with their message of marriage. Several times I have witnessed professions of faith, inclinations toward marriage, and feelings of good will toward a missionary fade away dramatically as soon as the missionary was out of hearing. I have heard apparently spontaneous middle-class attitudes and expressions spontaneously repudiated by lower-class informants when they came to trust me. This leads me to be highly skeptical of Goode's [3] and Blake's [4] thesis that lower-class people within the Caribbean regard the non-legal union (*living*, in Trinidad) and the resulting illegitimacy as deviant despite their high frequency.

In an influential paper Goode reconsidered a number of publications on Caribbean family structure as they bear on the question of the normative status of non-legal marital unions and illegitimacy.[5] The predominant conclusion of the researchers was that non-legal unions and the resulting illegitimate children are normative. However, Goode points to statements in the writings of these same researchers which are supposed to demonstrate that, despite their conclusions that non-legal marital unions and the resulting illegitimate children are normative, they are in actual fact deviant.

Most of the statements that are singled out by Goode [6] are of the following kinds: (1) that non-legal unions and illegitimacy are considered deviant by individuals who are not members of the lower class; (2) that the girl in her parents' house who becomes illegitimately pregnant is punished by her parents; (3) that non-legal unions are not as stable as legal marriages; (4) that most adults eventually do marry; and (5) that marriage is preferred to the non-legal union. Yet none of these statements constitutes evidence that the non-legal marital union and the illegitimacy resulting therefrom are considered to be deviant within the lower class.

The first three points need little comment. Obviously, if we are specifically concerned with values of members of the lower class, knowledge about the values of other classes is not directly relevant. If we are concerned with the non-legal union and the resulting illegitimate children, knowledge about attitudes toward illegitimate children who are not conceived within a non-legal union is not directly relevant. And finally, the argument that non-legal unions are less stable than legal marriages does not give us information about the normative status of the non-legal union.

What about the implications of the fact that most adults eventually marry? In Goode's words, "as individuals move through the life cycle, an increasing proportion are actually married, a phenomenon which would be inexplicable if the consensual unions were backed by a set of alternative norms." [7] But consensual or non-legal marital unions are backed by a set of alternative norms, and the explanation for the increasing proportion of married individuals in the older age groups is a simple one. As I have pointed out elsewhere, "Legal marriage and a non-legal union are not in opposition, but are, rather, two different types of acceptable marital patterns among the lower classes of the West Indies. . . . This is not to say that these two patterns are equally valued, nor that there are no regularities with respect to when one or the other pattern will be followed." [8] The fluidity of marital relationships that is symbolized by the non-legal marital union makes it possible for lower-class individuals to adapt to the economic uncertainties they face. The lower-class man's occupational and economic problems make it difficult for him to play the breadwinner role with ease; the non-legal marital union provides a flexible relationship within which a marital exchange is possible without the legal bonds of marriage.[9] It is in the later age groups, after a non-legal marital union has stood the test of time, that a marriage may be entered into in order to safeguard the legal rights of the wife and the children to the man's inheritance. Consequently, there is good reason for the rising proportion of individuals who are married in the older age groups, even though the non-legal marital union is normative and fulfills important functions within the lower class.

Perhaps the major defect in the arguments by Goode and Blake is the failure to distinguish between preferential and normative structure. They commit the fallacy of transforming preferential information into normative information. Information is presented that marriage is "preferred" to the non-legal union, that marriage is the "ideal," that marriage is "superior." This is used to bolster the conclusion that marriage alone is normative and that the non-legal union is deviant. For example, Blake asked the following question in Jamaica: "In general, for people in your position, do you think it is better to marry or just to live with a man (woman)?" [10] She reports that 83 per cent of the men and 83 per cent of the women "choose marriage unreservedly." On the basis of other unspecified questions in the interview she modifies the figure for women in order to be more conservative in her conclusions:

> 74 per cent of the women and 83 per cent of the men unreservedly choose marriage and are consistent in this point of view throughout. The remaining 26 per cent among the women and 17 per cent among the men are ambivalent toward marriage (i.e., choose it with reservations or elsewhere give evidence of ambivalence) with the exception of 3 women and 2 men who are negative.[11]

These data show a strong preference for marriage, but they do not permit the conclusion that "legal marriage is the only true union," [12] and they tell us very little about the normative status of the non-legal union.

Marriage may very well be the ideal pattern, or the preferred pattern; but to say that the non-legal union is deviant because marriage is preferred is clearly fallacious. It is also possible for the non-legal union to be normative, although less desirable than marriage.

In the 1962 data I collected, the evidence is very strong that marriage is preferred, and that the non-legal union (*living*) is normative. The data are presented in Table 8,[13] and include a breakdown by sex and social class. Looking only at the total sample in the right-hand column, we can see that for the three preferential questions (numbers 2, 3, and 5) the percentages favorable to *living* are 21, 28, and 29; for the three normative questions (numbers 1, 4, and 6) the percentages favorable are 81, 50, and 66.

In short, although marriage is preferable, *living* is on the

Table 8

PERCENTAGE FAVORABLE TO *LIVING* (NON-LEGAL MARITAL UNIONS) BY SEX AND CLASS

	UPPER LOWER	LOWER LOWER	TOTAL SAMPLE

1. Is it all right for a man and woman to live together in order to get to know each other's ways before they decide to marry?

	UPPER LOWER	LOWER LOWER	TOTAL SAMPLE
Female	38% (8)	73% (40)	
Male	75% (20)	98% (47)	
			81% (115)

2. Is it better for a man and woman who are very poor to get married, or is it better for them to live together common law?

	UPPER LOWER	LOWER LOWER	TOTAL SAMPLE
Female	0% (17)	16% (57)	
Male	15% (34)	37% (57)	
			21% (165)

3. Do you think that (1) living common law is better than marriage, (2) that marriage is better than living common law, or (3) that they both come as the same?

	UPPER LOWER	LOWER LOWER	TOTAL SAMPLE
Female	12% (17)	19% (57)	
Male	31% (36)	38% (57)	
			28% (167)

4. Do you think that living common law is a sin or not a sin?

	UPPER LOWER	LOWER LOWER	TOTAL SAMPLE
Female	24% (17)	36% (56)	
Male	61% (36)	63% (60)	
			50% (169)

5. A man and woman are thinking of getting married: (a) One person says they should marry right away, without having sexual intercourse before marriage. (b) Another says they should have sexual intercourse before marriage in order to get to know each other's ways. Which do you think is better? (If b) How should they get to know each other—by friending or by living common law?

	UPPER LOWER	LOWER LOWER	TOTAL SAMPLE
Female	6% (16)	27% (51)	
Male	21% (33)	44% (50)	
			29% (150)

	UPPER LOWER	LOWER LOWER	TOTAL SAMPLE

6. Some people are talking about marriage and living common law. (a) One person says that only *living* is good and that marriage is wrong; (b) Another says that only marriage is good and that *living* is wrong; (c) Another says that marriage is better but that *living* is also good; (d) Another says that *living* is better but that marriage is also good. Which is the closest to what you think?

	UPPER LOWER	LOWER LOWER	TOTAL SAMPLE
Female	41% (17)	58% (55)	
Male	63% (35)	83% (58)	
			66% (165)

Note: Bases of percentages are shown in parentheses. The first question was not added until after some of the interviews had been done. Other variations in N are due to cases in which the information was not ascertained. In question 3, answers (1) and (3) are coded as favorable to *living;* in question 5, answer (b), followed by a response that does not exclude *living*, is coded as favorable to *living;* in question 6, answers (a), (c), and (d) are coded as favorable to *living.*

whole considered to be normative. This emerges from a survey of lower-class respondents, many of whom were undoubtedly influenced by their knowledge of what was considered to be socially desirable from a middle-class perspective. The percentage normatively favorable to *living* that emerges from the survey is therefore a minimum figure. Equally important, the information obtained from informants through participant observation documents the lower-class acceptance of the *living* relationship.[14]

The manner in which the engagement letter fits into the pattern of marital relationships further substantiates the normative status of *living*. It also suggests the normative status of *friending*. When a letter is written, it involves the girl's parents and provides a measure of parental supervision over the relationship. As we have seen, however, such supervision is not used to insure the girl's marriage. It may, rather, be used to provide parental sanction for a *living* relationship. Nor does parental involvement safeguard the girl from sexual relations; rather, it sometimes provides parental sanction for premarital sexual intercourse within a *friending* relationship. In short, *friending* and *living* are part of the lower-class pattern of marital relationships. The existence of three marital relationships, the marital-shifting, and the fact that most *friending* or *living* relationships do not eventuate in marriage are not symptoms of disorganization. They are cultural adaptations that have developed under lower-class conditions.

A final point needs to be made. In discussing the engagement letter this chapter seems to emphasize marriage as a goal of all marital relationships. Marriage, without doubt, is the ideal. One variation of this ideal is to marry after spending some time *friending* and *living*. The engagement has been accommodated to this idealized sequence. In fact, however, the promise of the engagement letter is usually not fulfilled. Moreover, most *friending* or *living* relationships are not preceded by an engagement letter. The material in this chapter should therefore be related to the chapter titled "The Husband-Wife Relationship"; and the separate importance of *friending*, *living*, and marriage should be kept in mind.

NOTES

1. Other references to the engagement letter in the Caribbean area are found in: Melville J. Herskovits and Frances S. Herskovits, *Trinidad Village* (New York: Alfred A. Knopf, 1947), pp. 85–86 *et passim;* Keith F. Otterbein, "The Courtship and Mating System of the Andros Islanders," *Social and Economic Studies* 13 (June 1964): 282–301.

2. The use of the engagement letter is apparently of Spanish origin, and may have been introduced into Trinidad during the period of Spanish colonialism. According to the *Catholic Encyclopedia* (1st ed., s.v. "betrothal") "In Spain . . . a betrothal compact is considered invalid by the Church unless written documents pass between the contracting parties. This practice obtains in other countries also, but its observance is not necessary to validate the agreement." Herskovits and Herskovits (*op. cit.,* p. 294) refer to the practice as a reinterpretation of African patterns. The use of an engagement letter may well fit the contractual nature of certain African marriage patterns, and their involvement of kinsmen, but its source is probably not African. Cf. Isaac Schapera, *Married Life in an African Tribe* (Evanston: Northwestern University Press, 1966, first pub-

lished in 1940); A. R. Radcliffe-Brown and Daryll Forde (eds.), *African Systems of Kinship and Marriage* (London: Oxford University Press, 1950); Arthur Phillips (ed.), *Survey of African Marriage and Family Life* (New York: Oxford University Press, 1953); and Meyer Fortes (ed.), *Marriage in Tribal Societies* (Cambridge, Eng.: Cambridge University Press, 1962).

3. William J. Goode, "Illegitimacy in the Caribbean Social Structure," *American Sociological Review* 25 (February 1960): 21–30.

4. Judith Blake, "Family Instability and Reproductive Behavior in Jamaica," *Current Research in Human Fertility* (New York: Milbank Memorial Fund, 1955), pp. 24–41; and Judith Blake, *Family Structure in Jamaica* (New York: Free Press, 1961).

5. William J. Goode, *op. cit.*

6. *Ibid.*, pp. 24–26.

7. *Ibid.*, p. 24.

8. Hyman Rodman, "On Understanding Lower-Class Behaviour," *Social and Economic Studies* 8 (December 1959): 448–49.

9. Hyman Rodman, "Marital Relationships in a Trinidad Village," *Marriage and Family Living* 23 (May 1961): 166–70.

10. One could quarrel with the wording here. "For people in your position," coming from a middle-class interviewer, has a patronizing sound, and is perhaps not the best way of getting valid responses. Even more significant is the use of the word "just"—surely a possible indication to the respondent of which response is considered to be more socially desirable by the interviewer.

11. Judith Blake, *Family Structure in Jamaica*, op. cit., pp. 118–19.

12. *Ibid.*, p. 122.

13. Table 8 is a slightly adapted version of a table originally published by the author in "Illegitimacy in the Caribbean Social Structure: A Reconsideration," *American Sociological Review* 31 (October 1966): 673–83. The six preceding paragraphs, with minor alterations, are also reprinted from that article with the permission of the American Sociological Association.

14. Cf. David M. Schneider, *American Kinship: A Cultural Account* (Englewood Cliffs, N. J.: Prentice-Hall, 1968).

9. *Rules of Marriage and Residence*

What is fame for the man is shame for the woman.

COCONUT VILLAGER

HOW MANY WIVES should a man have? Where should he live after he marries? Is he forbidden to marry his mother's brother's daughter, or is she the preferred marriage partner? Who are his kinsmen? These are all cultural questions to which there are no universal answers. Every society has its own cultural rules that give at least partial answers to these questions. These kinship rules provide stability for the individual—for example, if he is expected to live with his wife at the home of her parents, then there need not be an agonizing decision about where to live each time a marriage takes place. Some of the kinship rules of Coconut Village are discussed in this chapter. All of them, unless otherwise specified, refer both to legal marriage and to customary marriage (*living*).

EXOGAMY

There is a preference, in Coconut Village, to enter into a marital relationship with a non-villager or a newly arrived villager. The preponderance of adult males in the village and the recent origin of the village (many villagers were born elsewhere and maintain non-village ties) contribute to the frequency of village exogamy. I expect that larger villages with a more equal sex distribution and older in origin would show a greater frequency of marriage within the village. But another factor which may lead a person to seek a wife elsewhere is that he and the other villagers know about the *friending* affairs of a girl in the village, and by entering a marital relationship with a non-village girl he is not troubled by such knowledge. As one informant put it:

Most fellas like to marry a girl of outside, don' mind
not knowin' the character of a girl outside; but when
here, they see all the action, they rather go outside.

The preferred marriage partner is a non-kinsman, although there is no objection to a distant kinsman. Because
of the presence of a considerable "East Indian" Muslim
population in Trinidad, with cross-cousin marriage preference, the question of marriage to a kinsman is almost always
taken by informants to mean marriage to a cousin, and is
looked upon without horror, but simply as "ridiculous." Many
informants are clearly aware of the practice of cousin marriage in the island, and talk of "the Indians" or "some others"
who do this. But the reaction to such marriage within the
informants' own group tends to be fairly uniform:

> You are a relative and let it be that; one way but not
> two ways.

*   *   *

> You have no right because you're both of the same
> blood.

*   *   *

> Around here they's take it up as a ridicule.

Occasionally, marriage to a first or second cousin takes
place, and the recollected reactions, while indicating the un-
desirability of such marriages, are not extremely severe:

> Two first cousins get marry and the aunt went to
> church to stop it. Was brother and sister children. But
> they did get married. (*And what happened?*) Every-
> body talk about it still; they look at children and say
> the children is cousins to the mother and father.

*   *   *

> (*Would a person usually marry a relative or a person
> who isn't a relative?*) Anybody, not bound to be a rela-
> tive, some people like a relative and some not. (*How
> about a cousin?*) Some people say you can' marry a

cousin, but I know people who marry first cousin, second cousin. (*What did the people do when that happened?*) Some does criticize, say I never would marry
a cousin, but you get criticism if you do right thing,
if you give a man a penny some come and say why give
him, he had his already and throw it away.

The reaction to brother-sister marriage, or to the marriage
of half-siblings, is more severe than that with respect to
cousins, and I have not heard of any such marriages. However, marriage with more distant kinsmen is not frowned
upon, and the hypothetical question about marriage to a
distant kinsman is often answered with the suggestion that
you might not even know that the person is related to you.
In addition, villagers would occasionally, and of their own
accord, add that you could not blame a person for marrying
a kinsman—even a close kinsman—if he didn't know that
such a kinship relationship existed.

(*Would a person marry a distant relative?*) People are
hardly likely to know a distant relative, a distant relative
doesn' mean a cousin. A cousin of mine's daughter had
a son who my daughter married, that's a distant relative, and I heard tell of him only.

*   *   *

(*Why would a person not marry a relative?*) I would
not marry my cousin. Nature will never exist to that
extent, it wouldn't love, knowing it's a relative, when
it come to a question of cohabitation, I don' feel there's
be any stimulation at all. (*How about if a person really
wanted to marry a cousin?*) I would look at that as ridiculous. I'm not charging you for something you don'
know, if you don' know it's okay, but if you know is a
cousin, then I charge him guilty.

NEOLOCAL RESIDENCE

It is the girl who usually moves from her village into the
village of her husband. In this way the man continues to

work at his job, which provides the financial support for the marital relationship. The man's job, however, is often irregular and poorly paid, and the marital relationship may falter if the man's employment situation worsens. An alternative pattern of residence is found in those cases where a woman owns her own house. The man moves into her home and is thereby spared the expense of acquiring a house, but his authority within the house is weakened when he does not own it.

In entering a marital relationship the boy and girl ordinarily move into a separate household, and the girl expresses this preference for neolocal postmarital residence by her expectation to be "put in a house." Furthermore, her decision about entering such a relationship takes into consideration the man's ability to acquire and maintain a separate household. However, where circumstances make it difficult to get their own household, they might still enter a marital relationship and live with the boy's family (patrilocal) or the girl's family (matrilocal) or they may live apart (dual residence).[1] These cases, however, are infrequent and the arrangement is considered temporary. If the marital relationship persists, the couple eventually will shift to their own household. The only strong preference is for neolocal residence: with regard to the other "expedient" types, matrilocal and patrilocal residence are preferred to dual residence; and some informants prefer matrilocal over patrilocal residence, stating that things might be more difficult when the mother-in-law and daughter-in-law live together. But aside from neolocal preference, the basic attitude is the "accordin'" one,[2] in which the informants stress that the particular circumstances of the particular people involved determine the residential pattern. The preference for neolocal residence, the acceptance of matrilocal, patrilocal, and dual residence, and the tendency for the latter three to shift to neolocal residence, are all illustrated below:

(*Where should a couple live when they get married?*)
I find they should live at them. But in some cases the

girl come and get pregnant, and the mother feel the
boy should marry the girl, but there is a shortage of
houses, and so they stay at boy's mother or girl's
mother. Sometimes they live good and get own place.
I know one case they get married and he stay at his
place and she stay at her place. She stayed at her sister's
and he at his mother's, and they have about five children.

* * *

(*When a couple decides to get married, where should
they live?*) They should live by themselves. Only in
certain cases a person would like to, but owing to circumstances can' get a place. But you find more peace
and quiet in your own place, you can lie as you like,
speak as you like. (*If you have to live with somebody is
it better to stay with the boy's family or the girl's family?*) It's as wide as it's broad, the one or the other if
you have no alternative. (*If they had a choice, at which
one would they be most comfortable?*) There is a great
amount of difference, my choice might be father, and
your choice might be mother, you have good father-in-
law and bad and good mother-in-law and bad.

* * *

(*Is it best to live near the boy's or near the girl's family?*) The further off from the family is quite better.
(*Where is it better to live if you have to, with girl's or
with boy's family?*) For him, better by his family, and
for the girl, better by her family. (*How about for both
of them?*) They could live at the boy's family, anyone
of the families, until they get a place.

* * *

If you take a girl home your mother does try to intrude
on the girl. Or if you live with girl her mother does try
to intrude on you. That's why I said you mus' live separate, so if you have a little misunderstandin', it home
at all you; but if at mother-in-law, you can' talk the
way you like, the mother-in-law and father-in-law is
there. Is one to rule the house, can' have two captain in
one ship.

MONOGAMY AND INFIDELITY

The marital relationship is ideally monogamic, whether we are considering the *friending, living,* or married relationship. In this way, the question of a child's paternity is not in doubt, and the proper parent-child relationships are established with the father recognizing and supporting his child. In actual practice, however, the onus of monogamic responsibility is placed upon the woman, and she is the one who ordinarily confines herself to a single partner at a time, particularly if she is *living* or married. The man, on the other hand, has a greater degree of freedom to establish extramarital *friending* relationships. One could say that the only difference between a single man and a married man is that the latter has a wife to remind him of the difference. This statement can probably be applied to other contemporary societies as well—but it may be somewhat truer of Trinidad because of the weaker sanctions against a man's extramarital relations. The following conversation, overheard in a taxi, gives us an idea of the man's position:

Woman: When I hear you married, I tell you in truth I really doubt it.

Man: I doubt it myself when I see myself in church.

Woman: I could expec' it of your brother, but I never think I see you marry.

Man: She catch me, man.

Woman: She catch you good, she catch you real good in truth. Where you livin'?

Man: We livin' in Sangre Grande.

Woman: But you mus' treat she nice, she a nice, quiet girl, you mus' not treat she bad.

Man: What you talkin'? Mus' still run around a little, yes.

Due to the presence of three distinct types of marital patterns, the villagers are able to keep the monogamic principle without losing the extramarital interest. A *legal* monogamic

Table 9
PERCENTAGE FAVORABLE TO INFIDELITY IN *FRIENDING*, *LIVING*, AND MARRIAGE BY SEX AND CLASS

	UPPER LOWER	LOWER LOWER	TOTAL SAMPLE
1. Is it all right for a man to have sexual intercourse before he marries?			
Female	63	37	
Male	69	81	
			62
2. Is it all right for a woman to have sexual intercourse before she marries?			
Female	50	29	
Male	56	74	
			51
3. Is it all right for a man to be *friending* with more than one woman?			
Female	18	10	
Male	36	30	
			23
4. Is it all right for a woman to be *friending* with more than one man?			
Female	0	2	
Male	14	13	
			8
5. Is it all right for a man who is living (common law) with a woman to be *friending* with someone on the outside?			
Female	29	7	
Male	25	20	
			17
6. Is it all right for a woman who is living (common law) with a man to be *friending* with someone on the outside?			
Female	6	3	
Male	11	8	
			7

	UPPER LOWER	LOWER LOWER	TOTAL SAMPLE

7. Is it all right for a man who is married to be *friending* with someone on the outside?

Female	6	5	
Male	11	18	
			11

8. Is it all right for a woman who is married to be *friending* with someone on the outside?

Female	0	0	
Male	0	5	
			2

Total Number of Respondents			
Female	17	59	
Male	36	61	
			173

bond is seldom transgressed; bigamy is a rare occurrence. But a casual *friending* relationship may exist side by side with a legal marriage or a *living* relationship. Such a casual *friending* relationship—*friending* on the outside, as the villagers would say—does not have the approval of the community and cannot be considered a form of marriage. Marital bonds, moreover, tend to be weak, and most persons have participated serially in several *friending* and *living* relationships. It is thus common to find a person who recognizes children by more than one spouse.

Attitudes toward infidelity were collected in the 1962 survey, with questions on *friending, living,* and marriage. The full set of data, broken down by social class and sex, are presented in Table 9. If we look at the percentages for the total sample, we can quickly see the over-all findings.[3]

Questions 1 and 2 are not on attitudes toward infidelity, but deal with the normative status of sexual intercourse before marriage. There are substantial numbers who state that premarital intercourse is all right for both men (62 per cent) and women (51 per cent). The rest of the questions deal with attitudes toward infidelity. Questions 3 and 4 are on *friending*—23 per cent approve of infidelity for men, and 8 per cent approve for women. These figures decline a little in the questions on infidelity within the *living* relationship (17 per cent approve for men, 7 per cent for women) and the legal marriage relationship (11 per cent approve for men, 2 per cent approve for women). One striking feature is the double standard that exists, with women expected to adhere to a code of fidelity in all relationships by a greater percentage of respondents. Another striking fact is that fidelity is expected by a very high percentage of respondents in all three relationships—*friending, living,* and married. The major differences are between the first two questions and the last six questions—the differences in expectations of fidelity within the three marital relationships in Trinidad are minor in comparison, although a slightly higher percentage do expect fidelity in marriage than in *living*, and in *living* than in *friending*.

THE PRINCIPLE OF FIDELITY

I have been discussing the *friending, living,* and married relationships as alternate forms of marriage, but in general it is not always clear what "marriage" is. This question is of little interest to members of a community, but it is of interest to anthropologists concerned with a universal definition of marriage.[4] It is also of interest to investigators whose research findings lead them to differ on whether consensual marital unions in certain societies are normative or deviant.[5] I have suggested elsewhere that we can use the principle of fidelity as one criterion (in addition to others, such as community approval of the relationship) for classifying a relationship as marriage.[6]

Sexual rights are one of the major elements that are acquired in the marriage process. These rights are either exclusively confined to the spouses, or are primarily confined to them, but with certain community-sanctioned exceptions.[7] As Fortes has put it, "what distinguishes the conjugal relationship uniquely from all other dyadic relationships, and isolates it as the core of the domestic domain, is the exclusive, or at the minimum privileged sexual rights and claims of the spouses on each other." [8]

This exclusive or privileged sexual relationship is generally supported by sanctions, and these are ordinarily more severe for women. Adultery is a trangression of the community expectations of this privileged relationship, and it is punished in varying ways, with varying degrees of severity, in different societies. I have referred to the privileged sexual relationship in marriage, the expectations of fidelity, and the sanctions against adultery as the "principle of fidelity." [9] Since this principle stems from, and supports, marriage, it is possible to use it when one is trying to distinguish between a man-woman relationship that is marriage and one that is not marriage. According to the principle of fidelity, we would have to say that the evidence points in the direction of including *friending* and *living*, as well as legal marriage, as forms of marriage in lower-class Trinidad. It will be of particular importance, in the theoretical chapters, to explore the functions served by these varying forms of marriage.

NOTES

1. George P. Murdock, *Social Structure* (New York: Macmillan, 1949). Cf. Paul Bohannan, "An Alternate Residence Classification," in Paul Bohannan and John Middleton (eds.), *Marriage, Family and Residence* (Garden City: Natural History Press, 1968), pp. 317–23.

2. See Chapter 12, p. 173.

3. A more detailed discussion of these data is available in Hyman Rodman, "Fidelity and Forms of Marriage: The Consensual Union in the Caribbean," in Gerhard Neubeck (ed.), *Extramarital Relations* (Englewood Cliffs, N.J.: Prentice-Hall, 1969), pp. 94–107.

4. E. R. Leach, "Polyandry, Inheritance, and the Definition of Marriage," *Man* 55 (December 1955), No. 199: 182–86; Kathleen Gough, "The Nayars and the Definition of Marriage," *Journal of the Royal Anthropological Institute* 89 (1959): 23–34; and Kathleen Gough, book review of *A Study of Polyandry*, *Man* 65 (January–February 1965): No. 23: 30–31.

5. William J. Goode, "Illegitimacy in the Caribbean Social Structure," *American Sociological Review* 25 (February 1960): 21–30; Judith Blake, *Family Structure in Jamaica* (New York: Free Press,

1961); and Hyman Rodman, "Illegitimacy in the Caribbean Social Structure: A Reconsideration," *American Sociological Review* 31 (October 1966): 673–83.

6. Hyman Rodman, "Fidelity and Forms of Marriage . . .," *op. cit.*

7. According to Murdock, "Taboos on adultery are extremely widespread though sometimes more honored in the breach than in the observance. They appear in 120 of the 148 societies in our sample for which data are available. In 4 of the remaining 28, adultery is socially disapproved though not strictly forbidden; it is conditionally permitted in 19 and freely allowed in 5." Murdock, *op. cit.*, p. 265.

8. Meyer Fortes (ed.), *Marriage in Tribal Societies* (Cambridge, Eng: Cambridge University Press, 1962), p. 8.

9. Hyman Rodman, "Fidelity and Forms of Marriage . . .," *op. cit.*

10. *Rules of Descent and Inheritance*

> *A formal arrangement of the more immediate*
> *blood kindred into lines of descent, with the*
> *adoption of some method to distinguish one*
> *relative from another, and to express the value*
> *of the relationship, would be one of the earliest*
> *acts of human intelligence.*
>
> LEWIS H. MORGAN

THE idea of our common descent from Adam and Eve emphasizes the relatedness of all mankind. An individual who sets out to trace his genealogical ties will find that he is related to a vast number of individuals. It is impossible to maintain active kinship ties with so many people. Rules of descent establish a manageable group of kinsmen for an individual. They specify that active kinship ties exist with only certain individuals with whom he is genealogically related. A rule of unilineal descent, for example, carves out special kinship ties for individuals who are related through a single line—fathers and sons are the link upon which patrilineal descent is built, and mothers and daughters the link for matrilineal descent.

The nature of the kinship relationship varies among different categories of kinsmen. An individual's relationship to his father may differ greatly from his relationship to his father's brother. The inheritance of property is one aspect of kinship ties: who inherits whose property? The rules of inheritance, for property not owned by a kinship group as a whole, establish the culturally correct individuals who inherit. These rules, to the degree they are generally accepted, minimize conflicts about the transference of property at the time of an individual's death.

BILATERAL DESCENT

The rule of bilateral descent applies in Coconut Village. This means that kinship bonds correspond perfectly to genealogical bonds and that each individual, with the exception of full siblings, has a different kinship group or kindred.[1] Since kinship bonds correspond to genealogical bonds, this opens up the possibility of an extremely large and unmanageable group of kinsmen. To avoid this, it is necessary to postulate that there is some definite point at which kinship relationships, traced genealogically, are no longer recognized. In Trinidad, as in the United States and many other bilateral descent societies, this is not altogether true, and the point at which kinship bonds end is quite indefinite. What actually happens is that each person's kindred is limited by his range of social contact.[2] In some societies, where kinship is a major preoccupation, kinship relations are traced in great depth. Due to the weakness of kinship ties in Coconut Village, descent is not extensively traced and the size of the active kindred is not large.

Since the kindred differs for each individual, with the exception of full siblings, there is no continuous base upon which a corporate kin group can be organized. As a result, the nuclear family becomes more important for the individual, and the kinsmen of the non-corporate kindred are generally less important. In contrast, where there are corporate kin groups, based upon unilineal or occasionally non-unilinial descent,[3] the activities of the group and the bonds it builds between its members make the nuclear family bonds less important.

Corporate kin groups also establish kinship ties that make the distinction between kin and non-kin much sharper than in a bilateral system with a series of interlocking kindreds. In a bilateral system, it is therefore likelier that close contact with a non-kinsman may involve the extension of kin-like status to that person, who is treated as a member of one's kindred, and perhaps addressed by a kinship term.[4] Some of the similarities between friends, neighbors, and kinsmen were discussed in Chapter 7; the terminological reflections of these overlappings between kin and non-kin will be discussed in the next chapter. Because of its vagueness about the boundaries of the kindred, we would expect that a bilateral kinship system is the one most likely to involve these kin and non-kin cross-overs.

In Coconut Village one's kinship descent is traced equally through the biological mother and father. For instance, the child's biological mother may not take care of her child, and she may not contribute to his support, but she is still the child's mother and the child will trace his descent through her. Similarly, the father may not live with his child, and he may not be supporting him, but the child will still trace his descent through the father. The fact that the sociological role of mother and father may be played by persons other than the biological mother and father in no way alters the rule of tracing descent through them. Although there is ideally an equal recognition of kin on both the mother's and father's side, the actual extent of recognition is established through contact with one's kinsmen. Since the father often does not enter into a stable marital relationship with the mother, the child ordinarily has more contact with, and stronger ties to, the mother's side of the family. The lesser importance of the father within the kinship system is illustrated by the following examples:

> (*What would most people say, between the mother's and the father's family, which do you think most people would prefer?*) Most of us think you get more appreciation on the mother's side. A boy might have a child with a girl and doesn't show that child any affection. But if your mother's sister give you something today and beat you nex' day, well she still aunt, she did give you something. Some of them, some fathers, you don' even know them.

> * * *

> (*Which side of the family would be more important between the family on the father's side and the family on the mother's side?*) Both side of the family can render assistance, if they want to do so. No choice between both of them, if both want to help, jus' as welcome. (*Who would usually help the child more?*) The girl's parents, usually. (*Why is that?*) The mother

would say is my daughter's child, is supposed to be my child, too.

The stress upon genealogical relationship as a basis for a kinship relationship is another factor which leads to a child's stronger bond with his mother's kin than with his father's kin. Since the identity of the biological father may be in doubt, the father's kin as well as the father will be chary about whether the child is related to them:

> (*Who would have more affection for a child, the mother's or the father's family?*) The mother will have more feelings for the child, the pains she know she bear. (*How about between the mother's and the father's family?*) The mother will say, that is my grandchild, but the man's mother, she might say the child is not the son's own, any man can make a child.

*   *   *

> (*What do people call a mother's sister?*) Some say auntie, some say tantie. (*And a father's sister?*) The same thing. Some people say they have more love for a sister child than for a brother child. (*Why is that?*) Because you're certain your sister child is hers, but his mother (*referring to the mother of the boy by whom the speaker's foster daughter had had a child*), she can' be certain, may be another boy's. (*Her foster daughter, in the meantime, was present and helping her to explain this to me.*)

This stress upon the biological tie of parenthood can thus be seen to relate to a variety of phenomena we have already noted—the father's doubts about whether a child is his, and his watchfulness and wariness; the use of the father's surname in everyday affairs, even though the child legally carries his mother's surname; and the double standard of behavior, in which premarital and extramarital relationships are more permissible for men than for women:

> (*What happens while friending, if the girl has a child and the father does not mind it?*) Still his child and

he is family to the child. But the girl must be seeing only one; if two, then maybe she doesn' know which is father. (*What would she do if she doesn't know?*) Well, would say is your child, but it may be mine. (*And who would be the family to the child?*) Well, if is my child, then I is family. (*And maybe the child doesn't know who is father?*) Well, not child's fault, is woman's fault. That's why is so important to have only one husband. If married to one and friendin' with another, may not know whose child it is. Woman may say is his child, and maybe he won' own it.

This leads to an interesting hypothesis about the relationship between the rules of descent and the rules of sexual behavior of a society.[5] Given the importance of the biological tie, we would expect a greater degree of premarital and extramarital sexual permissiveness in a matrilineal society (where descent is traced through the mother) than in a patrilineal or bilateral society. The reason for this is that a man's relationship to his sister's sons is of more importance to him in a matrilineal society than in a patrilineal or bilateral society, and his relationship to his own sons would be of less importance to him. Since he would have no doubts about his biological relationship to his sister's sons, regardless of the extent of sexual permissiveness, there may be less pressure for stricter sexual taboos.

INHERITANCE: LAW AND CUSTOM

Just as with the rules of descent, so with the rules of inheritance—there is both fixity and flexibility. Our major concern is with the customary workings of the rules of inheritance and with the villagers' attitudes about inheritance matters. These will give us information about family relationships in the village to add to what we have already learned in earlier chapters.

Custom and attitudes, however, do not operate in a vacuum. There are legal rules that pertain to inheritance, and custom interacts with these legal restrictions. The laws of Trinidad and Tobago make major provisions for (a) a wife or husband; (b) an unmarried daughter, or a married daughter if she is disabled; and (c) a son less than twenty-one years old, or a disabled son. "Reasonable provision for the maintenance" of these dependents is required. Where there is a surviving spouse and at least one additional dependent, and they contest a will, no more than two-thirds of the estate may be awarded to them by the court in fulfillment of the requirement for reasonable provision. Where there is a surviving spouse and no other dependents, one-half of the estate would be considered a reasonable provision. No provisions are made for any dependents other than those mentioned above. The court, however, is expected to consider the conduct of the dependent to the testator, and the testator's reasons for the dispositions he makes in his will. The law is therefore not altogether restrictive, and it permits customary rules to operate within fairly broad limits.[6]

The major point on which law and custom collide is in the definition of wife, husband, son, and daughter. The law recognizes only a legally married wife or husband, and only sons and daughters who are born to a couple in a legal union. Custom, however, also recognizes a wife or husband in a non-legal (*living*) union, and the sons and daughters of such a union. Controversy is therefore possible between a legal and a *de facto* wife, and between legitimate and illegitimate children. One villager, for example, expressed strong concern about what would happen to the land his father owned. He was one of more than twenty-five *outside children* of his father, who also had five legitimate children. His stated concern was that "the lawful children, they are not loyal, and they are liable to take all. And the child that is unlawful is deprived." In a case in which a man died intestate and his estate eventually was settled in court, the law found a compromise to the dispute:

> The lawful got the money, and the unlawful put in a claim because they are the ones that take care of the parents. And they win because the lawful children had to pay the unlawful ones compensation for taking care of the parents.

Despite the high potential for controversy, it is usually avoided. This is because customary rights and expectations take precedence over legal rights within the village. It is the personal relationship between people, and not the legal relationship, that is important. As a result, the non-legal wife who has lived with her *de facto* husband for many years has customary rights to the property. Similarly, "by customary right illegitimacy does not prevent a child from inheriting the property of its parents." [7] Since these customary rights are widely accepted, they mitigate conflict. For example, legitimate children who inherit property will often share it with illegitimate children of their own accord, because they are not supposed to deprive illegitimate children of a share of the inheritance. In one case, a man had five children, and only the last one was legitimate:

> When the father die he leave a house and twenty-five acres of land. And the lawful one get it. But she do right, and she get a solicitor to make up paper and divide the land proportionately to the others.

Legal solutions, under any circumstances, are not seen as ideal. As Harry C. Bredemeier points out, the law tends to be inflexible; it assumes that one side is right and the other wrong; and half of the people involved in litigation lose.

> The fact remains . . . that "the law" is for many people something to be avoided if at all possible. There is not a very good market for the law's output of justice; and— the other side of the same coin—the law is not widely regarded as the place to take one's conflicts, except as a last resort. [8]

Imagine how much more pertinent these general points become for lower-class Negroes in the West Indies who are subjected to English and other European laws that take little cognizance of their marital practices:

> As a general rule . . . the laws adopted in the West Indies were initially created for application to English institutions. Yet only a small proportion of these colonial

populations displays a culture pattern which approximates to that which underlies the English institutions. For the form and structure of many domestic unions in the West Indies differ fundamentally from those of the majority of English families. It is very common to find in the lower social class many domestic relationships of varying permanency which do not satisfy the legal requirements of marriage.[9]

Despite the general acceptance of customary practices in the lower class,[10] it is recognized that legal rights may interfere with what is customarily expected. As one woman stated, you can have "a lot of ups and downs with the government" (courts) before being able to claim the inheritance if your *de facto* husband dies. Unless the *de facto* relationship becomes *de jure*, it is possible for someone else to win legal rights to the inheritance that should, by custom, go to the non-legal wife. As a result, it is the issue of legality, rather than morality, that provides the major push toward marriage. A man is eventually expected to marry the woman he is *living* with, if they get along well, so that nobody else can lay claim to his property after his death. This produces some marriages at a relatively old age or when the man is on his deathbed.

If a man cannot marry the woman he is *living* with, because one of them is still married to another partner, then he is expected to make out a will leaving his property to her. It is a common practice for a man to exclude his legal wife from his estate if they separated after marriage and established permanent relations and homes outside the marriage. With evidential proof in court, the man's will is usually upheld and his *de facto* wife inherits the estate.

Although spouse and children are paramount in matters of inheritance, other kinsmen, and occasionally non-kin, may also be involved. This follows from the stress that is placed upon the personal relationship. The following examples indicate that the special relationship between the testator and the heir is an important consideration:

(*To whom would a man leave his things when he*

dies?) Sometimes to his children, or any other person who do for him when he sick.

* * *

(*Whom would a man leave his things for when he died?*) If he accumulated a certain amount, can leave it to a friend, a mother, a brother, it depend: if nearest of kin has happen to be livin' on friendly term or who know how to put it to use. If have a bad son and is wayward and always bring you to shame, perhaps think of somebody else, even though is your son.

* * *

I was in conversation with two men in the village. One mentioned an older man who lived a few miles from the village, saying: He would rather leave his money to a friend than to his children, except for one that showed some love to him. For the rest he would leave a glass of water and a shilling. (*Who should he leave it for?*) In his case he says if he get someone at least to care him, so when he dying he leave some for that person, because the children not worry with him.

* * *

A man in the village who had accumulated a considerable amount of property named his legal wife as the beneficiary for as long as she lives, and after her death his property was to be divided among all of his many children and grandchildren. According to a villager, these children (both legitimate and outside *children), and grandchildren (by his legitimate and* outside *children) will receive from two to five acres of land each, "according to how loyal the child or grandchild was to the old man."*

The point is that the individual may, within the limits imposed by law, exercise a good deal of choice in disposing of his money or his property. The primary obligations of an individual are to his wife (married or *living*) and to his children, whether by his wife or another woman; of secondary importance are the claims of a man's other kin; and lastly, the claims of non-kinsmen may enter the situation. These represent the range of possibilities open to the individual, and it is the nature of a man's relationship to his kinsmen and non-kin that influences his attitudes and his behavior.

NOTES

1. George P. Murdock, *Social Structure* (New York: Macmillan, 1949), p. 60.

2. *Ibid.*; Hildred S. Geertz, *The Javanese Family* (New York: Free Press, 1961), pp. 24–26.

3. See E. R. Leach, "Some Features of Social Structure Among the Sarawak Pagans," *Man* 48 (August 1948): 91–92; Ward H. Goodenough, "A Problem in Malayo-Polynesian Social Organization," *American Anthropologist* 57 (February 1955): 71–83; William Davenport, "Nonunilinear Descent and Descent Groups," *American Anthropologist* 61 (August 1959): 557–72; and Bernd Lambert, "Ambilineal Descent Groups in the Northern Gilbert Islands," *American Anthropologist* 68 (June 1966): 641–64.

4. Edward Norbeck and Harumi Befu, "Informal Fictive Kinship in Japan," *American Anthropologist* 60 (February 1958): 102–17; Geertz, *op. cit.*, p. 24; John A. Ballweg, "Extension of Meaning and Use for Kinship Terms," *American Anthropologist* 71 (February 1969): 84–87.

5. George P. Murdock, "Cultural Correlates of the Regulation of Premarital Sex Behavior," in Robert A. Manners (ed.), *Process and Pattern in Culture* (Chicago: Aldine, 1964), pp. 399–410.

6. *Trinidad and Tobago Revised Ordinances*, 1950, Chapter 8, No. 2, Wills and Probate, Section 90, pp. 1008–10.

7. K. W. Patchett, "Some Aspects of Marriage and Divorce in the West Indies," *International and Comparative Law Quarterly* 8 (October 1959): 675.

8. Harry C. Bredemeier, "Law as an Integrative Mechanism," in William M. Evan (ed.), *Law and Sociology* (New York: Free Press, 1962), p. 85.

9. K. W. Patchett, *op. cit.*, p. 666. Cf. M. G. Smith, "Social and Cultural Pluralism," in *Social and Cultural Pluralism in the Caribbean*, Annals of the New York Academy of Sciences, Vol. 83, 1960, pp. 763–77.

10. S. Comhaire-Sylvain, "The Household in Kenscoff, Haiti," *Social and Economic Studies* 10 (June 1961): 192–222.

11. *Kinship Terminology*

Part of the reciprocal behavior characterizing every relationship between kinsmen consists of a verbal element, the terms by which each addresses the other. Although some people commonly employ personal names even among relatives, all societies make at least some use of special kinship terms, and the great majority use them predominantly or exclusively in intercourse between relatives.

GEORGE P. MURDOCK

MOST OF US ask ourselves, at one time or another, whether to address John Smith as "John" or as "Mr. Smith." The choice of either term would, of course, depend upon our relationship to the man. For this reason it is often possible to learn something about the relationship between two people through the terms they use to address each other, or through their avoidance of terms of address. In everyday affairs the latter may happen simply because a person cannot decide whether "John" or "Mr. Smith" is more appropriate, and he may therefore refrain from using either. Clearly we cannot expect to know everything about a relationship once we have grasped its terminological handle. The term can only serve as a crude indicator of a complex relationship.[1] Nevertheless, it is possible, at times, to carry the analysis surprisingly far through a consideration of the terms of address used, particularly when there are also other data available about the nature of the relationship.

Although I have used a non-kinship example, kinship relationships are also illuminated by the terms of address. It is possible to learn about the kinship system in general through an analysis of the terms that are patterned rather than idiosyncratic. It will not add much to our knowledge of a kinship system to discover that one child calls its mother by her first name, but it could be extremely important to discover that many children do.

KINSHIP TERMS AND ROLE RELATIONSHIPS

For the most part I shall use kinship terms of address rather than terms of reference in order to highlight role relationships within lower-class Negro families in Trinidad. A term of address is used in speaking directly to a kinsman, and it is therefore more likely to be altered to correspond to the nature of the relationship between the kinsmen. For example, knowing that an aunt is frequently addressed not merely by an aunt term (e.g., auntie, tantie) but also by a mother term (e.g., mammy, mother) would suggest that in some ways both an aunt and a mother might play equivalent roles.

Even though the major part of the analysis will focus upon terms of address, I want to begin by considering some terms in general use in the village to *refer* to a group or collection of kinsmen. A term of reference is used to refer to a kinsman, or a group of kinsmen, when talking to a third person. The most frequently used term of reference for a collection of kinsmen in Coconut Village is "family," which may mean, quite simply, all of one's relatives or kinsmen, including grandparents, parents, aunts, uncles, cousins, siblings, etc. In the village, a family is not the group consisting of husband, wife, and children, as it sometimes is used in America or by the middle-class town dweller in Trinidad. Within Trinidad's Negro lower class there is no term that refers exclusively to the group consisting of husband, wife, and children. This suggests the relative lack of importance of the nuclear family. Moreover, the term "family" is not often used to refer to one's kinsmen as a group; it is usually used to refer to one's kinship tie to another individual, as in the expression "he is family to me." Even more significant, "my family" is often used to refer to a kinship relationship to one person, as in the expression, "he is my family." The implication is that kinship ties between particular individuals are more important than ties to a group of kinsmen.

Another term which may refer to a group of kinsmen is "home." There is a lack of consensus within the village about exactly what "home" means, and it can refer to non-kin as well as kinsmen. Ordinarily, the term refers to the group of people who live in the same household. This group consists of husband, wife, and children as the core, often with other kin, or non-kin, included. For instance, in replying to the expression, "How is home?" a person would discuss the welfare of those he is living with in the same household. Some informants, however, did not confine the term to those living together, but included those who visited freely in the household, whether friends or kin. These uses further document the overlapping of nuclear family, kinship, and friendship ties.

It has already been pointed out that there is a good deal of child-shifting and marital-shifting.[2] Alternative uses of the term "home" are therefore not surprising. The alternatives parallel the possibility of changes in household composition. They reflect the fact that (1) those who live together in the same household, regardless of kinship ties, have a special relationship; (2) those who visit freely within the household are potential household members; and (3) there is a strong personal element in the relationship between two kinsmen regardless of whether they share the same household or not. It therefore makes sense that a person's "home people" are those who are living in the same household with him, or in addition, those who visit the household freely.

Another relevant phrase is "home name." This is a nickname given a child by one of his kinsmen, and used as a term of address by those in the household, those who visit the household, kin and non-kin alike, and usually also by all others in the community. Briefly put then, the term "home" is often used to refer to the group of people living in the same household, and it reflects the intermingling of nuclear family members, other kinsmen, and non-kinsmen.

Considerable and varying use is made of kinship terms of address in non-kin relationships. "Pappy," "mammy," "auntie," "uncle," and variations of these are the terms most frequently used, and they may be used jocularly, as a sign of respect, or simply as a proper name. For instance, when a villager addresses someone of his own age range or younger, calling out, "Hey, pappy!" the usage is jocular and more

friendly than the very common "man" form of address between non-kin, as in "Is true, man?" or, "Come na, man."
The kin term is also used as a sign of respect to an "older
head," as when an older woman might be addressed as
"Auntie," or as "Ma Mary" by all the villagers. Finally, a
kinship term is at times used simply as a "home name": in
the village one young girl is known as "Tantie" by all, and
one man in his thirties as "Pap." This "name" usage also
shows up in terms of address used to kinsmen, where
terms like "Uncle Pappy" or "Tan' Tan' " (Aunt Aunt)
are used.

A variety of kinship terms are used to address certain kinsmen. We would expect that the largest number of alternative
terms would ordinarily be used within the most important
relationships. These terms would roughly correspond to the
different behavioral shades of the relationship. Although I
do not have the data to explore this correspondence in detail,
I do have a list of alternative terms of address for the mother,
father, aunt, and uncle. The alternatives noted for mothers
are the following: mammy, mummy, personal name (e.g.,
Ruth), mother, tantie, tantie plus the personal name (e.g.,
Tantie Ruth), auntie, mama, and ma. For father, the following terms are used: daddy, pappy, papa, pa, and dad.
There are also, of course, a variety of idiosyncratic terms,
but the above lists contain the terms most commonly used.
It is apparent that there are more alternative terms of address for a mother than for a father. There are also more
terms for an aunt than for an uncle. For instance, the following terms are commonly used for an aunt: tantie, Tantie
plus the personal name, auntie, Auntie plus the personal
name, the personal name alone, tan', and mammy. Uncle,
Uncle plus the personal name, and the personal name alone
are the only commonly used terms to address one's uncle.
In short, there are a good many more terms used in addressing a mother or aunt than a father or uncle, and this again
suggests the greater structural importance of the woman in
the kinship system.

A variant term of address to kinsmen of the preceding
generation is the use of the personal name or nickname.
This is not the dominant form of address as with members of

the contemporary or younger generations, but it is a more important variant than in the United States. The mutual use of the personal name by two kinsmen emphasizes the personal relationship between them, and the symmetry or equality of the relationship.[3] Kinship considerations are placed in the background. This variation is most frequently found in relationships with a mother or a mother's sister. It is not necessarily associated with a situation in which the children have been brought up by the mother's mother, thus sharing a sibling-like status with their own mother and mother's sister, and addressing their mother's mother by a "mother" term.[4] In the village, for example, one woman who has raised all of her children, and a grandchild, is addressed by name by all of them, as well as by all of the villagers. This terminological use is a further reflection of the greater degree to which personal relationships intrude upon kinship relationships within the lower-class family.

In the relationship between husband and wife the dominant term of address is the spouse's name. In addition terms such as "darling," "love," "doodoo," and "doo" are used, as well as a wide variety of nicknames; but the number of such terms used, as well as the frequency of their use, seems to be a lot less than in the United States.[5] Indeed, one informant stated that the use of a "sweet name" to a wife would draw a "Look, na, don' momaguy me" reaction. This suggests a less intense and less "romantic" relationship between husband and wife than in the United States.

Other terms that pertain to the marital relationship, such as "friending" and "living," have already been explained. In addition, I have touched upon the reference terms "husband" and "wife" within the *living* and married relationships. Someone who does not know whether the person he is addressing or referring to is in a *living* or married relationship may use the neutral term "madame," as in "Good afternoon, madame," or "How is the madame?" In the *living* relationship the terms "the mister" and "the lady" are sometimes used to refer to one's spouse, and the combination of a comprehensive and non-kinship term like mister or lady with a definite article rather than a possessive pronoun is indicative of the nature of the relationship. "Keeper" is also used as a term of reference, by both spouses, in the *living* relationship. This suggests the equality and mutuality of the relationship—the woman "keeps" the house, clothes, and cooking in order while the man "keeps" a sufficient amount of money flowing into the household to feed and clothe its members. The mutuality of this relationship is upset when one person does not live up to his "keeper" responsibilities. The other then tends to shirk his duties and perhaps to look about for another "keeper." There is a quick response to role failure: you're not your spouse's "keeper" unless your spouse is your "keeper."

THE DEVELOPMENT OF VARIANT TERMS

Up to this point I have dealt with kinship terms either implicitly or explicitly as a reflection of role relationships. I now wish to explore the accuracy of the association between role relationship and kinship term [6] through the consideration of a related question: How do the variant terms which cut across nuclear family and extended kin lines come into use in particular instances? How does one child come to address its mother as "mammy," one as "Ruth," and one as "tantie?"

One important way in which variant kinship terms are acquired is through the "principle of imitation." One person learns to address another by a variant kinship term by imitating the term used by a third person.[7] To make this point clear, let us consider a typical case. Of a woman's three children, two call her Tantie Nettie and one calls her Mummy, while all three of them call their mother's mother, "Mother." The woman's husband's mother lives next door to her, and her husband's sister's child lives there, i.e., the child lives with its own mother's mother. This child calls the woman's husband (the child's mother's brother) "uncle" and calls the woman "Tantie Nettie." The woman's second and third children are living with her and grew up in the household next door to their older cousin who calls their mother "Tantie Nettie." Through imitation of their cousin, they learned to call their mother "Tantie Nettie." In the meantime, the woman's first child, who is being raised by the woman's mother elsewhere in the village, and who is the same age as her cousin, had already come to call her mother "Mummy." All three children, in the meantime, call their mother's mother, "Mother," through imitating their own mother. In other words, through imitation two children call their mother "Tantie Nettie," while all three of them call their grandmother "Mother." The above principle, or process, of imitation is a very common one, and raises a number of important and interesting questions: When will a child imitate and when will it not? Whom will the child imitate? What of the association between the term of address and the role relationship where the principle of imitation is involved?

Unfortunately, my data were not collected with these questions in mind so that I cannot provide definitive answers. But I can offer some relevant comments. The first thing that is obvious is that the principle of imitation calls into question the association between the term of address and the structural relationship. If a term of address is *simply* adopted through imitating another person, we would not expect to find the term an index—even a crude index—of the role relationship involved. But a further complication arises. We cannot simply talk about adopting a term through imitation. It is necessary to specify *who* is being imitated, and *when* imitation would occur. Perhaps the answer is that you imitate a person with whom you are in close contact and who is using a term that "fits" the social relationship you have with the person to be addressed. The following questions and answers would summarize the process of adoption of variant kinship terms. How? By imitation. Whom? A person you are in close contact with. When? When it fits your relationship with the person to be addressed. Why? Because it fits.[8]

Although the above explanation of the principle of imitation appears to be adequate, I do not have the data to back it up. Moreover, in some instances the data refute the proposed explanation. For example, in the illustration given above, the woman's two children who were living with her used an "aunt" term (Tantie Nettie) in addressing her, while the child living with the woman's mother called her by a "mother" term (Mummy). We would, however, expect the opposite to be true if the process described above were in operation to "fit" together the term of address and the nature of the relationship. What is it that has gone awry?

Let us consider a point which has already been made— the general weakness of kinship bonds. To take an extreme and limiting case, if kinship were completely divested of all mutual obligations, kinship terms would be divested of all meaning as well. In such a case there would be no pressure to use a particular term of address for a particular kinsman, since all meaning would have been stripped from kinship terms and kinship ties. There would presumably be no inconsistency in adopting any kinship or non-kinship term to address a person (excluding the consideration of informal, non-kinship aspects of the relationship between persons). Although this is a limiting case, it does give us a clue to the lower-class kinship system in Trinidad. Since formal kinship bonds are weak, there is a tendency toward a random assortment of terms of address. As a result, the term of address does not always correspond to the nature of the relationship.

Kinship bonds in the village may be weak, but they are by no means devoid of meaning. A detailed study would undoubtedly reveal many consistencies in the process of adoption of variant kinship terms. That there is an organizing principle is, of course, obvious from the fact that the dominant, as opposed to the variant terms of address, clearly stress the structurally correct kinship bonds. Furthermore, the areas where we find the major use of variant terms—for example, "mother" terms toward mother's sister or mother's mother—reflect definite structural possibilities. Mother's sister and mother's mother may take over the mother role, and these variants clearly are not due simply to a random process.

A final point of interest is the extent to which the imitation principle may become generalized, so that everybody in the community uses the same term of address for a particular person.[9] For example, one woman in the village was addressed as "Becky" by almost everyone in the village, including her son and husband, although the young children in the village addressed her as "Miss Becky." Other than this the only terms used to address her were "Miss Edwards" and "Mistress Edwards" (after her first husband who died, and to whom she was married), but these terms were seldom used by residents of the village. Such widespread homogeneity in the use of a person's name gives further emphasis to the overriding importance of the personal element in kin and non-kin relationships.

TERMS OF ADDRESS AND TERMS OF REFERENCE

I have dealt with terms of address and terms of reference in analyzing kinship terminology, but with heavy emphasis upon the former. This is because terms of address are part of the relationship between two kinsmen; since there is ordinarily some flexibility about the particular term of address used, that term is apt to be more revealing about kinship behavior and relationships than is the term of reference. In contrast, a term of reference is not used directly to the kinsman in question, but is used to refer to him while talking to another party, who may or may not know the kinsman or have an independent relationship to him. For the sake of clarity, it may be necessary to specify to one's auditor the formal nature of the kinship connection. The term of reference is therefore less likely to correspond to the informal nature of the relationship. For example, I may refer to "my father" in talking to a great many people; in addressing my father, however, I may use "father," "dad," "daddy," or other terms indicating differing degrees of distance or intimacy.[10]

It is therefore necessary to modify the blanket statement Murdock has made about the greater usefulness of terms of reference over terms of address:

> Terms of reference are normally more specific in their application than terms of address. Thus, in English, "mother" as a term of reference ordinarily denotes only the actual mother, but as a term of address it is commonly

applied also to a stepmother, a mother-in-law, or even an unrelated elderly woman. Moreover, terms of reference are usually more complete than terms of address. It may be customary to use only personal names in addressing certain relatives, or a taboo may prevent all conversation with them, with the result that terms of address for such kinsmen may be completely lacking. Furthermore, terms of address tend to reveal more duplication and overlapping than do terms of reference. For these reasons, terms of reference are much more useful in kinship analysis, and are consequently used exclusively in the present work.[11]

The usefulness of the terms, however, would depend upon the kind of kinship analysis undertaken. It may be of extreme importance to note to whom besides the actual mother a "mother" term of address is used; it may also be crucially important to note to which kinsmen personal names are used in address and just where the duplication and overlapping of terms take place. In short, for certain analytic purposes, the terms of address are more useful than the terms of reference. The latter are more specific and complete, thus providing a better picture of the formal organization of kinship ties. Terms of address are more personal and variable, thus providing a better picture of the informal organization of kinship.

It is because terms of address provide a better reflection of role relationships that I have concentrated upon these terms. Not surprisingly, even though they do not always say so, when other investigators are primarily concerned with role relationships they have also concentrated upon terms of address.[12] It is in dealing with alternative terms of address that it is often possible to illuminate important structural features of a kinship system.

In Coconut Village we found that many terms of address cut across the boundary lines of the nuclear family: "mother" terms (mammy, mummy) are used for aunts and grandmothers (especially the mother's sister and mother's mother); "aunt" terms (tantie, auntie) are used for mothers; and occasionally "father" terms (daddy, pappy) are used for uncles. This fact, along with the use of kinship terms for non-kin, the absence of any clear-cut kinship terms referring to a kin group, and the occasional use of non-kin terms (e.g., Ruth, Mr. Everest) for mother, aunt, and uncle, further corroborate the structural point made earlier about the blur of boundaries between nuclear family, kinship, and community relationships. Moreover, the overlapping which exists between terms used to address mother, grandmother, and aunt reflects the structural possibility of the grandmother or aunt taking over the care of the child, while the lack of the same degree of overlapping between father, grandfather, and uncle terms indicates that an exchange of roles in these kinship relationships is less likely.

NOTES

1. David M. Schneider and George C. Homans, "Kinship Terminology and the American Kinship System," *American Anthropologist* 57 (December 1955): 1202.

2. Chapters 4 and 5.

3. Schneider and Homans, *op. cit.*, p. 1201.

4. Raymond T. Smith, *The Negro Family in British Guiana* (London: Routledge & Kegan Paul, 1956), p. 162.

5. Schneider and Homans, *op. cit.*, pp. 1202–3.

6. Robert F. Murphy, "Tuareg Kinship," *American Anthropologist* 69 (April 1967): 163–70.

7. Through imitation, one often learns the dominant term, too. For example, a child may imitate a friend who calls his mother "mammy," and address his own mother by that term.

8. Other complications can be introduced: If you are in close contact with two or more people using different but fitting terms, who will be imitated? Why does imitation sometimes occur and sometimes not occur? Who decides which terms fit a relationship?

9. Raymond T. Smith, *op. cit.*, p. 161.

10. Lionel S. Lewis, "Kinship Terminology for the American Parent," *American Anthropologist* 65 (June 1963): 649–52.

11. George P. Murdock, *Social Structure* (New York: Macmillan, 1949), p. 98.

12. Schneider and Homans, *op. cit.*; David M. Schneider and John M. Roberts, *Zuñi Kin Terms*, Notebook #3, Laboratory of Anthropology (Lincoln: University of Nebraska, 1956); Edward Norbeck and Harumi Befu, "Informal Fictive Kinship in Japan," *American Anthropologist* 60 (1958): 102–17.

PART FOUR

SOME THEORETICAL
CONSIDERATIONS

12. *The Circumstance-Oriented Man*

*Man to man is so unjus', we can' know which
one to trus'.*

COCONUT VILLAGER

UP TO NOW we have described family relationships and several cultural rules and patterns that illuminate these relationships. This chapter turns to a presentation and analysis
of some general characteristics that underlie family relationships among lower-class Negroes in Trinidad. These
general characteristics highlight the importance of the pressures and deprivations of lower-class circumstances in shaping family organization.

The following are the four general structural characteristics inductively derived from the data: (1) individualism—
narrowly defined as the extent to which the individual remains unbound by strong ties of kinship; (2) personalism
—the extent to which the content of a kinship relationship
grows out of interaction (instead of being prescribed by the
formal tie); (3) replaceability—the extent to which it is
possible to replace one person by another in a given kinship
role; and (4) permissiveness—the extent to which there
exist a variety of permitted patterns of behavior in a given
situation. All four of these characteristics are closely related
and each represents a continuum along which any group
can be ordered. Lower-class Trinidad would be at the high
end of the continuum for each characteristic.

INDIVIDUALISM

The lower-class individual in Coconut Village to a large extent remains unbound by strong ties of kinship. In comparison to individuals in other classes his behavior is less controlled by kinship bonds. For example, siblings are expected
to help one another, but the specific areas in which help is
expected are few. Aside from the pattern of housing a sibling

or (between sisters only) a sibling's child, the actual "help" relationship between siblings is largely devoid of content. Another sign of individualism is the tendency for terms of address to be selected at random. Since the kinship bonds are weak, the selection of specific kinship terms is less important. Of course, just as the random element in the choice of terms represents only a tendency of the kinship system, so the individualism represents only a tendency, albeit a much more dominant one than in most societies.

The person who is not strongly bound to his kinsmen often places his own welfare above theirs. As one informant said, "I myself have plenty of family, but I don' look for them, everybody more look for theirself these days." Within the political sphere the same attitude of "being out for oneself" is often expressed, and individuals frequently speak about some candidate who "was one of us, was crawlin' with us, but now he come high he en know us."

One basis for the husband-wife tie is an economic exchange: the wife provides household services such as cleaning, washing, and cooking, and the husband provides money to run the household. Beyond this, the nature of the economic relationship remains unspecified. The husband and wife usually save whatever money they can separately. If the wife works, she usually retains her pay for her own individual expenses, since her husband is supposed to pay for all household expenses. If they play in a *susu*, they ordinarily do so separately, as individuals. For example, the husband and wife from whom I rented a room in Coconut Village each ran his own *susu* and used his own money to take a *hand* in the *susu*. Animals such as pigs and chickens are almost always owned separately by the husband or wife, and not jointly. In all of these ways we see that individualism is characteristic of the husband-wife relationship.

Another interesting point sometimes arose when I asked a husband or wife for information about a spouse:

> (*What is your husband's name?*) *Elsie* (*calling to her husband outside the house*): John, what your name? The title does humbug me. *John:* Pierre. *Elsie:* Pierre.

(*And what is his age?*) *Elsie:* John, how much years you have? *John:* A two and a two. *Elsie (to John):* A two and a two, or a two and a one? *John:* A two and a two. *Elsie:* Twenty-two. (*And what is your husband's religion?*) *Elsie:* Anglican, I think. (*Calling out*), John, this thing does humbug me, what your religion? *John:* Roman Catholic.

*   *   *

(*What is your wife's title?*) *Denny:* Katie, what is your title, girl? *Katie:* Mitchell. (*And her son, how come he is Orville Williams?*) *Denny:* He carry the mother's title. *Katie (calling out from the next room):* Orville MacKay. (*N.B. Her name was Katie MacKay, later Mitchell when she was legally married. Her son was illegitimately born before her marriage, and his name is legally Orville MacKay, but he is known as Orville Williams, after his father.*) (*And how old is your wife?*) *Denny:* How old you is? *Katie:* I can' remember; I is . . . 32; yes 32. (*And her religion?*) *Denny:* Roman Catholic. (*And what is Orville's age?*) *Denny:* What about Orville's age? *Katie:* Going on seventeen.

These are villagers who spoke freely about kinship and other matters, but who were unsure about the kind of factual information I was requesting about the spouses they were *living* with. This, too, reflects the weakness and individualism of the marital bond.

In discussing parent-child relationships we must not forget that the socialization of the child ordinarily takes place within a kinship relationship, and often by the mother and father. Nevertheless, the social bond between parent and child is weak in comparison to parent-child bonds among middle-class and upper-class families. The son is often eager to leave his parents' home and to set up quarters for himself —to "take manship on my account" and to "live bachelor." In discussing their reasons for having children, parents often refer to the economic utility of the children—they can help out around the house, go to the *parlour* on a message, bring water from the river or wood for cooking. Lower-class children rarely remain in school after they are fourteen. A working child usually gives his parents some money from his pay and keeps the rest for himself, but there is no strong expectation that this will be done, and it is not always the case. A child may turn all of his money over to his parents, especially his mother, who will then use a part of that money to buy clothing for the child; or the child may keep all of the money for himself. Parents expect help from their children in their old age, and they often get some financial help or are taken into a child's household. But parents realize that such help cannot always be counted on, either because of financial inability or the child's unwillingness to help. Thus individualism is evident even in the parent-child relationship.

Individualism implies that kinship relations are set mainly in a person-to-person context which is not part of a larger sanctioning system. The sanctions which apply are primarily the responses of the other person in the kinship role relationship. Kinship ties are therefore carried out on a *quid pro quo* basis.[1] For instance, one informant stated her mother did not bring her up and did not contribute to her support, so that when she herself started to work she did not give any money to her mother, but to her aunt who brought her up. This was a perfectly acceptable line of behavior, and there were no pressures put upon her to give any money to her mother.

Ties to the nuclear family, kinsmen, and community members show a considerable degree of overlap in lower-class Trinidad. In some societies, it is possible to see one of these three groups as central. For example, the nuclear family has the greatest structural importance in the United States,[2] the extended family among the Tallensi,[3] and the community in the case of the Israeli kibbutz.[4] Ideologically, Coconut Village most closely approaches the modal United States case, but in practice radical changes have taken place so that the boundaries between the nuclear family, extended family, and community are not too clear. It is thus impossible to speak of the nuclear family as the central structural unit. One could make out a case for the household as the key unit, but even here it is necessary to hedge because of the quick changes which can take place in household composition and because of the individualistic relationships among household members.[5] In brief, it is more important to point to the individualism of the kinship system—the relative weakness of the kinship bond—than it is to point to any structural unit. Indeed, as I have already suggested, in lower-class Trinidad there is no strongly organized structural unit in the kinship system.

PERSONALISM

Personalism refers to the tendency for the normative and affective content of a relationship to grow out of the personal interaction between kinsmen. We would never expect the personal element to be absent in kinship relationships just as we would never expect two different individuals to fulfill a position in an organization in precisely the same way. But there is clearly a difference between a situation in which the official element is stressed and the personal element remains in the background, and one in which there are few official expectations and the individual is left to work out his behavior within a relatively unstructured relationship. Kinship relationships in many societies are fairly well defined, and an individual's kinship behavior is in considerable measure structured by his formal kinship role. The kinship situation in Coconut Village is not devoid of formal expectations, yet the meagerness of those expectations permits a considerable latitude for the individual. The personal aspect of the relationship between two kinsmen therefore plays an important part in influencing their behavior.

The alternate marital forms of *friending* and *living,* since they are not legally binding, make possible the formation and breakdown of husband-wife ties in accordance with personal factors. However, the formal requirements of a marital relationship remain important—fidelity is expected, especially of the wife; the husband is expected to provide for his family; the wife is expected to be a good housekeeper. If one of these expectations is not fulfilled, the marital relationship is under immediate danger of breakdown because the spouses operate on a *quid pro quo* basis. The marital attitude embraces the likelihood of separation. As a woman philosophically stated, "You *live* today and you part tomorrow." This attitude not only cushions the effects of a separation when it occurs due to deviance from the formal requirements; it also makes the occurrence of a separation likelier for idiosyncratic and personal reasons.

Zuñi kinship terms present an interesting parallel to Coconut Village. Schneider and Roberts have shown that Kroeber's basic insight about the importance of the person rather than his genealogical position explains the apparent irregularities in the use of kinship terms among the Zuñi.[6] Their use of kinship terms of address are patterned to a greater extent upon the actual role relationship between persons, and to a lesser extent upon the genealogical relationship. But the Zuñi differ from the Coconut Villagers in the other general structural characteristics of the kinship system, for individualism, replaceability, and permissiveness are not characteristic of the Zuñi.

It is obvious that the personalism of a kinship system is a relative matter, and that there is a greater degree of personalism pervading kinship relationships in lower-class Trinidad society than in most kinship systems. Fortes, for example, points to the personal nature of the *soog* or uterine bond among the Tallensi,[7] but there are also lineage bonds which involve a far lesser degree of personalism, and even within the *soog* relationship we find that there exists "a bond of mutual interest and concern uniting individual to individual . . . (in which) the model of the relations . . . is the affection, devotion, and strong feeling of mutual identification that prevails."[8] The Trinidad case, in comparison, involves a strong personal element in all kinship relationships, and one in which mutual dislike and avoidance might develop as readily as mutual affection and identification, without the strong feeling that this was wrong which is found among the Tallensi.

To take another example, Garigue, in a study of French Canadian kinship in Montreal, showed that there is selection and choice within a wide range of kinsmen according to factors like distance and personal likeability.[9] Urbanization did not reduce the kinship range to the nuclear family, but nuclear family ties still retained their priority:

> All informants reported their highest frequency of contact with their fathers and mothers and with their siblings, even if these lived in distant parishes in Montreal. Only when the degree of kinship was more remote did informants remark that geographical distances influenced contacts.[10]

In comparison, we find that the degree of personalism in Trinidad is more pervasive, and tends to include the parent-child and sibling bonds as well as the bonds between more distant kinsmen.

The chapter on kinship terminology delineated two practices that reflect the personalism of the system: the variant use of a kinsman's name as a term of address, and the use of kinship terms to non-kinsmen. The practices emphasize the importance of the informal (personal) aspect rather than the formal kinship aspect of a relationship. We have also seen that the personal nature of the relationship is used to decide the relative importance of one's friends and relatives: "Depends on how the person is to you"; "Those relatives far away, I can' rely on them"; "Perhaps it's accordin' to how they treat you." In short, although we must take note of the formal relationship, it is also necessary to emphasize its fluidity and the way in which the personal element may alter its form.

> (*What would people usually do when they decide to get married, or to be livin' together, where could they go to live?*) If they livin' with the family then they would go there, but is better alone, that way there are no ill feelings. (*What ill feelings would there be?*) Between you and your wife is no concern of theirs; they can quarrel, but if you en livin' there it doesn't matter, and then you can always say, I en livin' with you, na. (*If they have to go live with someone's family is it best to live with the girl's family or the boy's family?*) It's best with the girl's—well, accordin'; dependin'

on how the wife get along with the husband's family, or how the husband get along with the wife's family.

* * *

(*Which relatives would most people love?*) Most the mother and the father, some the mother more than father and some the father more than mother. (*Which side of the family, the mother's or the father's side, would most people love more?*) Well, is accordin', some will like the family by the mother and some by the father but I can' directly answer that; I can tell you who I love but I can' tell you for another. Some children love the mother and don' love the father and some love the father and don' love the mother. If he don' love that person, he might be able to give you just cause. I believe most children always love the father and mother more than the rest of the family.

Whether we are dealing with husband-wife, parent-child, sibling, or other kin relationships we find the same intrusion of personal considerations into the kinship bond. The favoritism practised among one's children, the readily alterable inheritance pattern, residential choice when neolocal residence is not possible, the relative loyalty given to one's social and biological parents, and more generally the strength of one's bond to any particular kinsman—all depend to a large extent upon the personal element.

REPLACEABILITY

Replaceability refers to the considerable leeway that exists for changing kinship roles. In the hypothetical extreme of this situation every person in the kinship system would be interchangeable, that is, could play any role. Of course, we do not find kinship systems of this sort, any more than we find jigsaw puzzles in which any piece can fit anywhere. Individuals and groups require a certain amount of consistency and patterning, both in terms of what is done and by whom. Age and sex place certain biological limitations upon what people can do, and societies impose cultural limitations in addition to the biological ones. In doing this, societies are not merely adding to an individual's limitations, but they are also adding to his skills and to organizational efficiency through patterns of specialization.

Although we do not find a kinship system in Coconut Village in which any person can play any kinship role, we do find a great deal of replaceability. But it is an organized system of replaceability. Certain kinsmen are more likely to replace each other. For instance, the mother's mother or mother's sister is more likely to take care of a child, when the mother does not, than is the father's mother or father's sister.

The characteristic of replaceability shows up most clearly in the husband-wife relationship and the parent-child relationship, where the inability to perform one's role adequately may result in a shift of role-players. Since there are no strong feelings with regard to the irreplaceability of a role partner, we find a great deal of marital-shifting and child-shifting:

> (*How do you come to live with a girl, in general?*)
> You meet the girl and talk with she and both in love
> and feel to go together. (*How long do you know her
> before livin'?*) A good time, a long time. (*Do you friend
> first, usually, or live first?*) Always friendin' first, you
> will be friendly first for some times with some girl,
> and you might be looking at each other, and get to-
> gether and bring her home after. (*Bring her home
> where, with your family?*) No, not with family. I was
> home with family, but when I take with she I get me
> own place. I had the girl here and she take all my
> chairs and wares, about three months aback. I come
> back from work one day and she take all my things and
> she gone. (*Why did she go?*) I don' know. (*You have
> any quarrels or row?*) I beat she the day before. (*How
> come you did that?*) She said I had other woman and
> bring a kind of row, and we start to fight . . . (*And
> how did you come to part with the girl you were living
> with in Sangre Grande?*) Other police fella take she
> away, and carry she some place else, quite in South.

She lef' me and go with the police fella. (*And what did you do after that?*) I take somebody else.

*   *   *

(*Where were you born?*) Cumana, there I born and grew to be a young man. I lef' about 15, was living with aunt in Cumana. (*And where did you go after that?*) Matura. (*How come you went to Matura?*) Well, I grew in Cumana to a certain age, then now I feel was to make a change, so I go down to Matura working, and also when my aunt took me she didn' live in Cumana directly, also in Arima, Oropouche, Guaico-Tamana, a year or two in different places. (*How come she moved?*) Is accordin' to livin', na, she live with a husband for a certain length of time and he leave she and she take with a nex' one.

*   *   *

(*What expenses would you have for children?*) Have to spend money on children, clothes, school books, have to pay for school. (*Who would pay for that?*) The father or the mother. (*Who is supposed to pay it?*) If the father alive, he, he's the man in house. (*What if he is with woman who had another man's child?*) O-ho! If he a good stepfather will treat them as his own children, but if he en good then they couldn' even live there, that mostly happen here. (*Where would they live?*) She have family, brother or sister, put them there, or with their father's family.

We have also seen, in discussing parent-child relationships, that if there is no daughter in the household, the son will be taught to do a girl's work, such as cleaning, washing, and cooking. Furthermore, when the father does not perform his task of *minding* the child, the job is taken over by the mother who may turn her child's care over to someone else. In both of these cases replaceability operates across sex boundaries to ensure that the required activities are carried out.

In discussing kinship terminology, I referred to the phenomenon of "generalized imitation" in which the same term of address comes to be used toward a person by all of his kinsmen and all the members of the village. For instance, one girl was called Tantie May by a nephew, and subsequently the same term of address was adopted by her own children and by all of the other members of the community. Although not extremely common, such undifferentiated terminology is indicative of the replaceability within the system.

In addition to the kinship system, the structural characteristics under discussion have significance for other areas of behavior. For example, replaceability is also characteristic of the occupational world of the lower-class villager, where the low level of skill required for most jobs can be quickly learned. Smith has written in the same vein about the British Guianese (Guyanese) villages he studied:

> Within the villages, the important fact is that to a very large extent any individual could replace any other individual in the occupational system without too much difficulty.[11]

When an individual's job skills are readily duplicated by others within a high unemployment economy, the worker is placed at a decided disadvantage. Union organization has not proceeded very far in Trinidad, and has not reached the coconut workers at all. Some of the villagers attempt to guarantee their job through personal ties with a coconut estate overseer, and they may lend him money, or try to get him to join with them in a *susu*. If the overseer joins in a *susu* with a group of villagers, he is interested in seeing to it that they can pay their *susu hand,* and he would therefore try to keep them working on the estate. Personal ties may thus become an important element in a work relationship as well as a kinship relationship.

PERMISSIVENESS

Permissiveness refers to a range of alternative patterns of behavior in a particular situation, and not merely a single prescribed pattern. For example, there are a variety of acceptable marital relationships which a lower-class person can enter. This is not true for a middle-class or upper-class person, who is expected to enter only one kind of marital relationship—a legal marriage. When we consider the patterns of inheritance, post-marital residence, care of children, use of kin terms, acceptance of illegitimate children, and acceptance of marital change, we also find that permissiveness is strong in Coconut Village. A man's wife and children usually inherit his property, but it is permissible for other kin or for non-kin to inherit in various circumstances; a mother usually takes care of her child, but it is common for the mother's mother, mother's sister, some other female relative of the mother or father, or a friend to take care of the child. These, and other examples, have all been dealt with in greater detail in previous chapters.

Let us also consider, at this point, the permissiveness involved in the use of kinship terms. This is one factor that contributes toward randomizing the use of kinship terms so that there is far from complete correspondence between the terms of address used and the nature of the relationships. I do not wish to recapitulate the arguments which were already presented in detail in the chapter on kinship terminology; rather, I wish to illustrate the way in which permissiveness is involved in the process of imitation:

A woman passed by and my informant called out, "Okay, auntie." She then told me: With her, we calls her aunt, she's a neighbor of ours, we jus' respec' her. You often call one another aunt, or uncle, and you nothing to them. (Why do you happen to call her auntie?) Her son, he don' call her mother or mammy, he jus' call her auntie, that's why we do. (How it is that her son calls her auntie?) Jus' as children does adopt their own names for parents, and you as parents doesn' take it away from them. For instance, I have an aunt and she has a little child and he calls her Deepull, I don' know where he gets that. (Does he always call her that?) He is 11 or 12 years old and he still call her that, but not all the time, sometimes. (Does anyone *also call her that?*) Now and then, if make joke or so. (*What does he call his mother most of the time?*) Tantie Verge. (*She is his mother?*) Yes, but he still calls her tantie, they goes to a strange place and he call her Tantie Verge and nobody knows she is his mother. (*How come he calls her that?*) He get the name from the elder niece and nephews.

* * *

(*How do you call your mother?*) Mother. (*And what does your cousin use when he wants to talk to your mother, how does he call her?*) Mother. (*How come he calls her mother?*) By jus' hearin' us call her mother, instead of calling her by her name. (*And your nieces, how do they call your mother?*) Mama. (*How come?*) On their own that's what they started to call her. (*And what do you call your father?*) Pappy. Everyone call him Pappy. (*Your cousin?*) Yes, and my nieces call him Pappy, too. (*Do any others call him Pappy?*) Well, the majority of my friends call him Pappy and they call my mother Tantie Bella or Miss Bella. (*How did they happen to use those terms?*) In Trinidad, when coming to you through a friend, if a friend call you daddy, you call him daddy, too.

* * *

My informant told me of several cases where a mother had shifted her child to the care of a relative or friend. (*What is the reason for that, why do the mothers do it?*) All of those, circumstances are just the same, the woman will disperse the child by finance; if not maintained by father she will go out to work. And you find some don' like the trouble, very often they don' like the child. A woman I know, gave it to a friend, it appears in her case she didn' want the trouble, and she friend hadn' no child and she bring up this child. But she know the mother and cling to the mother. (*How does she call the mother and the woman who cared for her?*) Call guardian any kind of name, christen the guardian, some call it mother, some tantie, and all kinds of insignificant names, you know. (*Do you know the name the child used in this case?*) Don' know this case, some cases call the guardian mother, and some cases christen the guardian and call it some kind of pet name and they don' sway them out of that, they keep on with the name, they don' force upon the child to call it any specific name, very often the child choose his own name.

Permissiveness is more general than the other characteristics we have dealt with. The existence of individualism, personalism, and replaceability can all be considered as aspects of the permissiveness of the kinship system, for it involves "permission" for the kinship bonds to be as fluid and elastic as these characteristics make them.[12] The interdependence of these characteristics is thus evident. Since the formal kinship bonds are weak (individualism) there is room for kinsmen to negotiate the terms of their relationship (personalism), and to terminate a relationship and enter a similar one with another person (replaceability).

THE CIRCUMSTANCE-ORIENTED MAN

A person's actions are influenced, among other factors, by the norms and the circumstances in which he finds himself.[13] In lower-class Trinidad the kinship norms are weak, and there is a good deal of permissiveness about patterns of behavior. In contrast, the pressure of circumstances is strong, and circumstances exercise a good deal of control over behavior. This orientation to circumstances enables the lower-class person to adapt to the hardships that he faces.

Individualism, personalism, replaceability, and permissiveness are all characteristics of the circumstance-oriented man.[14] Let us discuss individualism and personalism first. The weakness of formal kinship ties, and the importance of the personal element, give the individual greater leeway in adapting his behavior to his circumstances. There is a *quid pro quo* element in all kinship ties. Parents and children, for example, often view their relationship in personal terms which override the bonds of kinship. Parents explain their favoritism by indicating that some children "treat them nice" or are "more obedient" than others. Children point out that they can't love a parent who did not take good care of them. Husbands and wives are quick to react to the deviance of a partner. Middle-class patience in the face of deviance—the notion that the spouse will eventually straighten out, whether through time or through therapy—is rare. Because of limited resources lower-class people cannot afford to be patient. The pressure of circumstances is too strong and too immediate.[15]

Replaceability and permissiveness are also part of the orientation to circumstances. Marital-shifting and child-shifting are important patterns of replaceability. They provide for an exchange of individuals that enables a husband-wife and a mother-child relationship to continue in the face of adverse conditions. At the same time, the permissiveness of the system makes possible the unhampered operation of these patterns of replaceability. In this way lower-class people adapt to circumstances through alternate patterns of behavior that are more in keeping with the pressure of their circumstances.

The *accordin'* attitude is one reflection of the orientation to circumstances. It provides an excellent illustration of the fluidity of lower-class life. To question after question asking for the correct or expected behavior the villager would reply, "Well, accordin' . . ." and then suggest several alternative lines of behavior that might be taken, depending on the circumstances.[16] With this outlook, it is frequently possible for the villager to fit his behavior to the circumstances and to benefit from a flexible *accordin'* culture rather than suffer from a fixed Procrustean one.

It is important not merely to present the ethnographic data about lower-class family organization and values, but to understand and explain them. In the final two chapters we will seek such understanding and explanation. Chapter 13 moves us toward a theory of lower-class family organization, Chapter 14 toward a theory of lower-class values; and more will be said about the circumstance-oriented man in that context.

NOTES

1. Lee Rainwater, "Crucible of Identity: The Negro Lower-Class Family," *Daedalus* 95 (Winter 1966): 172–216.

2. Talcott Parsons, "The Kinship System of the Contemporary United States," *American Anthropologist* 45 (January–March 1943): 22–38; Talcott Parsons and Robert F. Bales, *Family, Socialization and Interaction Process* (Glencoe, Ill.: Free Press, 1955), pp. 3–33.

3. Meyer Fortes, *The Web of Kinship Among the Tallensi* (London: Oxford University Press, 1949).

4. Melford E. Spiro, "Is the Family Universal?," *American Anthropologist* 56 (October 1954): 839–46.

5. The household is "without a strictly determined structural pattern of its own." William Davenport, "Working Papers on Caribbean Social Organization: Introduction," *Social and Economic Studies* 10 (December 1961): 382. See also Chapter 7, note 2.

6. David M. Schneider and John M. Roberts, *Zuñi Kin Terms* (Lincoln: Lincoln Laboratory of Anthropology, University of Nebraska, 1956).

7. Fortes, *op. cit.*, pp. 37–40.

8. *Ibid.*, p. 37.

9. Philippe Garigue, "French Canadian Kinship and Urban Life," *American Anthropologist* 58 (December 1956): 1090–1101.

10. *Ibid.*, p. 1094.

11. Raymond T. Smith, *The Negro Family in British Guiana* (London: Routledge & Kegan Paul, 1956), p. 46.

12. For descriptive data suggesting similar characteristics, see Virginia Heyer Young, "Family and Childhood in a Southern Negro Community," *American Anthropologist* 72 (April, 1970): 269–88.

13. Leon Mayhew, "Action Theory and Action Research," *Social Problems* 15 (Spring 1968): 420–32; Talcott Parsons, *The Structure of Social Action* (Glencoe, Ill.: Free Press, 1949).

14. Very similar characteristics are attributed to temporary systems in which there is very high geographic mobility because of extensive job changes: Philip E. Slater, "Some Social Consequences of Temporary Systems," in Warren G. Bennis, Edgar H. Schein, Fred I. Steele, and David E. Berlew (eds.), *Interpersonal Dynamics*, revised ed. (Homewood, Ill.: Dorsey Press, 1968).

15. Oscar Lewis, *Five Families: Mexican Case Studies in the Culture of Poverty* (New York: Basic Books, 1959).

16. Flexibility and orientation to circumstances are also found among the Navaho due to "rapid change, resource instability, expanding population and territory, and the conflict between accumulation and kinship organization in a tribal society." David F. Aberle, "Some Sources of Flexibility in Navaho Social Organization," *Southwestern*

Journal of Anthropology 19 (Spring 1963): 7. Further work is needed to define and interrelate characteristics like "permissive," "flexible," and "loose," in regard to diverse societies and subsocieties, and to explain the conceptual likeness of these characteristics: cf. J. F. Embree, "Thailand—A Loosely Structured Social System," *American Anthropologist* 52 (April–June 1950): 181–93; O. R. Gallagher, "Looseness and Rigidity in Family Structure," *Social Forces* 31 (May 1953): 332–39; Pertti J. Pelto, "The Differences Between 'Tight' and 'Loose' Societies," *Trans-action* 5 (April 1968): 37–40; Symmes C. Oliver, "Individuality, Freedom of Choice, and Cultural Flexibility of the Kamba," *American Anthropologist* 67 (April 1965): 421–28; Ira R. Buchler and Henry A. Selby, *Kinship and Social Organization* (New York: Macmillan, 1968), pp. 79–80.

13. *Toward a Theory of Lower-Class Families*

One man's reasons are another man's ration-
alizations.

KENNETH BURKE

THE DETAILS of lower-class family life in Trinidad—or in
Mexico, Brazil, England, the United States—seem exotic to
a middle-class observer. Different forms of marital relationships and parent-child relationships have developed. People
speak out more forcefully and perhaps more realistically to
their friends, kin, and lovers. The popular songs' idealism:
"nature fashioned you and when she was done, you were all
the sweetest things rolled up in one," is replaced by the Negro
blues' realism: "you better get yourself to a blacksmith shop
to get yourself overhauled." [1]

Many of the details about lower-class Trinidad families
have already been presented. Some are peculiar to Trinidad,
or to Coconut Village, and have no significance for a theory
of lower-class family organization. Some, however, point to
behavior and attitude patterns that may have a bearing upon
a general theory of lower-class family organization. These
are presented below as seven major facts. They deal primarily with husband-wife and parent-child relationships—
partly because we have more information about these relationships and partly because they are the areas in which
general changes are likeliest to occur as a result of lower-
class circumstances.

THE FACTS TO BE EXPLAINED

How do we explain lower-class family organization? I shall
focus upon the Trinidad case, but inasmuch as the explanation is relevant to other societies it is a step toward a
general theory of lower-class family organization. The gen-

eral relevance of the Trinidad facts and their explanation must await additional cross-cultural research and analysis.

First of all, what are the facts about lower-class family organization in Coconut Village, Trinidad?

Fact 1: Husbands and fathers are often marginal members of the nuclear family.

Fact 2: Marital-shifting takes place frequently. During their lifetime, most people will be involved in several different marital relationships.

Fact 3: *Friending* takes place more often than *living*, and *living* more often than marriage. In other words, the more responsibilities a marital relationship involves, the less often it takes place.

Fact 4: There is a casual attitude between spouses.

Fact 5: The rate of illegitimate births is high. For all of Trinidad and Tobago it was 41.1 per cent of births in 1967.[2]

Fact 6: Child-shifting takes place frequently. It is usually the mother's mother or mother's sister who takes over the care of a child when the mother cannot.

Fact 7: There is no strong feeling that the biological mother must bring up her own children.

These seven facts summarize the major aspects of lower-class family organization in Trinidad. I recognize that some of the facts have been stated in a form that pertains too specifically to Trinidad, but this is because I am concentrating upon the description and analysis of Trinidad data. Fact 3, for example, refers to the frequency of specific types of marital relationships in Trinidad. Stated in terms that are more relevant to a general theory of lower-class families, it might read: Alternate marital forms develop that are more flexible and less binding than the dominant form of marriage.

THE MAN'S ROLE AS PROVIDER

The man's role as worker-earner lies at the center of an explanation of lower-class family relationships in Trinidad. The man is expected to work and to earn for his family; his status within the family hinges upon how adequately he provides. Unfortunately, the lower-class man is involved in much unemployment, underemploymˀˀt, poorly paid employment, and unskilled employment. Because of these handicaps in his occupational role he is frequently unable to fulfill his provider role. This situation is so all-pervasive that it has ramifications for the entire system of family and kinship organization.

The man's worker-earner role is crucial because it links the work and family worlds, in which the man plays two of the most important roles in his life.[3] The consequences for the man are particularly far-reaching when damage is done to him in this crucial joint role. He loses status, esteem, and income power, and this influences his position in the community and the family.[4] He is held in low esteem by the members of his own family when he is unable to fulfill their expectations of him as a provider. As a result, he often seeks gratification and relationships outside his family. This may be a factor in explaining the strong peer relations that develop within the lower-class community.[5] Male peers who are in similar circumstances are able to develop relationships through which it is possible to gain gratification. Similarly, in extramarital relationships a man may have sufficient resources available in order to provide adequately for another woman, if even only for a short period of time.

Does the weakness of the worker-earner role of the man and the concomitant lack of resources for the family lead to consequences that are universal in lower classes? Many others have described aspects of lower-class family organization in similar terms;[6] the evidence therefore clearly points to general patterns that extend far beyond the boundaries of Coconut Village or Trinidad. But the pattern does not seem to be universal. The type of society in which the forms of lower-class family life are importantly influenced by the man's role as worker and earner is a stratified, achievement-oriented society in which the occupational role is differentiated from family roles and in which the man is expected to be the family provider.[7] In a relatively homogeneous peasant society in which families work on the land as a group, or in ascriptive societies where the man's status within the family or community is less dependent upon his occupational status, we find a much lesser tendency for the development of new mating and family forms. In Greece, for example, where manhood is not defined in terms of earning capacity, the lower-class man suffers little loss of esteem within his family. Due to the instability of the Greek economy, unemployment has been frequent for highly educated and skilled men as well as for unskilled workers, and unemployment is not usually defined as personal failure.[8] In Guatemala, lower-class Indians show more nuclear family stability than lower-class Ladinos because of the economic importance the family has for the former in its work on coffee plantations.[9] In some communities the position of the lower-class man within his family rests on non-economic values;[10] in other societies these non-economic values are under assault because of a transition from ascription to achievement, social stability to social mobility.[11]

Even within the same society there are considerable differences between families in the importance attached to the male's earner role, and in their reactions to the loss of that role.[12] During periods of unemployment, for example, those men who view the male role as the dominant one within the family experience the lowest morale. Those who view the family in equalitarian terms, and who therefore presumably place less stress upon the importance of the male's dominant position as an earner, show higher morale.[13] In brief, there is less alteration of family structure attendant upon male unemployment or lower-status employment in those societies, or families within a society, which place less stress upon the male's earner role.

THE EXPLANATION

Two approaches are often used in explaining family patterns in the Caribbean. One approach is historically oriented and emphasizes the *origin* of a family pattern. What brought it about in the first place? Thus, we might trace the origin of the man's marginal position in the nuclear family to the system of plantation slavery.[14] The second approach is sociologically oriented and emphasizes the *function* of a family pattern. What part does it presently play in the over-all social system? [15] Both questions are relevant and related,[16] but I shall confine my attention to the functional form of explanation.

Fact 1: The lower-class man is in a marginal occupational position. As a consequence he is financially insecure. As a husband and father, however, his major responsibility is a financial one. He is unable to fulfill this major responsibility, and he is therefore unable to command the respect and obedience of his wife and children. Nevertheless, he is expected to be the major figure of authority in the household, and he may use physical force in an attempt to obtain reluctant obedience. As a result the man's role within the family is not a satisfying one. He is often a marginal or absent member of the nuclear family group. He spends more time outside the family with male (and occasionally female) peers who are similarly situated than he spends within the family. In interaction with these male peers he develops a group structure in which gratification is less contingent upon his performance in the worker-earner role. This group structure may take the form of a delinquent gang or a street corner group; in Coconut Village it was a group of talking, and occasionally drinking or draughts-playing, men.

Fact 2: Given the man's marginal role within the family, and the low degree of satisfaction in the husband-wife relationship, the frequency of marital-shifting is not difficult to explain. The husband may develop a *friending* relationship with another woman whose more modest financial needs he can temporarily meet, and from whom he gets the respect that is due a husband. This, of course, makes it more difficult for him to meet the needs of his first wife. In addition, his wife may develop a *friending* relationship with another man who will provide her with some of the extra money she needs. She does so, however, at the risk of breaking up her relationship with her first husband. In addition to the infidelity itself, the suspicion about infidelity may put an added strain upon the marital relationship. If the husband and wife also have *outside* children, these *outside* children will put an additional financial strain upon them. For all these reasons, marital separation and marital-shifting take place frequently.

Fact 3: The mutual advantages of a sexual and economic exchange between a man and a woman are constantly present. The man, however, finds it difficult or impossible to follow the dominant marriage pattern and to support a family in the expected manner. The result is the development of alternate forms of marriage that involve more limited responsibilities. The man seeks a marital relationship that will involve him in the fewest obligations. *Friending* satisfies this requirement and therefore occurs most frequently. It is usually a temporary relationship and it does not bind a man legally to support the woman he is *friending* with. It does bind him legally to support any children the woman bears him, if she can prove his paternity, but she would not often take the putative father to court.

The *living* relationship occurs next most frequently. Husband and wife establish a customary but not legal marital relationship by living together. The husband is not legally required to support his wife in the event of a separation, but he is legally required to support his children. As with the *friending* relationship, a legal divorce is not required to dissolve the relationship—and since such dissolutions are common there is a pragmatic value in avoiding a legal marriage. A legal marriage binds a man to support his wife and children, and marriage therefore takes place less frequently in the lower class.

Fact 4: Given the emphasis upon less binding marital relationships, and the frequency of marital-shifting, it becomes possible to explain the casual attitude between spouses. It would indeed be unwise to have an intense attachment to one's spouse if a separation is likely. The casual attitude keeps separations from being traumatic. These separations are taken in stride as part of the normal course of events. Of course the casual attitude between husband and wife also means that many relationships that could be "saved" are not. But a lower-class spouse is not oriented to-

ward the kind of marriage that a middle-class counselor
saves. They are more oriented toward the basic circumstances of life from which they can seldom escape, and a
middle-class marriage is a luxury that they may not be able
to afford.

Fact 5: Given the development of non-legal marital forms,
it is easy to explain the high rate of illegitimate births. The
many children born as a result of *friending* and *living* relationships are officially classified as illegitimate. They are
legally illegitimate, but not *socially* illegitimate. Lower-class
Coconut Villagers do not distinguish between legitimate and
illegitimate children except in relation to the laws of Trinidad and Tobago. Their own distinction, for a father, is between "children" and "*outside* children"; the latter are children that the father has had with a woman outside of the
living or married relationship he is in. But an *outside* child
is not stigmatized. Once again the attitude that has developed—the lack of stigma for illegitimate or *outside* children
—is appropriate to the circumstances. The high rate of illegitimacy and of *outside* children would make any associated stigma impractical. The basis for the high rate of
illegitimacy lies in a more fundamental economic fact, and
any tendency to emulate the middle class in its stigmatizing
attitude toward illegitimacy has been thwarted by the practical circumstances of lower-class life.[17]

Fact 6: Up to this point we have tried to explain the facts
about the lower-class family in Coconut Village on the basis
of the man's marginal economic position and his marginal
role within the family. The woman, for example, prefers a
legal marriage much more often than the man. Marriage
gives her the legal right to her husband's financial support
while he is alive and, more importantly, to his inheritance
when he dies. That the husband is the one who usually "has
his way," so that marriage is the least frequent relationship,
emphasizes the extent to which economic circumstances
have shaped the lower-class family. The woman accepts a
friending or *living* relationship, and some positive feeling is
associated with these relationships, because marriage is
viewed as impractical under certain circumstances.

What does the woman do, however, when she has children by a man and he leaves her? The separation may "solve" the man's financial problem if he stops supporting the woman and her children, or if he contributes less to their support after his departure. But what about the woman who is left with the children? It is on this point that we can explain the child-shifting pattern in Coconut Village. Since a woman is often left alone with her children, the child-shifting pattern provides her with a solution to her problem. She cannot both *care* and *mind* her children, and so she turns their care over to a female relative while she takes on the job of *minding* them financially. During the days of slavery the master was the child's "sociological father," and the mother was dependent upon the system of slavery rather than upon the child's biological father. With a strong public welfare program that emphasizes the ties between mother and child the child may have a "public welfare father," as is often the case with the Aid to Families with Dependent Children program in the United States. Such a program, especially before aid became available to children of unemployed fathers, complemented the structure of lower-class families, and reinforced the marginal position of the man in the family. In present-day Trinidad the child-shifting pattern serves the function of "sociological fatherhood"—it permits the redistribution of children into households where they can be taken care of, and it makes it possible for the mother of the child to work and to contribute financially to her child's support. In such a case the child may be "mothered" by a female relative of his mother and "fathered" by his mother.[18]

What about the so-called "matriarchal" structure of the lower-class family? This is often seen as the major characteristic of the lower-class family, but in my view its importance is grossly exaggerated.[19] It is true that a woman and some of her daughters and some of her daughter's children may live together. Nevertheless, such a matrifocal household is matrifocal by default, not by design.[20] The husbands of the daughters have not provided steady financial support for their wives and children; the daughters have therefore shifted their children to the care of their own mother (and the daughters may also move in with, or continue to live with, their own mother); a matrifocal household is the result. We must recognize the underlying processes of marital-shifting and child-shifting that lead to such a matrifocal household.[21] Too often this has not been done. We must also recognize that, in Trinidad at least, the woman may shift her child to a wide variety of other female relatives, and occasionally to a female friend or neighbor. In addition, there is a developmental sequence to the woman's marital history. She may move in and out of marital relationships with a number of men; some of her children may remain in a household with her; some may be shifted to the care of their mother's mother; some may be cared for by someone else. It is not a simple and stable matter of grandmother, mother, and child residing together.[22]

Fact 7: Given the frequency of the child-shifting pattern we can understand the lack of any strong feeling that it is the biological mother alone who must bring up her children. The mother's mother, mother's sister, and many others may, and frequently do, bring up the child. If there were a strong feeling that the mother should bring up her own child, it would be more difficult and guilt-provoking to turn one's child over to another's care. The lack of such a feeling makes it possible to maintain the child-shifting pattern, and therefore makes it possible for the woman whose husband has left her to arrange for the care of her child. Under such circumstances certain women at certain periods of time come to specialize in bringing up children, who may be their own or other's children. The older woman especially, who takes care of her daughter's children and who can count on some financial support from the parents of these children, tends to specialize in this child-rearing role.

According to my interpretation of lower-class family organization we have the following sequence: Man's occupational status → man's marginal economic position → man's marginal position in the family (and associated peer ties) → marital-shifting (and associated casual attitude between spouses) → woman's responsibility for the children → child-shifting (and associated attitudes about maternal care).

This explanation of lower-class family organization applies only to certain societies, but I believe it is the best explanation we have so far.[23] Further research and analysis will undoubtedly lead to modifications of the component parts of the theory.

SOME CLARIFYING COMMENTS

A major point that has to be made about this theory of lower-class family organization is that there is nothing inevitable about the sequence of events. The lower-class man in a marginal economic position may somehow manage to provide adequately for his family and play a central role within the family. The man in a marginal position within the family may remain in that role without shifting to another marital relationship. The man who does leave his wife may take his children with him, or provide adequately for them, so that his wife does not have to take financial responsibility for them. The woman who is left with the financial responsibility of her children may take care of them without child-shifting. In other words, we are dealing with tendencies in lower-class family organization and not with an inevitable sequence of events. There are alternative patterns to the sequence we have delineated. An important test of the theory is the relative frequency of such phenomena as marital-shifting and child-shifting in the lower and middle classes. That divorce-desertion-separation rates, illegitimacy rates, and rates of non-legal unions are often inversely related to social class in achievement-oriented societies is one set of evidence for the soundness of our theory of lower-class family organization.

I have made a number of statements about the development of practices or attitudes that are less guilt-provoking or more practical for members of the lower class.[24] These statements are of two kinds: they refer either to the development of practices that are in line with lower-class circumstances (e.g., marital-shifting is related to the man's economic position), or to the development of attitudes that are in line with lower-class practices (e.g., a casual attitude between spouses is related to marital-shifting). Behind such statements lies the idea that environmental circumstances, behavioral practices, and attitudes are in some degree of alignment with each other. I do not insist upon any set degree of alignment; nor do I insist that the alignments I have spelled out are the only ones possible. Social life is too complicated to permit such insistence.

What about the historical accuracy of the sequence I have set forth in the theory of lower-class families? It should again be emphasized that the theory is functional rather than historical—it is an attempt to explain the contemporary relationships of lower-class life rather than its historical development. Where I talk about "developments," I have in mind a development away from certain middle-class practices and attitudes toward the lower-class practices and attitudes under consideration. Whether such a development actually took place in certain lower-class groups is an empirical question requiring historical data that I have not attempted to collect. However, the historical approach, like the functional approach used in this book, is a legitimate one. One advantage of either the historical or functional approach is that it can also catapult us into the future—are the members of the lower class stuck with their behavioral patterns and attitudes because these are adaptive in lower-class circumstances? Or can members of the lower class overcome their lower-class circumstances? These questions will be dealt with in the next chapter.

NOTES

1. S. I. Hayakawa, "Popular Songs vs. the Facts of Life," *Etc.* 12 (Winter 1955): 83–95.

2. Trinidad and Tobago Central Statistical Office, *Population and Vital Statistics: 1967 Report* (1969).

3. Hyman Rodman and Constantina Safilios-Rothschild, "Business and the Family," in Ivar Berg (ed.), *The Business of America* (New York: Harcourt, Brace & World, 1968), pp. 311–35.

4. Jerome K. Myers and Bertram A. Roberts, *Family and Class Dynamics in Mental Illness* (New York: John Wiley, 1959); John H. Rohrer and Munro S. Edmonson (eds.), *The Eighth Generation* (New York: Harper, 1960); Martin Gold, *Status Forces in Delinquent*

Boys (Ann Arbor: University of Michigan Press, 1963); Robert Maisel, "The Ex-Mental Patient and Rehospitalization: Some Research Findings," *Social Problems* 15 (Summer 1967): 18–24; Hylan Lewis, *Culture, Class, and Poverty* (Washington, D.C.: Health and Welfare Council of the National Capital Area, 1967); Elliot Liebow, *Tally's Corner: A Study of Negro Streetcorner Men* (Boston: Little, Brown, 1967); Joan Aldous, "Wives' Employment Status and Lower-Class Men as Husband-Fathers: Support for the Moynihan Thesis," *Journal of Marriage and the Family* 31 (August 1969): 469–76; David A. Schulz, *Coming Up Black* (Englewood Cliffs, N.J.: Prentice-Hall, 1969).

5. William F. Whyte, *Street Corner Society* (Chicago: University of Chicago Press, 1943); Albert K. Cohen, *Delinquent Boys* (Glencoe, Ill.: Free Press, 1955); Gerald D. Suttles, *The Social Order of the Slum* (Chicago: University of Chicago Press, 1968).

6. Oscar Lewis, *Five Families: Mexican Case Studies in the Culture of Poverty* (New York: Basic Books, 1959); Raymond T. Smith, *The Negro Family in British Guiana* (London: Routledge & Kegan Paul, 1956); Lee Rainwater, Richard P. Coleman, and Gerald Handel, *Workingman's Wife* (New York: Oceana, 1959); Herbert J. Gans, *The Urban Villagers: Group and Class in the Life of Italian-Americans* (New York: Free Press, 1962); Lee Rainwater, "Crucible of Identity: The Negro Lower-Class Family," *Daedalus* 95 (Winter 1966): 172–216; Hylan Lewis, *op. cit.*; David Schulz, *op. cit.* See also Chapter 4, note 17.

7. Donald G. McKinley, *Social Class and Family Life* (New York: Free Press, 1964); Helen Icken Safa, "From Shantytown to Public Housing: A Comparison of Family Structure in Two Urban Neighbourhoods in Puerto Rico," *Caribbean Studies* 4 (April 1964): 3–12; Helen Icken Safa, "The Female-Based Household in Public Housing: A Case Study in Puerto Rico," *Human Organization* 24 (Summer 1965): 135–39; Eric R. Wolff, *Peasants* (Englewood Cliffs, N.J.: Prentice-Hall, 1966).

8. Constantina Safilios-Rothschild, "A Comparison of Power Structure and Marital Satisfaction in Urban Greek and French Families," *Journal of Marriage and the Family* 29 (May 1967): 345–52.

9. Richard N. Adams, "An Inquiry into the Nature of the Family," in Gertrude E. Dole and Robert E. Carneiro (eds.), *Essays in the Science of Culture* (New York: Thomas Y. Crowell, 1960), pp. 43–44.

10. A. H. Maslow and R. Diaz-Guerrero, "Delinquency as a Value Disturbance," in John B. Peatman and Eugene Hartley (eds.), *Festschrift for Gardner Murphy* (New York: Harper, 1960), pp. 228–40; William Madsen, *Mexican-Americans of South Texas* (New York: Holt, Rinehart and Winston, 1964); cf. Eric R. Wolff, *op. cit.*, pp. 62–65.

11. Melvin M. Tumin, *Social Class and Social Change in*

Puerto Rico (Princeton: Princeton University Press, 1961), pp. 180–84, 461, *et passim;* David Landy, *Tropical Childhood* (New York: Harper, 1965), pp. 148–54; Edward P. Dozier, "Peasant Culture and Urbanization," in Philip K. Bock (ed.), *Peasants in the Modern World* (Albuquerque: University of New Mexico Press, 1969), pp. 140–58.

12. See Mirra Komarovsky, *The Unemployed Man and His Family* (New York: Dryden Press, 1940); Ruth S. Cavan and Katherine H. Ranck, *The Family and the Depression* (Chicago: University of Chicago Press, 1938); E. Wight Bakke, *The Unemployed Worker* (New Haven: Yale University Press, 1940); William Haber, Louis A. Ferman, and J. R. Hudson, *The Impact of Technological Change* (Kalamazoo: Upjohn Institute for Employment Research, 1963).

13. Thomas Johnston, "Morale and Job Displacement: A Study of the Influence of Economic, Social, and Psychological Factors upon the Morale of a Sample of Displaced Newspaper Workers," M.A. thesis, Wayne State University, 1963, pp. 53–55, 75–76.

14. Fernando Henriques, "West Indian Family Organization," *American Journal of Sociology* 55 (July 1949): 30–37; Morris Freilich, "Serial Polygyny, Negro Peasants, and Model Analysis," *American Anthropologist* 63 (October 1961): 955–75.

15. Kingsley Davis, "The Myth of Functional Analysis as a Special Method in Sociology and Anthropology," *American Sociological Review* 24 (December 1959): 757–72; Robert Brown, *Explanation in Social Science* (Chicago: Aldine, 1963), pp. 109–32; Carl G. Hempel, *Aspects of Scientific Explanation* (New York: Free Press, 1965), pp. 297–330.

16. Vera Rubin, ed., *Caribbean Studies: A Symposium*, 2nd ed. (Seattle: University of Washington Press, 1960); Sidney W. Mintz, "Foreword," in Norman E. Whitten, Jr., and John F. Szwed (eds.), *Afro-American Anthropology* (New York: Free Press, 1970), pp. 1–16.

17. See Chapter 14 for further discussion of norms and values.

18. Edith Clarke, *My Mother Who Fathered Me* (London: George Allen & Unwin, 1957).

19. A matriarchal society is one in which the women are normatively expected to hold formal authority within the kinship system. This is emphatically not the case in lower-class Trinidad (or anywhere else), and those who discuss lower-class matriarchies are, at the least, confusing behavioral patterns and normative patterns. See also Elizabeth Herzog and Hylan Lewis, "Children in Poor Families: Myths and Realities," *American Journal of Orthopsychiatry* 40 (April 1970): 375–87.

20. From a "women's liberation" perspective, the marital power that lower-class women acquire is ironic. They are not normatively expected to acquire such power, but they often do. This power, however, does not make them freer to "develop their potential," but places additional burdens upon them. Lower-class women are so tied up with

mundane matters and in coping with deprived circumstances that they have not yet become part of the women's liberation movement.

21. Households may also be said to display varying degrees of matrifocality depending upon the amount of power the woman has within the household. And, in achievement-oriented societies, lower-class women do have more marital power than women of other classes. See Hyman Rodman, "Marital Power in France, Greece, Yugoslavia, and the United States: A Cross-National Discussion," *Journal of Marriage and the Family* 29 (May 1967): 320–24; Nancie L. González, "Toward a Definition of Matrifocality," in Norman E. Whitten, Jr., and John F. Szwed (eds.), *op. cit.*, pp. 231–44.

22. Raymond T. Smith, *op. cit.*, Chapters 5 and 6.

23. This explanation borrows heavily from the literature on lower-class family organization, and particularly from the writings of Hylan Lewis, Lee Rainwater, and Raymond T. Smith. I am also aware of my indebtedness, not always footnoted, to Lloyd Braithwaite, E. Franklin Frazier, Herbert J. Gans, Oscar Lewis, Elliot Liebow, S. M. Miller, M. G. Smith, and Talcott Parsons.

24. For further details, see Chapter 14.

14. *Toward a Theory of Lower-Class Values*

The reports of life among the poor emanating from policemen, judges, and welfare workers are the domestic equivalent of portrayals and assessments of indigenous lifeways by colonial administrators or missionaries.

CHARLES A. VALENTINE

THERE HAS BEEN a tremendous upsurge of interest in poverty and its prevalence among certain national (or racial, ethnic, regional) groups. In the Western hemisphere this interest has focused primarily upon Afro-Americans. Several current questions in the domain of culture and values are of intense theoretical and practical concern: Do the differences in behavior of the poor, or of Afro-Americans—insofar as there are differences—represent merely situational adaptations to different circumstances? Or is there a separate culture of poverty? Or a separate Afro-American culture?

THE CONTROVERSY

Differences in behavior are interpreted by some investigators as situational,[1] and by others as subcultural.[2] The situational perspective stresses that although the behavior is different, the values are similar. The behavior is simply adaptive to the (lower-class or black) situation. The subcultural perspective stresses that the values, as well as the behavior, are different. These issues have a strong practical import: The existence and strength of a separate black culture would provide a strong ideological rallying point for separatist organizations among Afro-Americans, while its absence would lend ideological support to racially integrated organizations.[3] The existence and strength of a separate culture of poverty (in the negative sense in which it is usually portrayed) would suggest government programs aimed at alter-

190

ing lower-class values, while its absence would suggest programs to alter the situation and increase the opportunities for social mobility.[4]

I do not intend to deal with the issue of an Afro-American subculture, but to focus upon the question of a lower-class culture, or culture of poverty.[5]

THE FACTS TO BE EXPLAINED

Before elaborating upon the controversies about lower-class culture, let us present the Trinidad facts that need to be explained:

Fact 1: Legal marriage is the preferred marital form, but alternative marital unions are also included within the normative range.

Fact 2: Legitimate childbirth is preferred, but illegitimate children born within an alternate marital union are normatively accepted.

Fact 3: There are strong individualistic and personal (*quid pro quo*) elements in all kinship relationships. These kinds of relationships are both empirically and normatively expected.•

Fact 4: Kinship relationships are characterized by replaceability and permissiveness. These characteristics are also empirically and normatively expected.

Many other details about the values of lower-class families in Trinidad have been presented throughout this book. Some are special cases of the four facts listed above—the favoritism parents show to some children and the expectation that young children will help with household tasks are instances of Fact 3. Other details, such as the value placed upon verbal sparring and topical commentary through calypsos (Appendix 1), are uniquely Afro-American, and do not have special relevance to a theory of lower-class values. These kinds of creative elaborations are of utmost importance for understanding that Afro-American cultures are not merely examples of lower-class culture.[6] Since the major focus of these theoretical chapters is the *class*-related features of the subculture, I have made special efforts elsewhere to include comprehensive details of family life and values that some readers will want to look at from different perspectives.

ADAPTATION AND CULTURAL MODIFICATION

The key to an explanation of lower-class values in Trinidad lies in the interdependence of behavior and values. Values are not always good predictors of behavior because of the pressure of circumstances. A man's behavior in certain situations may be radically different from his stated values.[7] Nevertheless, a man's values and behavior are not completely independent. Schumpeter has said that "the class situation may so specialize members of the class that adaptation to new situations becomes all but impossible."[8] Insofar as that is so, man's predicament may lead him to maladaptations such as mental illness. But man, on the whole, is an adaptive creature, and he may bring his behavior into alignment with conditions despite opposing values. Man is also a creature of some coherence, and he may resist changing his behavior; if his behavior does change, he may subsequently modify his values.[9] The process may also go in the other direction, with value change leading to behavioral change; or there may be a mutually interacting process of incremental change between values and behavior.[10]

The interaction of conditions, values, and behavior is especially interesting among lower-class individuals. Let us assume that at some earlier point all individuals shared the dominant values of the society.[11] Lower-class individuals would then face the problem, identified by Robert K. Merton, of being unable to perform in accordance with society's dominant values because they lack resources to offset the pressure of environmental conditions.[12] One result, initially, would not involve any value changes, but would merely involve behavioral adaptation to the situation. Through time, however, the interdependence of behavior and values would lead to value modifications. Some lower-class individuals could conceivably drop their allegiance to middle-class values and develop uniquely lower-class values that are in harmony with their lower-class situation. Others could retain the middle-class values, and simultaneously develop additional values that would be more closely related to lower-class circumstances. Finally, some individuals might drop their allegiance to middle-class values without developing other values, and thus orient themselves pragmatically in at least some areas of life.

In sum, there are at least four possible kinds of responses that lower-class individuals may take to the Mertonian problem (and even these categories ignore the complexity of the response patterns, of how we know when an adaptive response becomes a value, or when a waning value is no longer a value):

Response 1. *Middle-Class Values:* Lower-class individuals share the middle-class values and have not developed any alternative values.

Response 2. *Lower-Class Values:* Lower-class individuals have abandoned the middle-class values and have developed their own values.

Response 3. *Value Stretch:* Lower-class individuals share the middle-class values and have also developed alternative values.

Response 4. *Pragmatism:* Lower-class individuals have abandoned all values in a particular area and act in the light of circumstances.

Lower-class people may adopt any one of the four alternatives, and since they are in a process of adapting to dominant values and deprived circumstances, they may change through time from one alternative to another. Each alternative involves a rather different life style. It is therefore not in the least surprising to find controversies about whether there is a lower-class culture and about its characteristics.

The major focus of the controversy between situationalists and subculturalists, until very recently, has been upon Responses 1 and 2. Response 1 is situational in the sense that differences in lower-class behavior are not accompanied by differences in cultural values. Response 2 is subcultural in the sense that it implies a uniquely integrated system of lower-class values. The data suggest, however, that Responses 3 and 4, although usually neglected, are extremely important alternatives within the lower class. By focusing upon these responses we can both clarify the nature of the controversy and explain some of the lower-class values in Trinidad.

THE EXPLANATION: LOWER-CLASS VALUE STRETCH

The lower-class value stretch is a response of members of the lower class to a situation in which circumstances make it difficult or impossible for them to behave in accordance with the dominant values of an open-class society. The following is an elaboration of the assumptions and hypothesized relationships that enter into the theory of the lower-class value stretch.[13]

1. In an open-class society the possibility of mobility is open to all.
2. The values of the dominant social classes (including the possibility of mobility for all) are promulgated to all members of the society.
3. Members of the lower classes have difficulty in behaving in accordance with some of the dominant values because of inadequate resources.
4. Members of the lower classes therefore show more "deviance" from some of the dominant values.
5. As a result, in order to minimize negative sanctions, members of the lower classes are less committed to some of the dominant values than are other members of society.
6. Furthermore, some members of the lower classes develop alternative values that are in accord with their circumstances, so that their actual behavior is likelier to be rewarded. What is deviant from the point of view of the dominant values is normative from the point of view of the alternative values.
7. The development of alternative values is a continuing process; some lower-class members are socialized into accepting them from childhood, others come to accept them later in life, while others never accept them.

8. The major form taken by the system of values that thus develops in the lower class is the "lower-class value stretch."

By the value stretch I mean that the lower-class person, without abandoning the general values of the society, develops an alternative set of values. Without abandoning the values of marriage and legitimate childbirth he stretches these values so that a non-legal union and illegitimate children within that union are also desirable (Facts 1 and 2). The result is that the members of the lower class, in many areas, have a wider range of values than others within the society. They share the general values of the society with members of other classes, but in addition they have stretched these values, or developed alternative values, which help them to adjust to their deprived circumstances.

The above assumptions and implied relationships are not new,[14] but they make explicit what has remained largely implicit in the literature—that the value stretch is an important response within the lower classes. As with the theory of lower-class family organization, the sequence of events is not inevitable, and the historical accuracy of the sequence is an empirical question that I have not pursued, but that will, I hope, be pursued by others.

THE EXPLANATION: PRAGMATISM

A number of investigators have emphasized the pragmatic and adaptive quality of lower-class behavior.[15] This response parallels the sequence of events hypothesized in the development of the lower-class value stretch up to item 6. At that point, instead of developing alternative values that are more in accord with their circumstances, lower-class members become still less committed to the dominant values of the society. Eventually in some areas of life they react to circumstances pragmatically rather than normatively; they are neither guided nor hampered by allegiance to any set of values.[16]

Facts 3 and 4—the individualistic, personal, replaceable, and permissive elements in kinship relationships—can be explained as aspects of the pragmatic orientation of lower-class individuals. These kinds of kinship relationships are one lower-class answer to the deprivations of life. They provide the flexibility that makes it possible to emphasize or de-emphasize the relationship to any kinsman, depending upon circumstances. They also provide the flexibility to choose among a range of alternative patterns of behavior, depending upon circumstances.

The lower-class man is not other-oriented or inner-oriented—but circumstance-oriented.[17] David Riesman dealt with middle-class men who could chart their course without regard to the vagaries of the weather. Guided by radar, the other-directed man's ship steers a fairly stable course, dictated by the (admittedly changeable) signals received from his peers. Stabilized by a gyroscope, the inner-directed man's ship maintains an even keel on a course determined by his parents' internalized standards. The circumstance-oriented man, however, is at sea in a boat. He cannot ignore the weather. Relying upon a sail, the circumstance-oriented man's boat rides a choppy course that reflects the changing winds. He cannot be too much bound by inner standards or others' standards because this would divert him from his major task. He must steer a course according to the circumstances about him. Not being bound by formal kinship ties, and with freedom to emphasize the personal element in kinship relations, the lower-class person is better able to meet life's exigencies.

FUTURE IMPLICATIONS

What are the future implications and practical applications of our theory of lower-class values? To return to a question asked earlier: Are members of the lower class stuck with their adaptive behavioral patterns or can they overcome their lower-class circumstances?

In my opinion the culture and personality of members of the lower class are not altogether determined by the circumstances of lower-class life. Individual ability or creativity, or parents or friends or kinsmen who are especially able or creative, can set a lower-class person on a track that leads him to surmount rather than adapt to lower-class circumstances. Similarly a cultural tradition that is antagonistic to the characteristics of lower-class life, or that sets a heavy store by family solidarity and educational advancement, can propel many of its adherents out of their lower-class circumstances. Perhaps that is why Jewish, Greek, Armenian, Maltese, Chinese, and Japanese immigrants to the Americas have been so mobile and have moved so quickly out of the lower class.[18] Perhaps that is one reason why Negroes in the Americas—whose cultural traditions were largely destroyed during the days of slavery—so often manifest the lower-class characteristics in archetypal form.[19]

A NEW PERSPECTIVE

The theories we have presented put a new perspective upon lower-class family life and values. As the middle-class critic sees lower-class life it is characterized by "promiscuous" sexual relationships, "illegal" marital unions, "illegitimate" children, "unmarried" mothers, "deserting" husbands and fathers, and "abandoned" children. These are typically viewed in a gross manner as, simply, *problems* of the lower class. According to our perspective it makes better sense to see them as *solutions* of the lower class to problems that they face in the social, economic, and perhaps legal and political spheres of life. This means that the typical member of the lower class is faced with a chronic economic problem that spawns a series of related problems. Part of the solution to these problems is to be found in the nature of lower-class family life and values. By permitting certain practices (e.g., marital-shifting and child-shifting) and by developing certain relationships (e.g., *friending, living*) the lower-class person is able to solve some of the problems that he faces because of his deprived position in society. Of course, the new family forms do not solve all of his problems, and they may bring other problems in their wake.[20]

It must be remembered that words like "promiscuity," "illegitimacy," and "desertion" are not part of the lower-class vocabulary, and that it is misleading to describe lower-class behavior in this way. These words have middle-class meanings, imply middle-class judgments, and should not be used to describe lower-class behavior—unless, of course, our intention is to judge this behavior in a middle-class manner in order to bolster a sagging middle-class ego. For this reason I have coined terms that do not convey middle-class moral judgments—marital-shifting and child-shifting. I have also used the Trinidadian terms, where appropriate—*friending, living, outside* children. In this way I believe we have moved toward a better understanding of lower-class family life in its own context. We have avoided some of the middle-class biases. And we have come to see how the patterns of lower-class family life and of lower-class value modifications help the lower-class person adapt to the chronic deprivations he faces.

NOTES

1. Although they discuss other approaches, the basic orientation of these investigators is situational: Hylan Lewis, *Culture, Class and Poverty* (Washington, D.C.: Health and Welfare Council of the National Capital Area, 1967); Elliot Liebow, *Tally's Corner: A Study of Negro Streetcorner Men* (Boston: Little, Brown, 1967); Louis Kriesberg, *Mothers in Poverty: A Study of Fatherless Families* (Chicago: Aldine, 1970).

2. The basic orientation of the following investigators is subcultural: Fernando Henriques, *Family and Colour in Jamaica* (London: Eyre & Spottiswoode, 1953); Walter B. Miller, "Lower Class Culture as a Generating Milieu of Gang Delinquency," *Journal of Social Issues* 14 (1958), No. 3: 5–19; Edward Banfield, *The Unheavenly City: The Nature and Future of Our Urban Crisis* (Boston: Little, Brown, 1970); Oscar Lewis is also subculturally oriented—see Chapter 1, note 5.

3. Harold Cruse, *The Crisis of the Negro Intellectual* (New York: William Morrow, 1967); Harold Cruse, *Rebellion or Revolution* (New York: William Morrow, 1968); Bennett Berger, "Black Culture or Lower-Class Culture?" in Lee Rainwater (ed.), *Soul* (Chicago: Aldine, 1970), pp. 117–28; Robert Blauner, "Black Culture: Lower-class Result or Ethnic Creation?," in Lee Rainwater, *op. cit.*, pp. 129–66.

4. For a great deal of relevant material, see the papers by Daniel P. Moynihan, Peter H. Rossi and Zahava D. Blum, S. M. Miller

and Pamela Roby, Otis Dudley Duncan, Herbert J. Gans, Lee Rainwater, and Walter Miller in Daniel P. Moynihan (ed.), *On Understanding Poverty: Perspectives from the Social Sciences* (New York: Basic Books, 1968).

5. A subculture or biculture of poverty might be a better term: see the discussion in Chapter 1. The material in this chapter borrows from the following three articles I have written: "The Lower-Class Value Stretch," *Social Forces* 42 (December 1963): 205–15; "Illegitimacy in the Caribbean Social Structure: A Reconsideration," *American Sociological Review* 31 (October 1966): 673–83; "Controversies About Lower-Class Culture: Delinquency and Illegitimacy," *Canadian Review of Sociology and Anthropology* 5 (November 1968): 254–62.

6. Bennett Berger, *op. cit.*; Robert Blauner, *op. cit.*; Virginia Heyer Young, "Family and Childhood in a Southern Negro Community," *American Anthropologist* 72 (April 1970): 269–88.

7. Irwin Deutscher, "Words and Deeds: Social Science and Social Policy," *Social Problems* 13 (Winter 1966): 235–54; Gordon H. DeFriese and W. Scott Ford, Jr., "Open Occupancy—What Whites Say, What They Do," *Trans-action* (April 1968): 53–56; Melvin L. DeFleur and Frank R. Westie, "Verbal Attitudes and Overt Acts: An Experiment on the Salience of Attitudes," *American Sociological Review* 23 (December 1958): 667–73.

8. Joseph A. Schumpeter, *Imperialism and Social Classes* (New York: A. M. Kelley, 1951), p. 220.

9. Bernard Berelson and Gary A. Steiner, *Human Behavior: An Inventory of Scientific Findings* (New York: Harcourt, Brace & World, 1964), pp. 506–7; Seymour S. Bellin and Louis Kriesberg, "Relationships Among Attitudes, Circumstances, and Behavior: The Case of Applying for Public Housing," *Sociology and Social Research* 51 (July 1967): 453–69; Leon Festinger, *A Theory of Cognitive Dissonance* (Evanston, Ill.: Row, Peterson, 1957).

10. Ira L. Reiss, *The Social Context of Premarital Sexual Permissiveness* (New York: Holt, Rinehart and Winston, 1967), Chapter 7; Herbert J. Gans, "Culture and Class in the Study of Poverty: An Approach to Anti-Poverty Research," in Daniel P. Moynihan (ed.), *On Understanding Poverty, op. cit.*, pp. 201–28; Lee Rainwater, "The Problem of Lower-Class Culture and Poverty-War Strategy," in Daniel P. Moynihan (ed.), *On Understanding Poverty, op. cit.*, pp. 229–59.

11. See Reinhard Bendix, "The Lower Classes and the 'Democratic Revolution,'" *Industrial Relations* 1 (October 1961): 91–116; Robert K. Merton, *Social Theory and Social Structure*, revised ed. (Glencoe, Ill.: Free Press, 1957), pp. 131–94.

12. Robert K. Merton, *op. cit.*

13. This formulation has been influenced by George C. Homans, "Bringing Men Back In," *American Sociological Review* 29 (December 1964): 809–18.

14. For similar ideas see: Raymond T. Smith, *The Negro Family in British Guiana* (London: Routledge & Kegan Paul), p. 149; Lloyd Braithwaite, "Sociology and Demographic Research in the British Caribbean," *Social and Economic Studies* 6 (March 1957), p. 534; Hyman Rodman, "The Lower-Class Value Stretch," *op. cit.;* Ulf Hannerz, *Soulside: Inquiries into Ghetto Culture and Community* (New York: Columbia University Press, 1969); Lee Rainwater, "The Problem of Lower-Class Culture and Poverty-War Strategy," in Daniel P. Moynihan (ed.), *On Understanding Poverty, op. cit.*

15. Hylan Lewis, *op. cit.;* Elliot Liebow, *op. cit.;* Robert E. Staples, *The Lower Income Negro Family in Saint Paul* (Saint Paul, Minn.: Urban League, 1967).

16. My analysis of lower-class responses makes use of ideal types, and these abstractions obviously cannot capture the total reality. Pragmatism is not the same as chaos, anarchy, or amorality. For example, a pragmatic orientation in one area may be influenced by values held in related areas. Similarly, a more general system of values would usually be needed to lend support to the negotiated interpersonal transactions that characterize pragmatism, similar to the non-contractual elements of contract clarified by Emile Durkheim.

17. David Riesman, *The Lonely Crowd* (New Haven: Yale University Press, 1950).

18. Nathan Glazer, "Social Characteristics of American Jews," *American Jewish Yearbook* 56 (New York: Jewish Publication Society of America, 1955), pp. 3–41; Fred L. Strodtbeck, Margaret R. Mac-Donald, and Bernard C. Rosen, "Evaluation of Occupations: A Reflection of Jewish and Italian Mobility Differences," *American Sociological Review* 22 (October 1957): 546–53; Bernard C. Rosen, "Race, Ethnicity, and Achievement Syndrome," *American Sociological Review* 24 (February 1959): 47–60; Martin Gold, *Status Forces in Delinquent Boys* (Ann Arbor: University of Michigan Press, 1963); T. Scott Miyakawa, *Protestants and Pioneers* (Chicago: University of Chicago Press, 1964).

19. The adaptive and cultural developments among Afro-American groups have heretofore largely occurred in response to their situation in the larger society. Recent events increasingly suggest that Afro-American cultural developments are becoming more autonomous, and that cultural (as well as social, political, and economic) strengths will lead to more Afro-American unity and social class mobility: see Harold Cruse, *The Crisis of the Negro Intellectual, op. cit.*

20. Hyman Rodman, "Family and Social Pathology in the Ghetto," *Science* 161 (August 23, 1968): 756–62.

APPENDICES

1. Calypso Selections

> "Poverty must have its pleasures, my child,"
> said the old woman, laughing. "Suffering needs
> singing and drinking, otherwise it feeds on us.
> He's a tough customer, but he isn't going to
> make a meal of us. We'll eat him up."
> NIKOS KAZANTZAKIS

THE CALYPSO SELECTIONS add further documentation to some of the topics of this book about Trinidad: poverty and unemployment; race, class, and color discrimination; Negro and Indian friction; the cosmopolitan basis for harmony; the husband-wife relationship; the concern with a wife's infidelity and deceit; the father's marginal role in the family; and the physical punishment of children. None of the calypsos are reprinted in their entirety, and, shorn of their rhythm, the printed page captures only a skeletal image of this art form that originated in Trinidad. The reader will have to visit Trinidad during the Carnival season to savor the full flavor of the calypso. At the same time he will have the opportunity to see a pre-Lenten spectacle that is unmatched anywhere in the world.

The calypsonians in Trinidad are, with some exceptions, lower-class Negro men who write their own words and music and sing and play their own songs. The calypsos are a commentary on many aspects of life in Trinidad. They are usually topical and humorous, with a great many sexual *double entendres*. For the most part, they present a lower-class viewpoint, or a Negro viewpoint, or a male viewpoint.

I do not suggest that the calypsonians are a representative lower-class group, nor that the calypso selections I have made are in any way representative. But there are many more selections, not included here, that are variations on the themes illustrated in this appendix. On the whole these selections buttress parts of the presented description of lower-class life and lower-class family organization.

The source for most of these calypso selections is the series of "souvenir booklets" in which many of the Carnival season's best calypsos are compiled. I have corrected obvious typographical errors, and I have occasionally added punctuation or changed the spelling of words in order to clarify the meaning of some of the calypsos. Other than that I have reprinted the selections as they were originally printed.

It should be remembered that many changes have taken place in Trinidad in the past ten or twenty years. The topical references in the calypsos do not all pertain to the current situation. As a result, the date each calypso was first sung is given. The Federation of the West Indies was in existence only from 1956 to 1962, and one of the issues faced by the federated islands was the search for an acceptable site for the Federal capital. These, and some other topical references, may not always be clear to the reader unfamiliar with Caribbean or Trinidad affairs. Some help is available in Appendix 2, which explains most of the words whose meanings are not obvious from the context.

POVERTY AND UNEMPLOYMENT

Members of the lower class are well aware of their deprived position in society. Although there have been many political changes since the 1950's, as detailed in Chapter 2, the problem of poverty and unemployment is still severe.

How Can Starvation Fight Federation
Small Island Pride (*1949*)
> Relax and take this seriously
> Let's concentrate on ah hungry family
> A poor mother with two young babies
> Finds herself on morning times without tea
> And just imagine the poor father aint working no way . . .
>
> I'm appealing to the Government
> To find us some kind of employment
> We can't depend on our Councillors
> And the bigger shots always turn out failures

They always preaching how they move motions for me
    and you
And got us pending and we can't see what the hell they do
Once they could wake up in the morning and find butter
    on their bread
They don't care if poor people dead.

High Cost of Living
Lord Eisenhower (*1953*)

I don't know what's going on in this country
But the things going from bad to worse daily
I hearing men with money complaining
How they fed up with this high cost of living
So just imagine a poor man life to-day
With a family to mind, a house rent to pay
When that man draft a plan and that plan should fail
He must try thiefing and that is jail.

We Want Better Condition
Tiny Terror (*1954*)

Under these life condition I cant live in this island (*twice*)
The constant raising of food price not nice
And many days I cant buy my rice
So in my opinion
Some body bound to die here for starvation
No No No Government we cant take it so
No No No give the people free passport and let them go.

Yearly Happening
Lord Eisenhower (*1954*)

The higher authorities should be more than glad
To ease the present situation in Trinidad
For there are hundreds of people around the place
Daily depression staring them in their face
No employment, no real means of living
Some of us walking the street half-naked and starving
Oppress by grief and perpetual misery
Through neglecting us to aid a next colony.

Dream of the Food Register
Lord Superior (*1956*)
> Last night ah lay down ah feeling bad
> But listen what a funny dream I had
> I dreamt this world was made over
> And everybody had a food register
> It was placed upon your forehead very neat
> And will register everything you eat.
> So what ever you eat for lunch or dinner
> It used to show on the register
> I see the saga boys were badly fed
> Theirs only used to show mauby and sweetbread.

> You can take it from the Superior
> The sagas never like the register
> What ever they eat you compel to know
> Because the register was there to show
> Sometimes you'll see them picking their teeth
> You will believe they eat
> Is smart they smart believe me
> They could eat an ostrich, ah fuss they hungry.

Unemployment
Mighty Bomber (*1967*)
> I had it really hard
> The unemployment situation in Trinidad
> Thousands of people like me and you
> So much responsibilities but no work to do
> With families to mind we cant be at peace
> So you see that why the crime wave bound to increase.

RACE, CLASS, AND COLOR DISCRIMINATION

Discrimination against Negroes was common in Trinidad until the mid-1950's. Since 1956, however, local control of government by the People's National Movement, a predominantly Negro-supported party, has eliminated discrimination against Negroes in most areas. Nevertheless, discrimination against the poor is still common.

Sin and Damnation
Vivian Comma (1954)

What a calamity
How the people suffering in this colony (*repeat*)
They suffer from a disease that's spreading on and on
It is a lighter skin is better than a darker one
And it has made us despise each other
Even hating our Mothers and Fathers.

So if you say the lighter your skin the better for you
Well then those lighter than you are better off than you
But I say that is sin and damnation
Placing such importance in pigmentation.

Guardian Beauty Contest
Attila the Hun (1955)

I for one was never disappointed
From the time that the contest started
For I have seen many a brown skinned miss
Who were the quintessence of loveliness
But in the backyard hear a judge remark
Shes really lovely but she too dark
And it is with chagrin despair and pain
You see another flat back white woman get it again.

So it is time that our forces we enlist
And put an end to all this stupidness
Let us tell them all immediately
With protest from all over the country
That when a beauty contest they are judging
There must be no question of colour or skin
And if no regard for our views are shown
Then let us leave the white people business alone.

For this Guardian Competition
Is nothing but real discrimination
One thing in this world will never be seen
Is a dark skinned girl as Carnival Queen.

All Courts Should Have Jurors
Lord Eisenhower (1956)

> That is why all courts should have jurors
> Some magistrate does try case by favour
> Well it becomes a style of the town
> When you wrong in court you wrong, you right you still wrong.
>
> Some magistrate doesn't got no reason
> I'll tell you why and how that does happen
> Some times they suffering from wife trouble
> And come to court to pass it on people
> Especially if you dumb to the laws
> And you haven't got a lawyer to fight your cause
> They'll take away you rights and claim that wrong
> And if you argue at all they would send you down.
>
> I know ah big shot name Mr. Bubble
> Once got himself in a serious trouble
> He give a fête and invite his honour
> And put him to dine with his eldest sister
> The day of the case ah so shock to know
> Magistrate was in powers to try case so
> Mr. Bubble tell a lie and get off scotch free
> And the complainant get three months in custody.

Coloured Cricket
Lord Cypher (1956)

> If ah should catch my son playing cricket
> Waip wap is licks with the wicket
> For I can bet the last of my dollar
> The game is played according to colour
> But ah dont care who may vex or please
> It's a daily occurence in the West Indies.

NEGRO AND INDIAN FRICTION

The major racial friction in Trinidad is found between the two major racial groups—Negroes and Indians. The Negroes and Indians are also divided by religious and political differences. The Negro-Indian friction in Trinidad is mild in comparison, say, to Negro-white friction in the United States. It has also been mitigated by a shared history of subjugation, either in slavery or indentured labor, and by the occasional cooperation between Dr. Rudranath Capildeo, former leader of the Democratic Labour Party, and Dr. Eric Williams of the People's National Movement. (In the calypsos below, the latter is referred to as "Willie" and as "the doctor" and the former is referred to as "the mad scientist.")

The Changes of the Indians
Mighty Cobra (1954)
> I'm begging the higher authorities to check up on the
>   Indians seriously
> Long ago it was the Indians toting load
> Otherwise with a broom they sweeping the road
> But if you tell them so they'll tell you you're wrong
> The Indians and them they own half the town.

William The Conqueror
Mighty Sparrow (1957)
> I am no politician
> But I could understand
> If it wasn't for brother Willie
> And his ability
> Trinidad wouldn't go neither come
> Long ago we used to vote for roti and rum
> Nowadays we eating the Indian and them
> Then we vote P. N. M.

Income Tax
Lord Superior (1957)
> Tax them doctor tax them
> Tax them like you are mad
> Lord Superior say
> Dont care who feel bad
> Down to the street girls
> You should make them bawl
> Check every Yankee man that they call
> And buss tax on them and all.

It have some old Indian people
Playing they like to beg
This time they got one million dollars
Tie between their legs
I'm telling the doctor
I am talking the facts
Is to chop loose the capra with a sharp axe
And haul out your income tax.

The United Indian
Mighty Striker (*1959*)
I will bet money by the thousands
Nobody unite as the Indians
It's hard for Negro to do
But not the Indians, believe is true
The people really have a mind
I could prove it every election time.

If they can't spell a-t, they going up for election
If they can't spell b-a-t still they voting the man
Could be a-b-c Harrylal, believe what ah say
Or never-go-to-school Ramlol, they voting the man on
    election day.

Every election Negro can't get a vote from Indian
Poor Ramcharan was in trouble with his own Indian people
Although Ramcharan is an Indian they throw him down
    Federal Election
The Indian tell him to go and hide because he gone across
    on the Negro side.

Election Violence
Mighty Christo (*1961*)
Whip them P.N.M. whip them
You wearing the pants
If these people get on top is trouble
And we aint got a chance
Now we faring better
Since we got we Premier
We living in contentment
So who we want? P.N.M. government.

Ah hear up in Couva
They attack a minister
And one Ramadeen
Try to thief a voting machine
Well that was ignorance
But he didn't have a chance
So they send him to Carrera
And when he come out is straight back to Calcutta.

The Mad Scientist
Nap Hepburn (*1962*)
Well ah glad the election over
And the doctor come back in power (*repeat*)
It was a hard fight
Platform speakers saying what they like
One side was offering education
And the next side revolution.

From Trinidad and Tobago the doctor had to go
Only in the rural districts support the mad scientist
The election was at hot pace
Some deceitful people vote race
But all who vote race I have one thing to say
That the doctor come here to stay.

THE COSMOPOLITAN BASIS FOR HARMONY

There is harmony as well as friction in Trinidad. The following calypso selections stress the mixed descent of many Trinidadians, and their cosmopolitan basis for cooperation.

What's Federation
Small Island Pride (*1956*)
The Trinidadian ask the Grenadian
If she could tell her what is federation
The Grenadian said, girl, federation is ah combination of
    generation
She said because me mother was ah Grenadian
Who married me father ah Trinidadian
Ah made two children one for ah Chinese man

And the other one for a St. Lucian
When you contact all these generation
The answer to that is federation.

Trinidad Carnival
Mighty Sparrow (*1957*)
The biggest bacchanal
Is in Trinidad Carnival (*repeat*)
All you got to do when the music play
Take your man an break away
Regardless of colour creed or race
Jump up and shake your waist
This is the spirit of Carnival
It is a creole bacchanal
So jump as you mad this is Trinidad
We don't care who say we bad.

Federated Islands
Mighty Bomber (*1959*)
There's a task before us
We must fight dominion status
Free trade and free movement
And have a sound devoted government
So to speak we want to accomplish
We must forget everything about racial business
Giving our leaders their every need
Regardless of colour, their class or creed.

Calypso Animals
Mighty Chiang-Kai-Shek (*1960*)
Some might vex because ah singing this song,
But ah want to show them I ain't wrong;
Ah don't care they say ah making trouble
Ah man and his name bound to resemble.
I jump in the Calypso fête
And call myself Mighty Chiang-Kai-Shek.
The reason why it's plain to see
That I have the appearance of a born Chinese.

Me grandma from Venezuela,
Me father, well he from China.
Me mother a Grenadian,
And the result was me a Calypsonian.

SEX AND MONEY

In an established marital (*living*) relationship the man is expected to earn the money and the woman is expected to take care of the house. Their sexual relationship goes without saying. In a more casual relationship between a man and a woman, however, money is exchanged for sex, and this is illustrated below in a variety of ways:

Seven Day Mopsy
Lord Eisenhower (*1956*)

>The lord was in love with a seven day mopsy
>That was thrills for me
>She wont light a fire on Saturdays
>Only living on bread, sweet water and praise
>And on those nights if ah touch her or anything
>She'll turn her back towards me and start to sing.

>Well the next week end which was my final visit
>I well enjoy it
>As ah reach that night she start to hug and squeeze me
>Expecting money
>Ah good eat and drink she out black is white
>As ah finish ah get up and say good night.

>When she notice in truth no money to come
>She hold me in her arms and she start to hum
>I am yours heart and soul I am yours etc.
>I say yes Mavis you mine for as I can see
>But you is seven days you cant spend anglican money.

Theresa
Mighty Sparrow (*1957*)

>You worse than a dog Theresa
>Girl you break me heart

This morning you take me dollar
Now you playing smart
This morning you come we talk we business quiet and soft
Ev'ry time ah come you making excuses and trying to put
    it off.

Now make up your mind Theresa
I ain't making joke
I don't want to use me razor
But this thing won't work
Give me back me money or else
Settle up socially
Nobody yet never take me money
And making old style on me.

Glasses Women
Growling Tiger (1959)

I remember some time at Morvant
I met a beautiful girl and her name was Ramona
Talking in conversation
She said she loved me dearly but what compensation
She wanted to test her eyes
Forty-five dollars glasses I sympathize
But she was owing rent and the hair dresser
And complaining about her old grandmother.

Women and Money
Mighty Conqueror (1962)

When a poor man see a woman and he like she bad
He have to be like if he mad
And tell she he have house and property
But if he only play honest and tell she the truth
He cant conquer the old brute
Not he, because he brokes and a'int have no money

So when you see a pretty woman
With a ugly ugly man
It ain't hard to understand
That he have the things to make she happy
She don't care what she friends and them say bout she
Once she's getting the money

The man could be ugly like sin
But the money is damn good looking.

Cockset Paper
Little Mystery (*1965*)
    I tried my best to convince she
    That it's good currency;
    Ah show she the One, the Five and the Ten.
    She said, "Little Mystery, all right then."
    She enquired from the neighbourhood
    And found out the money was good.
    Well, from then when ah bring me pile
    If you see how she grabbing it with a smile.
    She bawl out "One ting ah like with you Mystery,
    You does give me plenty money,
    But right now ah have a hot head
    Ah owe the store on me Simmons bed."

UNFAITHFUL WIVES

Lower-class men in Trinidad are strongly concerned about the fidelity of their wives. Colorful phrases are sometimes used to refer to a wife's infidelity, for example, "someone's putting pepper in your rice," or "there's more in the mortar besides the pestle." The calypso selections below are about unfaithful wives in *living* and married relationships.

Mary I Disgust
Lord Kitchener (*1944*)
    Mary I tired and disgust
    Don't boil no more fig for me breakfast (*repeat*)
    Thirty dollars for the fortnight you spending
    What the devil you doing in the kitchen
    Ah go cut your salary
    For good jockey riding me race for me.

    Darling is a long time ah notice
    Some botheration in me business
    'Cause when ah knock off from duty

Ah always meet you rample and sleepy
But ah can't get to bounce de superman
That have me business in such condition
Ah go chop like a grass cutter
And the Government go charge me for manslaughter.

Mamma Has a Chinese Man
Lord Melody (*1951*)

I was living with a Chinese girl in the country
That was misery
I married the craft in nineteen-forty
We had two children one died unfortunately
Went to work and come back, I feeling so bad
I meet the child crying in the middle of the yard.

Daddy ma beat me today
Because I didn't want to go and play
A chinky eye man with a big big head
Was lying down upon the bed.
I said your mother has a Chinese man
Mama has a Chinese man
Your mother has a Chinese man
Trespassing upon my plan.

Boxum Boxum
Mighty Panther (*1954*)

A school master and a yard boy in conversation
In the district want to know who is the better man
The boy said school master I know more girls than you
The school master said no my son that aint true
He said this argument we can over come
Any girl pass you or I we will say Boxum

The first girl that pass was Boxum Boxum
The second one each of them said Boxum
What made the school master feel so blue
When his wife pass the boy shout out Boxum too.

Little Watchman Willie
Small Island Pride (*1955*)

Well slow, slow, slow the boy father advancing

But louder and louder the boy shouting
Mammy, Mamma daddy coming
She said stop him but don't say what is happening
Well the boy starts to feel uneasy
Fly inside the bush to help his poor mammy
I cannot explain what the poor child see
But he shout daddy a man on you' property.

A Sailor Man
Mighty Sparrow (1957)
Since I married Dorothy
She have me going crazy
Well is butt like fire
I cant take it no longer
No no no I cant stand the pressure
Like she want me to commit murder.

She have a sailor man
And she have a Chinese man
She leave the Chinese man
For a black old ugly police man

Everyday is a complain
Like she want to burn down Port-of-Spain
And if I raise my hand at all
You surprise to hear how she would bawl
It's the same behavior
Horn like fire
I cant take it no longer
You know I nearly dead with tabanca.

My Federal Troubles
Mighty Wrangler (1958)
Trouble with me and Iris
And this Federal business
Man trespassing on my land
And the old talk was we are a nation
But ah start threatening like ah mad
Ah don't want no nation inside me yard

Monday was ah Jamaican
Tuesday was ah Vincentian

Catch a Bajan in me bedroom next night
He say he looking for the Federal site.

The Message
Mighty Power (*1961*)
Ah hear good evening, good evening (*repeat*)
Is here Monica living
I say yes, but she gone to the grocery
If you want you could wait for she
Ah never hear more in my life
Ah man give meh this message to give me own wife.

He tell me to tell she dont disappoint he
Meet him by the Savannah at eight-thirty
Please Power please give this message to she
He tell me to tell she dont keep him waiting
Long as the other evening.

Worse Than That
Mighty Bomber (*1963*)
Me wife began to make row with me
How you could insult me family
He does come to visit me now and then
Is me father son and me mother friend
He was cold and she had the fever
So with vicks they rub one another
Both of them still lie down on me bed
Is now ah get red.

Woman Better than Man
Lord Blakie (*1967*)
I started laughing, she said what you laughing for
Ah say I could remember the same thing with my girl Dor
She had a next man, and for no reason
The first day I came and ketch him home, she said was she
    cousin.

MISTAKEN PATERNITY

The concern about whether the husband is also the father of his wife's child can be seen below:

No Darling This Child Aint Mine
Invader (1942)
    Miss Daisy you must be crazy
    Why you brought me up for bastardy (*repeat*)
    After you mamaguy me and take my money
    And still sleeping in William bachy
    When the baby born stick your grind
    No darling that child aint mine.

    Now listen how this Miss Daisy
    Wanted to use her head on me
    It wasn't quite two weeks since we got in friendly
    She declared she was in baby
    But I hear the gossip and hear the rumour
    It was for a Yankee soldier.

Gossipmongers of Trinidad
Mighty Dictator (*1951*)
    And the calypsonian
    Is the biggest gossipmonger in the island
    An Indian couple up Belmont
    Make a white baby I'm sure you heard the stunt
    What a loving father
    He said his wife was drinking milk of magnesia
    I tried my best to help him out too
    I say she watch up at the sky so the eyes get blue.

Que Sera, Sera
Mighty Pretender (*1958*)
    Me and the girl was living kinda happy
    Til I took home a friend by the name of Louie
    A certain fella from Caripito

With a slight resemblance of Valentino
She tumble a pair of children on me
The image of my good friend Louie.

Mildred Don't Cry
Small Island Pride (*1959*)

Ah think ah go run
Every time ah go and come is a different son
And what hurting me
Every children she make none resemble me
The first child she make is for a old French man
The second one resemble an Italian
Now ah fetch her in the arms of the Lord Melody
What the hell she go make but a damn monkey.

Sparrow Christening
Lord Melody (*1961*)

The food that they served was sicking
Roti, corn-beef, and green plantain
The grandmother refuse to hold the kid
She say the child have a white man forehead
So the godmother and the godfather
Grab a car and went back to Morvant
That was the talk in Petit Valley
How the Sparrow christen a next man baby.

The child ain't resemble the great grandfather
The child ain't resemble the great grandmother
The child ain't resemble Sparrow at all
He say they exchange the child in the hospital.

Child Father
Mighty Sparrow (*1963*)

Child father well they mamaguy me
Child father well ah go half kill somebody
Them wahbeen women in true they making me hop
But unless you lick them down this nonsense won't stop.

They does run about with Tom, Dick and Harry
And when they dead out, Lord they looking for me,

Hear them telling Bim and Bam how Sparrow is dey man
Couple days dey telling me they making a baby.

Bad Neighbours
Mighty Shadow (1965)
> My neighbour name Julian
> Have me in big confusion (*repeat*)
> I can't leave my girl friend and go to work
> Julian always home with some old talk
> Now Lilian have a son
> It come out the image of Julian.

> When you leave your wife at home
> With your neighbour alone
> She does get accustomed to him
> She will start calling him fancy
> Names like Doo Doo Darling
> And if she only fall with a belly pain
> She want somebody to rub she down
> And when he finish rub with his
> Soft candle you whole bed rample.

A FATHER'S FAILURES

A man should support his wife and children. The following selections point out that this is what is expected of a husband-father, even though he often does not fulfill his obligations.

Advice to Calypsonians
Lord Creator (1959)
> The calypsonian of today
> Throwing 'way they money in every way
> And from the time they get the money
> They looking for Jean and Dorothy
> To give them all the money that they make in the tent
> And they poor wife ain't have a cent.

> But not me my money is to buy a house and land
> For my wife and all my family

For when I'm becoming an old man
I want to settle in luxury
I'll help out poor people to the end
'Cause they are my friend
This throwing way money must stop
And help your children that coming up.

Father's Love
Mighty Viper (*1961*)

Let's us sit and wonder
How many children love their Father
I think its a perfect shame
Children calling their Father by his name
It is hard to be a Father
For your children to call you Tom, Roy or Jagader
So it grieves me day and night to see
Children honouring their Mother so gratefully
And their Father they always neglect
Not even a teaspoon full of respect.

Yes a mother love is great
But a father love we cannot underestimate
For mammy may be home nursing the baby
While daddy may be bursting stone in a quarry
So you see dad have to work and mind the children
That they may grow up good women and men
So ah sure the public will agree with me
For love greater than those is hard to see.

Shakespeare the Madman
Nap Hepburn (*1962*)

William Shakespeare again,
I would prove where he was insane,
On this quotation ah must attack,
He said there are four things that come not back,
Ah spoken word, ah neglected opportunity,
I know is five which prove he was crazy.
The fifth was me pa leave since ah was small,
And up to now me pa enh come back at all.

Low-Minded Men
Mighty Bomber (*1962*)

> Is a long time ah studying this thing
> Fools for women, rum drinkers and gambling
> Some men have their children and wife to support
> And they go about life not knowing its worth
> Leaving their children and wife to starve
> And when they reach home not a cent they have.

BEATING CHILDREN

Mothers, fathers, or their substitutes, often beat children to enforce obedience, or at least to punish what is regarded as bad behavior.

Who Stole the Bake?
Lord Melody (*1951*)

> A baptist preacher living peacefully
> With two little children in Lavanty
> His work was selling sweepstake
> So one evening he roast up some bake
> Went to sleep and get a bake missing
> So he wake up the children and start asking.
>
> Jonah? yes pa; you take a bake here? no pa
> Well one gone, one gone, one gone
> The power fly up in the old man head
> Raff a belt and nearly killed the poor children dead
> With whap! whap-whap! whap! whap-whap!

Mamma Look a Booboo
Lord Melody (*1956*)

> Mamma look ah booboo, they shout
> The mother told them shut up your mouth
> That is yuh daddy. O no
> My daddy cant be ugly so
> Shut yuh mouth go away
> Mama look ah booboo dey.
>
> I coulden even digest my supper

Due to the children behavior
John, yes Pa, come here a moment
Bring the belt yuh too damn curgelent
Daddy is James start off first
No daddy is Joyce who start to curse
Ah drag my belt from off me waist
If yuh see races out the place.

Mother Day Calypso
Striker (*1958*)

Last Mother's Day they happy all about
Poor me ah had to hosh op my mouth
Little children from East to the West
Said how they mother she try her best
Nice treatment for so, everybody say
And they start out singing on Mother's Day.

M is for the million things she gave me
O means that she is only getting old
But all my mother used to give me heaven knows
Is to kneel down on grater with plenty blows.

World's Laziest Man
Mighty Dougla (*1961*)

Since ah was small is the same thing
My grandmother complaining
That ah so lazy she couldn't make no hand of me
If she beat me to make me work she only making joke
She could beat me till she beat off all me clothes
Ah too lazy to brakes from blows.

2. *Glossary of Trinidad Creole English Terms*

> *There is a certain cultural self-satisfaction in the discovery that we shall not only bequeath cultural heritages of steelband calypsos, pitch lake, and carnival, but our children will speak a language which belongs to them. . . .*
> *In the same way that English has as its main linguistic pillars a Roman-French-Saxon-Germanic origin, so Trinidadianese rests on a foundation of African-Spanish-French-English base, with English taking precedence over the other three.*
>
> C. R. OTTLEY

BOTH STANDARD ENGLISH and Trinidad Creole English are currently spoken in Trinidad. The latter is the dominant language of lower-class individuals, but it is understood and spoken by many other Trinidadians who also speak standard English. Trinidad Creole English developed as a result of historical events that blended West African, Spanish, French, and English influences. The French patois which was important in Trinidad from the late eighteenth century to the early twentieth century was a major ingredient, and the migratory contacts with other West Indian islands led to a good deal of sharing in the development of the various Creole languages throughout the Caribbean.[1] The East Indian migration to Trinidad led to the incorporation of some Hindu terms as well.

The glossary below covers all of the Trinidad Creole English terms used in this book that may be unfamiliar to the non-Trinidadian, and it also contains some terms that are not used in the book in order to give the reader a better idea of the language's vocabulary. However, grammatical construction, pronunciation, and etymology are only imperfectly rendered in this glossary and in the examples throughout the text; my major focus is lower-class family organization and not language, and the reader interested in the latter should consult other sources.[2]

The spelling of Trinidad Creole English terms has not become standardized,[3] and the spelling inconsistencies in this book mirror the inconsistencies of the language. Wherever possible I have used local spelling preferences. The lack of standardization is illustrated by *en*, which is sometimes spelled *ain', ain't, en, ent*, or in other ways. I have tried to cover some variations by giving cross-references in the glossary. But without a standardized orthography for Trinidad Creole English the glossary cannot cover everything. Some spellings, especially of short words, are occasionally based upon the native pronunciation of standard English terms, for example, *dey* for *there* or *their* (or *they*), or *ting* for *thing*. These kinds of spellings are used in some of the calypso selections, but there are too many variations and idiosyncrasies to try to cover them all in the glossary. Trinidad Creole English spelling is more frequently used in this book for the shorter and more common words, because the Creole English spelling of these words has become more standardized.

Some of the terms still in use in Trinidad are listed by the *Oxford English Dictionary* as archaic or obsolete. *Mistress, horn*, and *well* are examples. Some of the terms have dropped the initial syllable from the standard English word, such as *press* for *oppress* and *maphrodite* for *hermaphrodite*. Some terms are uncommonly used elsewhere, but are the preferred terms in Trinidad, for example, *fête* and *bacchanal*. Finally, there are some terms which have been adopted from standard English but altered in meaning—*humbug, curry-favour*, and *ignorant* are examples.

NOTES

1. See Frank A. Collymore, *Notes for a Glossary of Words and Phrases of Barbadian Dialect*, 2nd ed. (Bridgeton, Barbados: Advocate Co., 1957).

2. Frederic G. Cassidy, *Jamaica Talk: Three Hundred Years of the English Language in Jamaica* (London: Macmillan, 1961); Douglas Taylor, "The Origin of West Indian Creole Languages: Evi-

dence from Grammatical Categories," *American Anthropologist* 65
(August 1963): 800–814; Morris F. Goodman, *A Comparative Study
of Creole French Dialects* (The Hague: Mouton, 1964).

    3. My glossary was prepared independently of these other
glossaries of Trinidad terms: Macaw, *Notebook* (Port of Spain, Trinidad: Trinidad Publishing Co., 1960), pp. 95–96; C. R. Ottley, *Trinibagianese*, 2nd ed., Vol. 1 (n.p., 1966); C. R. Ottley, *Trinibagianese*,
1st ed., Vol. 2 (n.p., 1966).

*Note: When words defined in this glossary appear in
other definitions they are printed in small capitals.*

ACCORDIN', according to the circumstances, depending upon the
    situation, e.g., "Does a child love its mother more or its father
    more?" "Well, accordin'; sometimes the mother and some-
    times the father."

ADVANTAGE, v., to take advantage of, e.g., they like to advantage
    you too much.

AGAIN, adv., else, more, any more, further, e.g., what have you to
    say again? or, I don' love you again.

AH, (1) pron., I, (2) indefinite article, a.

AIN'T, AIN', see EN

ALL WHERE, in all places that, e.g., he was assured of support
    all where he spoke.

APPA, APA, OPPA, OPA, n., man who believes he is a child's father,
    although he is not, e.g., you only apa, you en papa (source:
    perhaps Spanish *opa*, foolish).

AS, prep., like, e.g., my neighbor is as family to me.

AS MAN, man to man, e.g., speaking as man, I was 'fraid that
    day.

ASK ME, NA, that's so true, you can say that again, e.g., "She fas',
    yes." "Ask me, na."

BACCHANAL, n., scandal, orgy, e.g., that court case was a bac-
    chanal.

BACHELOR, adv., alone, singly, e.g., He (she) livin' bachelor.

BAD-JOHN, n., rogue, lawless youth, e.g., too many bad-johns
    attendin' the races.

BAD-TALK, v., to speak ill of, e.g., don' bad-talk me when I go.
    (Also used as a noun.)

BAKE, n., a local pancake, *roti*.

BASKET, TO GIVE SOMEONE A, to flatter someone jokingly, e.g.,
    don' give me a basket, na.

BASODEE, adj., confused, dazed, bewildered, e.g., he got basodee in front the crowd.

BATCHIE, BACHY, n., a place where a man lives alone; a place to which a girl can be brought for sexual intercourse, e.g., I have a batchie fix up.

BEHIND, prep., after, e.g., He always behind me to do so-so-so.

BHAGEE, BHAJI, n., a spinach-like dish made from the leaves of the dasheen (source: Hindi).

BLACK IS WHITE, freely, without restraint, e.g., they cursing black is white.

BOBOL, n., trickery, corruption, underhandedness, graft, e.g., it have too much bobol in government, man. *Bobolist*, n., one who practices bobol.

BOOBOO, n., (1) an insect; (2) any frightful thing, e.g., mama, look, a booboo dey.

BOOTOO, n., stick, baton, police truncheon.

BOSS, adj., superb, outstanding, e.g., that pig is boss.

BOUNCE UP, v., to come upon, to meet suddenly.

BRAKES, v., to shield, make excuses, beat around the bush, e.g., I find he brakesing a lot.

BRASS-FACE, adj., brazen, bold, e.g., she too brass-face.

BREAK AWAY, v., dance, JUMP-UP.

BROCKO, adj., lame, e.g., He have a brocko leg.

BROCKOGEE, n., a person who is lame.

BUFF, v., censure, reprove, scold, e.g., they buff her all the time. Buff, n., chiding, reprimand, scolding, e.g., he gettin' buff for so! (source: contraction of *rebuff*).

BUS', v., do suddenly; do severely.

BUS' DUT, v., run away, run like hell.

BUS' ONE'S SKIN, BUS' ONE'S TAIL, to beat, to hurt, e.g., come here now or I bus' you' skin.

BUTT, v., to strike with the head or horns; to cuckold.

CAPRA, n., Indian cloth or garment, e.g., turban or dhoti.

CARE, v., to raise, bring up, GROW.

CARRERA, n., the island off Trinidad where the Trinidad and Tobago prison is.

CATCH ONE'S SKIN, CATCH ONE'S TAIL, to have a lot of difficulty, e.g., I catch my skin till I finish that.

CHAC-CHACS, n., maracas, small round calabashes with wooden handles containing seeds and used to beat a rhythm.

CHOKE VEIN, vague term used to "explain" a pain, e.g., look me foot, it have a choke vein.

CHOOK, see JUICK.

CHOOPS, CHUPSE, see STCHOOPS.

CHUT, interj., expression of annoyance or disgust, e.g., Chut! What you beat he for?

CLEAR, adj., fair, light, e.g., his skin clear, clear.

COCOYEA, n., the central strip of a coconut leaf. *Cocoyea broom,* the broom made from these strips.

COME, v., to be, to become, to turn out, e.g., if you is married or livin', it come as the same; the more she come big, the more stupid she come.

COMESS, n., scandal, confusion, disturbance, e.g., stay away, it have too much o' comess in that (source: perhaps a contraction of *commerce*).

COOLIE, n., (derogatory) East Indian.

CRAFT, sometimes CRAF' or CRAFF, n., girl friend, attractive girl, e.g., I married the craft in 1965.

CREOLE, n., a native of the West Indies, especially a Negro as opposed to an East Indian. To be *creolized,* to become like a Creole in behavior or values.

CROSSES, n., troubles, e.g., look at me crosses, na.

CURRY-FAVOUR, v., to show favoritism, e.g., the teacher curry-favour for he (source: modification of standard English).

DANDAN, n., dress, e.g., I have a pretty dandan.

DEAD, v., die, e.g., you must dead sometimes.

DEY, there, their, or they.

DIABLESSE (pronounced: jabless), n., in Trinidad folklore, a beautiful woman with one cloven hoof who lures men into the forest and then disappears (source: French, *diablesse,* she-devil).

DID (plus infinitive), to indicate past time, e.g., he did want it for heself, or, he did go yesterday.

DOES, v., get(s) along, e.g., they does well with everyone.

DONE (plus infinitive), to indicate past tense, with a sense of finality, e.g., he done los' already.

DOODOO, DUDU, DOO, DOOD, DOODS, n., an affectionate name used to address someone (source: French, *doux,* sweet).

DOUENNE, n., the spirit of an unchristened child (source: possibly Spanish, *duende,* elf, ghost).

DOUGLA, DOGLA, n., a person of mixed Negro and East Indian descent.

DRAUGHTS, n., checkers (British term).

DROP, n., lift, ride, e.g., will you give me a drop to Sangre Grande?

EASE ONE UP, to let one off easily, e.g., she ask her teacher to ease she up.

EAST INDIAN, n., a native of India, or his descendant.

EH-EH, interj., expressing surprise, wonder, e.g., Eh-eh! I didn' see you there, man.

EN, sometimes ENH, ENT, AIN', AIN'T, neg., am not, do not, did not, does not, e.g., I en like it there, it en have nothin'.

FAMILY, n., relative(s), e.g., he is family to me.

FEELINGS, n., affection, tenderness, e.g., Mothers have more feelings for the child than fathers.

FÊTE, n., a festive occasion (source: French, *fête*).

FINANCIAL, adj., paid up, e.g., the society does give you sick benefits if you financial.

FIND, v., think, e.g., Is too warm, you don' find so?

FIRE, v., to drink an alcoholic beverage, e.g., Come on, man, le' we fire one.

FOR SO, (1) for no special reason, just like that, e.g., he was doin' it for so. (2), in abundance, e.g., there was roti for so at the wedding.

FRANCE, n., hell (usually in phrases), e.g., Go to France! or, What the France!

FREENESS, n., a free fête with lots to eat and drink, e.g., they have a freeness up the road.

FRESH-UP, adj., rude, forward, aggressive, e.g., she too fresh-up.

FRIEND, v., to be involved in a relationship entailing sexual intercourse and other mutual obligations, but not living together. *Friending*, pres. part., *Friendly*, adv., *Friend, Boyfriend, Girlfriend*, n.

FRONTISH, adj., pushy, forward, e.g., he always frontish when people visit.

FUSS, AH FUSS, interj., e.g., Fuss, I tired, or, Ah fuss, I hungry!

GALVANISE, n., corrugated galvanized iron sheets, e.g., they usin' galvanise for the roof.

GET IN ONE'S SKIN, to urge one on, e.g., she get in his skin to marry she.

GETTING-IN, n., the period between first meeting a girl and starting to FRIEND with her; v., the process of establishing a FRIEND-ING relationship, e.g., He gettin-in with she.

GROW, v. trans., to raise, bring up, e.g., my aunt was the one that grow me; v. intrans., to be raised, e.g., I grow at my aunt.

HAD WAS, v., had, e.g., I had was to get it.

HAND, n., a share or part of a SUSU, e.g., he have two hand in that susu.

HAUL YOU' SKIN, HAUL YOU' TAIL, move on, scram!

HE, pron., him., e.g., What you worryin' with he for?

HOLD STRAIN, be patient.

HOME NAME, a pet name, an affectionate name used in the home and often elsewhere, e.g., Doodoo is my home name, my christened name is Catherine.

HORN, v., to cuckold, e.g., she horn the man.

HOT, adj., wild (used with boy or girl), e.g., I never think I see that hot boy marry.

HOT SHIRT, n., a loud shirt.

HOW, a greeting, e.g., John, how!

HUMBUG, v., to keep back, bother, trouble, e.g., this foot does humbug me.

HUSBAND, n., the man a woman is living with, e.g., is he your married husband?

I WISH, I'd never do that, NEVER HAPPEN (source: from the expression "I wish I do that, le' me dead.").

IGNORANT, adv., bad, e.g., stop actin' ignorant.

IN YOUR NUMBERS, in large numbers, e.g., turn out in your numbers to hear Victor Bryan tonight.

IN-LAW, sometimes used for step-relationship, e.g., mother-in-law for stepmother.

IS, v., are, e.g., we is no fools.

IS, it is, is it? e.g., "Is God what doin' that"; "Is true?"

IT HAVE, is there? are there? there is, there are, e.g., "It have how many people livin' there?" "It have only one."

JAB, n., devil (source: French, *diable*, devil).

JAMET, n., prostitute.

JUICK, JOOK, CHOOK, v., stick, push, pierce, e.g., she juick she finger in she throat.

JUMBIE, n., ghost.

JUMP-UP, n., a dance done to calypso tune; v., to do this dance.

JUST NOW, adv., soon, e.g., I comin' just now.

KEEPER, n., the person you are LIVING with, e.g., he (she) is my keeper.

KNOB, n., one of the pieces used in playing draughts.

LAGAHOO, n., a man who turns into a beast to do harm to people; in general, a person you can't trust (source: French, *loup-garou*, werewolf).

LAGNIAPPE, n., a bonus, something extra, e.g., four mangoes for twenty cents and one as lagniappe.

LEEPAY, v., to cover tapia walls with a thinner, whiter mud to make them smoother (source: Hindi).

LEF', v., leave, e.g., he want to lef' me home.

LICKS ONE'S SKIN, LICKS ONE'S TAIL, to beat badly.

LIKE, as if, it seems that, e.g., from that day, like he have me in mind.

LIKE FIRE, a great deal, much, e.g., we drank rum like fire.

LIME, v., to watch and enjoy an event from outside, e.g., to lime a fête.

LIVE, v., to be in a LIVING relationship with. LIVING, adj., indicates a relationship between a man and woman in which they live together and have mutual obligations to each other, although they are not married. LIVING, pres. part., e.g., we en married, we jus' LIVIN'.

MACO, n., busybody, gossip.

MADAME, n., a married woman, or one who is LIVING; often used to address a woman whose marital status is unknown.

MAKE, v., to bear, to have, e.g., to make a baby.

MAKE JOKE, to joke, e.g., don' make joke, man.

MAKE MESSAGE, to buy the groceries, to shop.

MAKE OLD STYE, to show off; to fool.

MAMAGUY, v., to flatter and deceive, e.g., don' mamaguy me.

MAN, n., a common term of address, usually friendly, e.g., I didn' see you, man.

MAPHRODITE, MORPHADITE, MORPHADIZE, n., hermaphrodite; occasionally, homosexual.

MASH, v., to step on, knock down, beat, crush, e.g., mash the brakes, or, I'll mash you if you do that.

MASHED-UP, adj., bad, painful, e.g., a mashed-up feeling.

MASTER, adj., best, e.g., oil is good, but saffron is master.

MAUVAISE-LANGUE, n., BAD-TALK, malicious rumor (source: French).

MELONGENE, n., eggplant (source: possibly French)

MELT, v., run away, disappear, e.g., when trouble start, he melt.

MIND, v., to take care of financially, e.g., to mind a child.

MIND, TO HAVE IN, to think of with evil intent, e.g., since that happen, he have me in mind.

MISS, n., used to address a single girl, and often to address a married woman as well. Also, a sign of respect to any woman, as would be used by a servant or a small child.

MISTRESS, n., used to address or refer to a married woman, e.g., good morning, Mistress Jones (source: "archaic" English survival).

MOOMOO, n., a silent person, e.g., he just sat there like a moomoo (source: French, *muet,* dumb, mute).

MORE THAN, besides, other than, e.g., you mean you have no other educated members in the island more than P.N.M.?

MORPHADITE, MORPHADIZE, see MAPHRODITE.

NA, NAH, NUH, used as a stress in talking, pleading, threatening, etc., e.g., I want to go, na; I ask you a question—answer, na.

NANCY-STORY, n., a fairy tale, a fabrication, an untruth (source: West African, *Anansi story,* a folk tale about Anansi, the spider).

NARA, n., a stiffness or pain of the abdomen or stomach.

NENNEN, n., godmother; CATCH YOUR NENNEN, to have a lot of trouble.

NEVER HAPPEN, that will never happen.

NEXT, adj., other, e.g., He is married, but he livin' with a next woman.

NOW, adv., shortly, e.g., Ah comin' now.

OBZOKEE, sometimes OBSUKKY, OBZOCKY, adj., ugly, dilapidated, shabby.

OL' MAS', OLE MAS', adv., (1) awry, wrong, e.g., he made his plans, but everything turn ol' mas'; *play ol' mas'*, do something in a ridiculous manner, e.g., what she doin' in that dress, she playin' ol' mas'?

OLD HEAD, n., an elderly person, one who has lived in a particular place for a long time.

OLD STYLE, see MAKE OLD STYLE.

ON TERMS, on good terms, e.g., the two of them not on terms at all.

ONE TIME, adv., at the same time; now, rather than later, e.g., do that one time, man.

ONLYEST, ONLIEST, adj., only, e.g., that was the onlyest shirt I had.

OUTSIDE CHILD, a child had with someone other than the person one is LIVING with or married to.

OY, interj., a greeting. e.g., Man, oy!

PAN, n., a steelband instrument made of an oil drum and tuned in sections to play musical notes.

PAPPY-SHOW, v., to open to ridicule, e.g., "You dance well." "Don' pappy-show me, man, I know I can' dance."

PARLOUR, n., a small store selling SWEET DRINKS, SWEETS, cigarettes, and a variety of other small items.

PIQUANT, n., thorn, e.g., a piquant JUICK me in the foot (source: French, *piquant*, prickle).

PITCH OIL, n., kerosene.

PRESS, v., oppress, e.g., that man does press you too much.

PULL, v., to get along, e.g., the Smiths and the Edwards doesn' pull at all.

PUSH FIRE, v., incite, cause trouble, e.g., she like to push fire and then run.

QUEEN, n., an elderly, respected woman.

QUITE, all the way, e.g., He come quite from Matelot.

RAMPLE, v., rumple.

RANGO, adj., wild, undisciplined, e.g., He's a real rango type.

RAP, n., clap, applause, e.g., give the ol' man a rap, na.

RATHER, v., prefer, e.g., I rather a girl child than a boy child.

REACH, v., take, go with, e.g., wait a minute, I'll reach you there.

ROTI, n., an Indian pancake.

SAFE, n., a receptacle used to store food and provisions (source: British).

SAGA BOY, n., a man about town, a boy who is popular with the girls.

SCIENCE, n., the art of black magic, e.g., I wouldn' meddle with he, na, he know too much o' science.

SEE, v., agree, e.g., I don' see with you at all.

SEE ONE'S SKIN, SEE ONE'S TAIL, to have a lot of trouble.

-SELF, suffix, exactly, right, e.g., I livin' here-self since 1960.

SHE, pron., her, e.g., he always beatin' she.

SO-SO-SO (from two up to eight or more so's may be used consecutively), this and that, a variety of things, e.g., he come up to me and he say so-so-so-so.

SOUCOUYANT, n., a woman who turns into a ball of fire and sucks people's blood.

STCHOOPS, STUPES, expression of disdain, mild disgust, e.g., when I suggested that she visit them, she said "stchoops." The sound is much more frequently used than the word (source: probably West African [onomatopoeic] from the sound made sucking one's teeth).

STEELBAND, n., a band made up of differently tuned steel PANS.

STUDY, v., to be interested in, to be concerned about, to be thinking of, usually with evil intent, e.g., maybe he tell you he forgive you, but he still studyin' that.

SUCK ONE'S TEETH, to say STCHOOPS.

SUSU, n., (1) an institution in which a number of persons take hands, contributing the same sum of money every specified period for each hand; each person draws all of the money successively. (2) a loose woman, e.g., she a susu, man, everybody in that (source: Yoruban, *esusu*, a financial arrangement similar to [1] above).

SWEET, adj., inebriated, drunk, e.g., Look, Jack sweet for so!

SWEET, SWEETIE, n., candy (source: British).

SWEETBREAD, n., a bread made with sugar, grated coconut, raisins, or other sweet ingredients.

SWEET DRINK, n., a soft drink, a carbonated beverage.

SWEET MAN, n., a man with whom a woman is FRIENDING outside of a married or LIVING relationship.

SWEET NAME, n., a pet name.

TABANCA, n., heartache, especially over a spouse's infidelity.

TAKE IN, v., fall ill suddenly, e.g., if I take in, she will call a doctor.

TAKE WITH, v., to start to FRIEND with or to LIVE with, e.g., I take with she last year.

TANTIE, TANT, TAN', n., aunt (source: French).

TEA, n., breakfast, the morning meal.

THROW, v., to pay money into a SUSU, e.g., I throw my two dollars every fortnight, and then when I draw my hand I can do something with the money.

T'IEF, v., thieve, steal, e.g., she t'ief me money.

TITLE, n., surname.

TOO BAD, very much, a great deal, e.g., I like that too bad, man.

TOUCHOUS, adj., touchy, concerned, interested in, e.g., a boy does be more touchous about the money he give his parents than a girl.

TRUE, FOR TRUE, is that the truth? that is the truth, e.g., I must be getting old for true, or, "I say he dead, man." "True?"

TRUST, TRUS', adv., on credit, e.g., give me the bread trust.

USES, v., used, e.g., he uses to call me John.

VEX, v., to get vexed, to get angry with, e.g., I fuss, I vex!

WAHBEEN, WHABEEN, n., promiscuous woman, prostitute.

WANT, v., need, e.g., the house want repairs.

WELL, adv., very, e.g., he well right, or, he well bad.

WIFE, n., a woman that a man is LIVING with or married to, e.g., if you livin' under one roof with she, she your wife.

WORRY, v., to take seriously, to be concerned about, e.g., don' worry with he, na, when he drunk he en know what he sayin'.

YES, used for emphasis, e.g., she fas', yes; he goin' to win, yes.

ZABOCA, n., avocado.

Index